KW-482-261

Nice (p54)

Mercantour National Park (p243)

PROVENCE & THE CÔTE D'AZUR

THE JOURNEY BEGINS HERE

There's the Provence and Côte d'Azur of magazine covers and social media posts: vast plains ablaze with lavender, striped beach umbrellas against the dazzling blue of the Mediterranean. Then there's the Provence and Côte d'Azur you might not have met yet: little-known ski resorts and alpine villages with rich pastoral traditions.

Chrissie McClatchie

@chrissie_mcclatchie

Growing up with a French mother in Australia, Chrissie spent many childhood holidays in the south of France. She moved to Nice just after graduating from university; 15 years later she's still there.

My favourite experience is a weekend escape in the **Parc National du Mercantour** (p243), where I can swap the crowds of the coast for empty alpine trails in under 90 minutes. Total bliss.

WHO GOES WHERE

Our writers and experts choose the places that, for them, define Provence and the Côte d'Azur.

My favourite experience is cycling the **Monts de Vaucluse** (p208). It has lighter traffic than other areas of the Luberon, with plenty of backroads that let you zigzag between villages. I love the wild valleys and hills on this side of the Monts de Vaucluse, and the quiet villages like **Venasque (p208)**, which lie at the edge of the typical traveller's loop.

Ashley Parsons

@enselle.voyage

Ashley is a travel and adventure writer. She currently splits her time between Provence and the French Alps. Follow her travels on horseback, bike, foot or train.

My go-to experience is a local lunch of razor clams and wine in **Les Goudes (p141)**, followed by a walk into the wild and a dive into the Med.

Michael Frankel

Michael is a Marseille-based freelance writer who lives for the slow doors of a hotel room clicking behind him as he makes his way down to the street.

HEMIS / ALAMY STOCK PHOTO ©

STÉPHANE DEBOVE/SHUTTERSTOCK ©

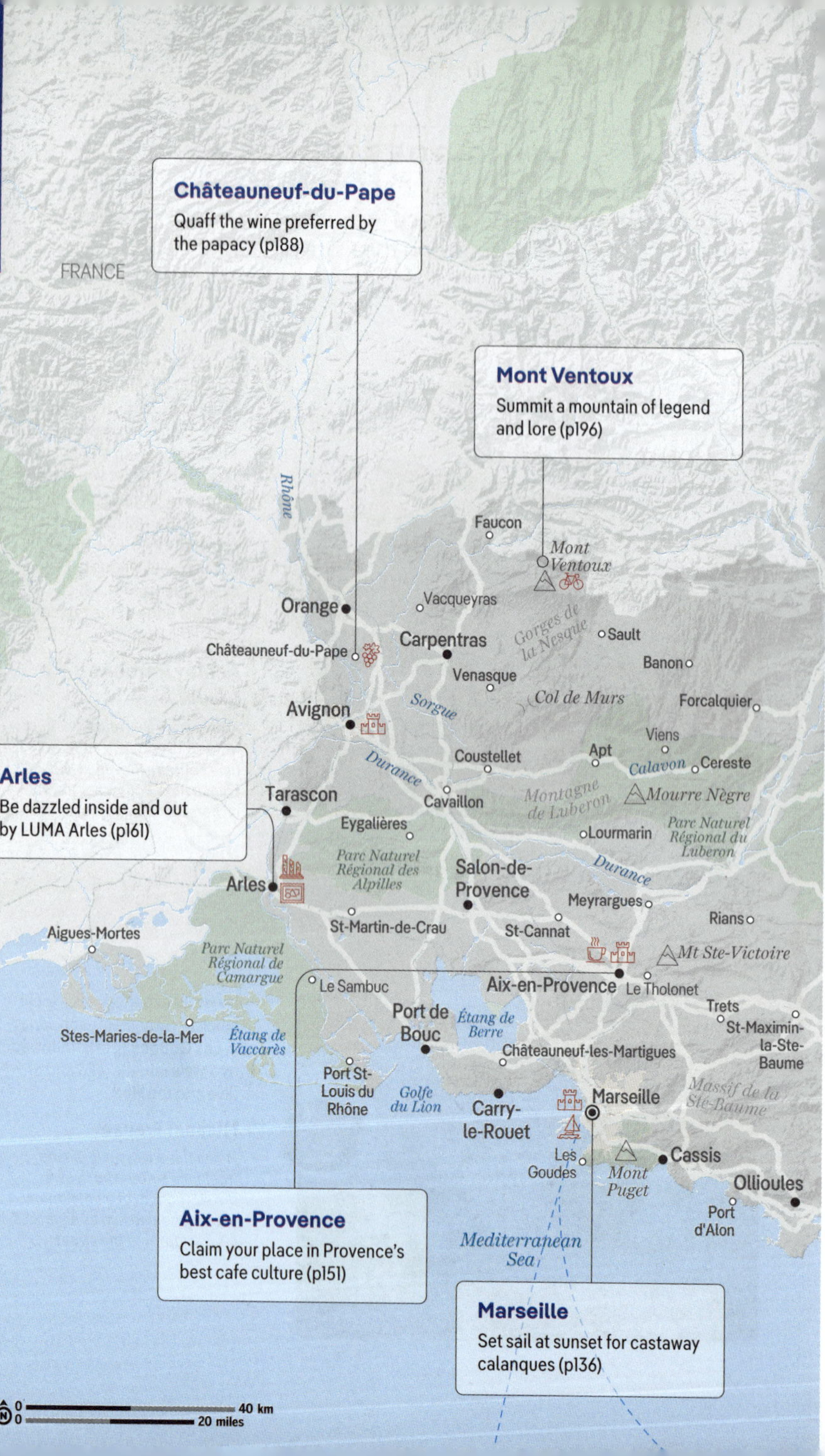

Châteauneuf-du-Pape
Quaff the wine preferred by
the papacy (p188)

Mont Ventoux
Summit a mountain of legend
and lore (p196)

FRANCE

Rhône

Faucon

*Mont
Ventoux*

Orange

Vacqueyras

Châteauneuf-du-Pape

Carpentras

Sault

Banon

Venasque

*Gorges de
la Nesque*

Col de Murs

Forcalquier

Avignon

Sorgue

Coustellet

Apt

Viens

Cereste

Calavon

Arles
Be dazzled inside and out
by LUMA Arles (p161)

Durance

Tarascon

Cavaillon

*Montagne
de Luberon*

Mourre Nègre

Lourmarin

*Parc Naturel
Régional du
Luberon*

Eygalières

*Parc Naturel
Régional des
Alpilles*

Arles

Salon-de-
Provence

Durance

Meyrargues

Rians

Aigues-Mortes

St-Martin-de-Crau

St-Cannat

*Parc Naturel
Régional de
Camargue*

Le Sambuc

Aix-en-Provence

Le Tholonet

Mt Ste-Victoire

Trets

St-Maximin-
la-Ste-
Baume

Stes-Maries-de-la-Mer

*Étang de
Vaccarès*

Port de
Bouc

*Étang de
Berre*

Châteauneuf-les-Martigues

Port St-
Louis du
Rhône

*Golfe
du Lion*

Carry-
le-Rouet

Marseille

*Massif de la
Ste-Baume*

Aix-en-Provence
Claim your place in Provence's
best cafe culture (p151)

Les
Goudes

*Mont
Puget*

Cassis

Ollioules

Port
d'Alon

*Mediterranean
Sea*

Marseille
Set sail at sunset for castaway
calanques (p136)

0 ___ 40 km
0 ___ 20 miles

Moustiers-Ste-Marie
Breathe in the season's lavender fields (p242)

Monaco
Tuck into fresh seafood from Monaco's last fisherman (p96)

Nice
Immerse yourself in Belle Époque detail (p54)

Île de Porquerolles
Hike, cycle and swim in a Mediterranean paradise (p114)

Bormes-les-Mimosa
Buckle up for a floral winter road trip (p119)

FRANCE

ITALY

La Mortice

Lac de Serre-Ponçon

St-Paul-sur-Ubaye

Le Lauzet-Ubaye

Barcelonnette

L'Ubaye

La Tête de la Sestrière

La Foux d'Allos

St-Étienne-de-Tinée

Mont Mounier

Punta Marguareis

Col de Tende

Barles

Reserve Geologique de Haute Provence

Parc National du Mercantour

Le Boreon

Tende

Digne-les-Bains

Bléone

Thorame-Haute

Col de St-Michel

Guillaumes

Mont Bégo

Annot

Var

Villars-sur-Var

l'Arpette

St-Andre-les-Alpes

Lac de Castillon

FRANCE

Gorges de Daluis

Gorges de la Vésubie

Auvestre

Collet Barris

Rougon

St-Martin du Var

Menton

Verdon

Grand Plan de Canjuers

Bargème

Loup

La Colle Loubière

Èze

MONACO

Parc Naturel Régional du Verdon

Montmeyan

Châteaudouble

Grasse

St-Laurent-du-Var

Nice

Côte d'Azur

Col de la Grange

Lac de St-Cassien

Antibes

Cotignac

Cannes

Châteauvert

Argens

Le Muy

Mt Vinaigre

Îles de Lérins

Le Luc

Agay

La Sauvette

St-Raphaël

Cuers

Collobrières

Les Issambres

Golfe de St-Tropez

Massif des Maures

Domaine du Rayol

St-Tropez

Côte d'Azur

Hyères

Bormes-les-Mimosas

Port d'Hyères

Mediterranean Sea

Porquerolles

RED, WHITE & ROSÉ

When the ancient Greeks planted France's first wine grapes in the soils around newly founded Massalia (Marseille), the seeds of Provence's prized wine tradition were sown. Today, over 80% of all wine made here is rosé, and the pink flows year-round on sunlit cafe terraces. There's so much more to the region's winemaking than one colour, however; it extends from the deep reds of the Vaucluse to boutique 'Made in Nice' whites.

Vineyard Visits

Phone ahead to ensure that someone will be there to welcome you at the cellar door, especially for smaller vineyards. Tasting fees are common.

Cooperative Spirit

If you find yourself short on time but want to get a feel for the region's wines, plan a visit to the local wine cooperative.

Rosé Time

To go to the heart of Provence's famous rosé, visit the Maison des Vins de Côtes de Provence in Les-Arcs-sur-Argens.

Châteauneuf-du-Pape (p188)

PLAN YOUR TRIP

BEST WINE EXPERIENCES

Sip the elixirs of medieval popes at ❶ **Châteauneuf-du-Pape** (p188) and take a new favourite home; these complex reds only improve with age.

Fall under the spell of Beaumes-de-Venise at ❷ **Domaine de Ferme St-Martin** (p193) in the Ventoux. Tastings are hosted by a sommelier and a hypnotist.

Admire the supreme panoramas from ❸ **Domaine des Masques** (p158), just 15km outside Aix-en-Provence.

Meet the small monastic community with a surprising viticultural tradition on the ❹ **Île St-Honorat** (p80) off the coast of Cannes.

Decide for yourself if Coco Chanel really found inspiration for her iconic logo at ❺ **Château de Crémat** (p63) in the hills of Nice.

DEYMOSHR/SHUTTERSTOCK ©

Gorges du Verdon (p239)

WATER WORLDS

The calm Mediterranean Sea is as pretty as a picture, but don't just admire the view. You can tailor the day's activities to match your mood: relaxed afternoons on a skippered sailboat, easy swims with a snorkel and mask off undeveloped islands or deeper dives down to moody shipwrecks.

In Season

Easter is considered the traditional starting point for the diving season, which runs until October. Boats shutter up for winter, though locals swim year-round.

Pointus

A delightful splash of colour and character, *pointus* are the region's traditional wooden fishing boats. Spot them in ports from Marseille to Menton.

BEST WATER EXPERIENCES

Set sail in search of dolphins on a replica 16th-century sailing boat in ❶ **St-Jean-Cap-Ferrat** (p70).

Relax into yachting life or go for a spin on a crewed catamaran in the ❷ **Golfe de St-Tropez** (p104).

BYO snorkelling gear to the ❸ **Écomusée Sous-Marin de Cannes** (p81), where sculptures dot the ocean floor.

Run the rapids of the ❹ **Gorges du Verdon** (p239) for Provence's best rafting and canyoning.

Rig the sails then tuck into a vegetarian brunch on board the *pointu Coco*, departing from ❺ **Marseille** (p141).

CITY LIFE

From the cosmopolitan grit of Marseille to the shiny glitz of Monaco, Provence and the Côte d'Azur's urban centres warrant your time and attention. Inside these bustling cityscapes, you can dine on inventive cuisine, search for street art and while away the hours on a shaded cafe terrace. Expect plenty of history, but also a taste of what the future holds.

BEST CITY LIFE EXPERIENCES

Wake up with an appetite in ❶ **Nice** (p61); from lavender croissants to smashed avo on toast, an inventive breakfast and brunch scene is simmering.

Sink into cafe culture at one of the many outdoor terraces in ❷ **Aix-en-Provence** (p153). Dark sunglasses are a requisite for people-watching.

Find yourself framed by street art on Cours Julien in ❸ **Marseille** (p136), where a sunset *apéro* can easily morph into a night out.

Grab a seat at a charming bar on rue des Teinturiers in ❹ **Avignon** (p185) and settle in for happy hour.

Join the afterwork crowd for festive Friday night drinks and organic beer at the harbourfront ❺ **Brasserie de Monaco** (p97).

The Principality

Smaller than New York's Central Park and with a population of just 36,000, Monaco is the world's second-smallest country and one of its most dense (p92).

Golden Hour

Terrace tables fill up come 5pm with groups of friends catching up for an early evening apéritif, known colloquially as *apéro* (p62).

Home Brew

An exciting craft beer scene is brewing. Swap out your usual choice for a local drop flavoured with regional ingredients, like lemons from Menton (p89).

11

ARTS & CRAFTS

Cézanne in Aix-en-Provence, Van Gogh in Arles, Matisse and Chagall in Nice, and Picasso here, there and everywhere. The quality of light and the way it colours the landscape has long made Provence a muse for the masters. Marvel at their work in museums, chapels and even the homes they once lived in. A wealth of other arts-and-craft traditions, from fine ceramics to outdoor galleries and even nature's own pigments, await.

Wild Art

The Route de l'Art Contemporain (Contemporary Art Route) is an open-air art tour through the prehistoric Réserve Géologique de Haute-Provence, which starts in Digne-les-Bains (pictured above, p234).

Sure Bet

Before the high rollers descend at 2pm, Monaco's Casino de Monte-Carlo opens for self-guided tours through the lavishly decorated, gilded, Belle Époque gaming rooms (p96).

Handcrafted

Leather sandals in St-Tropez, blocks of *savon de Marseille* in Salon-de-Provence and ceramics from Vallauris are all souvenirs to treasure.

BEST ARTS & CRAFTS EXPERIENCES

Follow in the footsteps of Pablo Picasso, who made the potter's village of ❶ **Vallauris** (p87) and the village of Mougins home.

Spot Frank Gehry's striking ❷ **LUMA Arles** (p161) from a distance: it's a steel-clad tower and inspiring cultural palace.

Be dazzled by the eye-catching monochrome rounds of the ❸ **Fondation Vasarely** (p156) in Aix-en-Provence, dedicated to optical art.

Hike into the ochre-tinted swirl of cliffs, fairy chimneys, cirques and hills of the terracotta ❹ **Colorado Provençal** (p218).

Join the cool crowd and check out the latest modern art exhibition at ❺ **Villa Noailles** (p114) while taking in the view over Hyères.

MARCO BOTTIGELLI/GETTY IMAGES ©

Calanque d'En-Vau((p147)

ISLANDS & CALANQUES

Get ready to embrace barefoot adventures along powder-white beaches and refreshing swims in shallow waters. Local ferry services shuttle residents and visitors to and from sun-kissed islands, which are blissfully serene and car-free. On the mainland, don't miss Marseille's marvellous *calanques* (inlets).

My Calanques

Download the My Calanques app for hiking routes, traffic updates, flora and fauna guides and practical information at your fingertips.

Rubbish & Plastic Free

Cannes' Îles de Lérins are garbage bin free; visitors must take all rubbish back to the mainland with them. BYO water bottle to the Îles d'Hyères.

BEST ISLAND & CALANQUE EXPERIENCES

Sun yourself on the daydream beaches of the ❶ **Île de Porquerolles** (p115) off Hyères.

Hop on the ferry to Château d'If and ❷ **Îles du Frioul** (p143), rocky islets in the bay of Marseille.

Spend a day at your very own castaway bay in ❸ **Calanque d'En-Vau** (p147).

Catch the Train de la Côte Bleue and skim Marseille's coast to ❹ **Calanque du Jonquier** (p150).

Swap the bustle of Cannes for the pine-fringed hiking trails of the ❺ **Îles de Lérins** (p80), a short ferry ride from the mainland.

INLAND VILLAGES

Medieval builders knew a thing or two about building to last: standing tall over the countryside and witnesses to centuries of history, Provence's hilltop villages have withstood wars and invasions. Today, the only threat to peace comes from tour buses in summer, although many villages in the hinterland remain refreshingly low-key.

Look for This Label

Les Plus Beaux Villages de France is a label that recognises France's most beautiful villages; there are 18 (and counting) in Provence and the Côte d'Azur. (p72)

Bistrot de Pays

Taste your way through Provence's rural restaurant scene. The Bistrot de Pays organisation champions rural bistros that serve up local produce at reasonable prices. (p235)

No Access

High, hard-to-access rocky outcrops were prime real estate in the early Middle Ages as coastal dwellers moved to hilltops to defend themselves against Saracen attacks.

BEST VILLAGE EXPERIENCES

Eat your way through ❶ **Saignon** (p210), a laid-back village perched high above Apt with a generous share of top restaurants.

Hide out in ❷ **Cotignac** (p123), a charming village in Provence Verte with an exciting gourmet and cultural scene.

Scale to the top of ❸ **Ste-Agnès** (p72), the highest coastal village in Europe, where a medieval garden sprouts from 10th-century ruins.

Make ❹ **Moustiers-Ste-Marie** (p242) your base to visit the lavender fields of the Plateau de Valensole; don't leave without visiting its ceramic workshops.

Board the Train des Merveilles for a cinematic route from Nice to ❺ **Tende** (p74), an alpine village in France's most easterly corner.

NATURE ALL AROUND

No matter where you are in Provence and the Côte d'Azur, you're never too far from nature's embrace. You can set off on foot along rugged shoreline trails, pause to cool off in the glassy sea, hike to mountain reserves to observe wildlife or tackle majestic mountain summits by bike. At the heart of it all is the sublime Gorges du Verdon, where sport and nature meet in the shadow of sheer limestone cliffs that rise from turquoise waters.

Animals Crossing

Wildlife-spotting opportunities include marmots, chamois and ibex in the Parc National de Mercantour, vultures in the Gorges du Verdon and rare butterflies around Dignes-les-Bains (p243).

Visitor Limits

To preserve the unspoilt feel of the Île de Porquerolles, visitor numbers are limited to 6000 per day from the end of June to the beginning of August (p114).

Seeing Stars

Sometimes the best experiences stir after dark; low light pollution makes the Alpes-de-Haute-Provence a magnet for stargazing (p234).

❶ ❷ ❸ ❹ ❺

BEST NATURE EXPERIENCES

Tackle the ride at the top of many cyclists' bucket lists, ❶ **Mont Ventoux** (p196), a windswept mountain steeped in centuries of lore.

Go fossil spotting at the ❷ **Réserve Géologique de Haute-Provence** (p234), Europe's largest protected geological reserve.

Take your pick from hiking, cycling, driving, canyoning or rafting the deep ❸ **Gorges du Verdon** (p237).

Breathe in the fresh mountain air and set off in search of alpine wildlife just 1½ hours from Nice in ❹ **St-Martin-Vésubie** (p74).

Slow down in the ❺ **Camargue** (p169), a vast shimmer of salt flats and marshlands where pink flamingos, black bulls and wild horses roam.

FLOWERS & GARDENS

From rows of purple lavender stretched as far as the eye can see to the delicate rose and jasmine fragrances that underlie the world's most recognisable perfumes, so much of Provence's identity is intertwined with its floral bounty. Breathe in the smells and soak up the traditions in the region's vast fields and manicured gardens.

Lavender Versus Lavandin

Real lavender grows at altitude, is slightly greyer and a key ingredient in perfume. *Lavandin* is a long-stemmed hybrid used to scent household products.

The Rite of Spring

The gardens of the Côte d'Azur throw open their gates to welcome visitors during the month-long Festival des Jardins de la Côte d'Azur in April.

Purple Power

Hilltop Tourrettes-sur-Loup is known as the village of violets; it breaks out in every shade of purple in early March for the annual Fête des Violettes (p86).

BEST FLOWER AND GARDEN EXPERIENCES

Don't miss Provence's iconic **❶ lavender fields** (p210) but choose sustainable visits.

Set off on the coastal **❷ Route du Mimosa** (p119), a 130km winter road trip framed by golden blooms.

Breathe in the scents of the world's greatest perfume flowers at the **❸ Jardins du Musée International de la Parfumerie** (p88).

Find a peaceful corner of Monaco in the **❹ Roseraie Princesse Grace** (p95), an English-style garden with over 6000 rose bushes.

Wander the breezy gardens of **❺ Domaine du Rayol** (p117), where each corner of the park is cultivated with species from arid ecosystems around the world.

LIVING HISTORY

Wherever you look, you'll find relics of Provence and the Côte d'Azur's rich history on display, from the earliest imprints of human settlement carved by hand in caves to imposing Roman arenas where gladiators once fought to the fortified Gothic palace the medieval papacy called home. Belle Époque buildings and art deco detailing are tokens of modern times and tell the story of how the southeastern coast of France grew into a must-visit destination for early travellers.

Boom at Noon

No, you're not hearing things. Every day at midday, a cannon rings out across Nice. A tradition dating from the late 19th century, today's cannonball is a firework (p56).

Did You Know?

There is only one team in Marseille: Olympique de Marseille (OM). They're the only French football team to have lifted the Champions League trophy (p140).

True Story

Follow the comings and goings of the emigrants of Barcelonnette at the Musée de la Vallée and in the village's Mexican villas (p244).

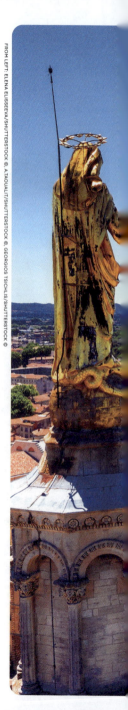

BEST HISTORY EXPERIENCES

Wander the World Heritage listed streets of ❶ **Nice** (p54) and step back into an era when winter was the high season for travel.

Scrape back layers of time at the ❷ **Palais Princier de Monaco** (p94),where careful restoration work is revealing Renaissance frescoes.

See if you can answer the mystery surrounding 40,000 enigmatic Bronze Age rock engravings in the ❸ **Vallée des Merveilles** (p74).

Feel the Roman legacy as you walk the streets of ❹ **Arles** (p164) – a one-time economic, political and cultural centre in a sprawling empire.

Lose yourself in the churches, gardens and abbeys that stand testament to the time the papacy swapped Rome for ❺ **Avignon** (p186).

FLAVOURS OF PROVENCE

Whether you're hungry for gastronomic dining or street food that sets your taste buds sizzling, Provence and the Côte d'Azur's kitchens have you covered. Marseille overflows with global flavours, while chefs in Nice are reinventing the city's traditional cuisine. Fresh, seasonal flavours rule the coast; inland, the mountain air is paired with heartier fare. Whether breakfast, brunch, lunch or dinner, there's always someone bringing something new to the table. So make sure you pack your appetite.

Black Gold

The truffle season runs from mid-November to mid-March; an estimated 70% of French truffles sprout from the soils of the Vaucluse. Carpentras is the truffle hub (p190).

Markets

Provence knows how to throw a market, from fragrant weekly events to speciality markets that shine a spotlight on a particular product in season.

Who Does It Best?

Is the best *panisse* (chickpea fritters) from Marseille or Nice? Sample both cities' offerings and decide for yourself.

BEST FOOD EXPERIENCES

Savour the flavours of a forgotten pastoral cuisine at ❶ **Auberge St Martin** (p76) in La Brigue.

Confuse your sweet tooth with a scoop of charcoal-flavoured vanilla ice cream at ❷ **Vanille Noire** (p139) in Marseille.

Immerse yourself in the Camargue's rice culture during a visit to the ❸ **Maison du Riz** (p170). You can even stay the night.

Warm up after a day on the slopes with a delightfully decadent ❹ **Fondue de l'Ubaye** (p245) created from three alpine cheeses.

Feast on catch-of-the-day from the last of Monaco's traditional fishers, Eric Rinaldi, at ❺ **Pêcherie U Luvassu** (p98).

REGIONS & CITIES

Find the places that tick all your boxes.

The Vaucluse & Luberon

MOUNTAINS, WINE & SUNSHINE

Avignon blends papal history with modern theatre. Too-pretty-to-be-true Gordes is the essence of Provence in a bottle. Saddle up to summit Mont Ventoux or slow down on country lanes weaving through scented lavender fields. Fill your basket with fresh produce at markets in Carpentras and sip your way through Châteauneuf-du-Pape.

p178

The Vaucluse & Luberon
p178

Bouches-du-Rhône
p131

Bouches-du-Rhône

FOLLOWING THE RIVER TO THE SEA

France's second-largest city is the gritty, multicultural melting pot of Marseille. First settled by the Greeks, today it's the gateway to hidden coastal *calanques* (inlets), Aix-en-Provence's cafe culture, the wetlands of the Camargue, Arles' Roman monuments and a timeless landscape that inspired Van Gogh and Cézanne.

p131

Alpes-de-Haute-Provence

FROM ALPINE VALLEYS TO FIELDS OF LAVENDER

Buckle up for white-knuckle adventure in the Gorges du Verdon, clip onto a via ferrata in Digne-les-Bains, trace fossilised footprints in the Réserve Géologique de Haute-Provence and ski the slopes of the Ubaye Valley. The southern Alps is Provence like you never imagined it.

p227

Alpes-de-Haute-Provence
p227

Côte d'Azur & Monaco
p48

The Var
p100

Côte d'Azur & Monaco

WHERE THE MOUNTAINS MEET THE MEDITERRANEAN

Nice is the big city coming of age while Cannes and Monaco deliver all the five-star glamour. Mougins, Èze and other perched villages conceal artists' studios and fine-dining tables. The gardens of Grasse perfume the world. The mountain scene is gloriously off-radar.

p48

The Var

BEACHES, HILLTOP VILLAGES & THE SEA

From the blingy beach clubs of St-Tropez to the laid-back surfer vibe of Hyères' Presqu'île de Giens, there's a beach to suit everyone in the Var. Pale pink rosé flows forth from inland vineyards. Provence Verte brims with stylish villages and lush green landscapes.

p100

ITINERARIES

Hilltop Villages & Market Towns

Allow: 5 days **Distance:** 105km

The Vaucluse and the Luberon are storybook Provence: dreamy hilltop villages, vineyard-strewn plains, buzzing produce markets and vintage 2CVs chugging along country lanes. From Carpentras, this unhurried route coils east through antique towns, lavender-framed abbeys, unreal ochre-red landscapes and serene frescoed churches before arriving at sweet Reillanne.

① CARPENTRAS ⏱1 DAY

Your Luberon road trip starts with a gastronomic bang in the shady squares of **Carpentras (p190)** where aromas of fresh truffles and juicy strawberries fill the air, depending on the season, and a bright Provençal market pops up every Friday morning, no matter the time of the year. Spend the afternoon among the sun-drenched vineyards of the Ventoux, just a short drive out of town.

② L'ISLE-SUR-LA-SORGUE ⏱1 DAY

Where cobblestones meet canals, **L'Isle-sur-la-Sorgue (p202)** oozes Provençal charm. Traditional *négro chin* wooden boats and water wheels stand testament to the town's rich past while the antique shops that line the narrow streets speak of its modern-day status as one of France's premier destinations for antique lovers.

🔺 *Detour:* Uncover the source of the River Sorgues in Fontaine-de-Vaucluse. ⏱ *5 hours*

③ GORDES ⏱1 DAY

In a country not lacking in the beautiful villages department, **Gordes (p206)** is often voted as the most attractive of all. Decide for yourself if this Luberon stunner takes your top place, although be prepared to share the winding lanes with busloads of tourists in the height of summer. Stretch your legs on the 3km walk to the Abbaye Notre-Dame de Sénanque, a 12th-century abbey surrounded by blooming lavender.

COLORADO
Provençal

Reillanne

Saignon

④ COLORADO PROVENÇAL ⏱ 1 DAY

Beat the heat by setting off early for the **Colorado Provençal (p218)**, an awe-inspiring landscape of fairy chimneys and desert rocks tinted rust, crimson and burnt orange between Roussillon and Rustrel. A busy ochre quarry between the 1880s to the late 1950s, the site is now a unique hiking destination with two family-friendly (but not pram-friendly) trails. Hiking boots, hat, sunscreen and water are obligatory.

⑤ SAIGNON ⏱ ½ DAY

Get a feel for traditional Provençal life in **Saignon (p210)**, a lovely village above Apt that overlooks the Luberon and beyond to Mont Ventoux. Capture the best views by following the short trail up to the castle ruins and the Rocher de Bellevue, then wind back down to admire fading frescoes inside the 12th-century Église Notre-Dame de Pitié. Stock up on picnic supplies in the village.

⑥ REILLANNE ⏱ ½ DAY

Raise a toast to the end of the journey at Café du Cours, a lively restaurant-cafe in the centre of **Reillanne (p211)** with a popular live music program. Sunday's Grand Marché de Reillanne is one of the best in the region and transforms the quiet perched village into a feast of zero-kilometre produce: olive oil, farm-fresh eggs, chickpeas and melt-in-your-mouth tomatoes.

Moustiers-Ste-Marie (p242)

ITINERARIES

Provence's Alpine Heart

Allow: 6 Days **Distance**: 214km

Take roads less travelled as you drift deeper into the Alpes-de-Haute-Provence. Cut across sun-drenched plateaus bursting with purple lavender, contemplate brilliant night skies, kit up for white-knuckle adventures and recover in thermal cures as you embark on this action-packed drive that curves north from Banon to Barcelonnette.

① BANON ⏱ ½ DAY

Begin this inland itinerary in **Banon (p235)**, an attractive hilltop village overlooking lavender fields and best known for its eponymous goat's cheese that comes rustically wrapped in a chestnut leaf. Pick up a precious parcel at either the Tuesday or Saturday morning markets; add in a baguette, tomato, charcuterie and some in-season fruit and *voilà*, your picnic lunch *à la provençale* awaits.

② ST-MICHEL-L'OBSERVATOIRE ⏱ ½ DAY

The small village of **St-Michel-l'Observatoire (p234)** is a stargazer's delight. See what constellations you can spot with the naked eye, or spend a summer night in the company of experienced English-speaking astronomers at the Centre d'Astronomie.

🦅 *Detour:* Watch for soaring birds of prey along the well-marked 13km hiking trail that starts and ends in Revest-des-Brousses. ⏱ 3 hours

③ VALENSOLE ⏱ 1 DAY

For a few weeks in late June and early July, the vast 800-sq-km Plateau de **Valensole (p240)** explodes with the purple hues of lavender bloom – your chance to snap the quintessential Provence photo. Lavender farms are open year-round for distillery tours, souvenir shopping and to explain the key differences between the region's two main crops: *lavande* and *lavandin*.

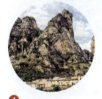

④ MOUSTIERS-STE-MARIE ⏱ 2 DAYS

Huddled beneath sheer cliffs, the stonewashed village of **Moustiers-Ste-Marie (p242)** oozes Provençal chic. Devote a day to mooching around cobbled streets and learning more about the local ceramic traditions. Set off early for an action-packed second day in the Gorges du Verdon, whether hiking, cycling, rafting or canyoning.

⑤ DIGNE-LES-BAINS ⏱ 1 DAY

Choose your own adventure in **Digne-les-Bains (p230)**: either relax into the famous healing baths that once cured Napoleonic soldiers or clip onto the via ferrata climbing route that starts just outside the town. The capital of the Alpes-de-Haute-Provence was also the home of intrepid traveller Alexandra David-Néel.

⑥ BARCELONNETTE ⏱ 1 DAY

Take in the dramatic alpine views as you cross over mountain passes en route to **Barcelonnette (p243)**, the friendly village dotted with sumptuous Mexican villas – so named after emigrants to Mexico returned in the late 19th century. Set off on a hike into remote pastures. Once the sun sets, tuck into one of the valley's famous three-cheese fondues.

PLAN YOUR TRIP · **ITINERARIES**

Coastal Provence

Allow: 7 days **Distance**: 314km

The natural beauty and diverse landscapes of coastal Provence reveal all their splendour on this shore-hugging route through the Bouches-du-Rhône and Var. Heading east from Stes-Maries-de-la-Mer, encounter windswept marshlands teeming with wildlife, rocky coves, towns rediscovering their groove and endless stretches of sandy beaches.

STES-MARIES-DE-LA-MER ⏱ 2 DAYS

Start off in **Stes-Maries-de-la-Mer (p172)**, a seaside town of wide beaches, ice-cream shops and Roma pilgrimages. Hire a bike to explore the haunting landscapes of the Camargue wetlands, with pink flamingos and cowboys. Track birds of prey with your binoculars at the Parc Ornithologique du Pont de Gau nature reserve.

🐾 *Detour: Break for a lunch with a side serve of Roman history at Arles.* ⏱ *5 hours*

CARRY-LE-ROUET ⏱ 1 DAY

Next stop is the Côte Bleue (Blue Coast), a pine-scented coastal stretch of limestone coves, walking trails and long-horned goats west of Marseille. Base yourself in **Carry-Le-Rouet (p150)**, a quiet fishing port now a popular holiday resort and the spot to feast on hand-plucked *oursins* (sea urchins), particularly during February's beloved Oursinades celebrations. Cool off in the translucent waters of the Parc Marin Côte Bleue, a designated marine park.

CASSIS ⏱ 1 DAY

Bypass busy Marseille for laid-back **Cassis (p148)**, a chic fishing village and the gateway to the majestic Parc National des Calanques. Lace up your hiking boots (and pack your swimsuit) to tackle the trail to Calanque d'En-Vau and back. Reward your efforts with a glass of AOC Cassis, Provence's first wine appellation, on a terrace overlooking the photogenic waterfront.

④ HYÈRES 🕐 1 DAY

Visitors too often drive straight through **Hyères (p113)** on their way to the Îles de Porquerolles – it's their loss. Today, the hip Villa Noailles modern art gallery and a cluster of cool dining options are bringing this resort town back to life. Don't miss the medieval *vieille ville* (old town) high above the modern centre.

🔄 *Detour: Ditch the car for the Îles de Porquerolles (p114), a short ferry ride from Hyères.* 🕐 *1 day*

⑤ GRIMAUD 🕐 1 DAY

Seven kilometres separates **Grimaud (p109)** from Port Grimaud and a full day allows you to see both. Quilted in bright bougainvillea, medieval Grimaud is perched high above the Golfe de St-Tropez; the modern pleasure port dates from the 1960s and is a pretty place to spend a few hours mooching around Venetian-inspired canals and bridges.

🔄 *Detour: Hop on a Bateaux Verts for a day trip to St-Tropez.* 🕐 *1 day*

⑥ ST-RAPHAËL 🕐 1 DAY

Savour this last length of road (in winter, a stretch of the scented Route du Mimosa) as it clings to the coast through lovely Ste-Maxime, energetic watersports hub St-Aygulf, and Fréjus with its impressive Roman ruins. Where Fréjus ends, **St-Raphaël (p112)** begins. Lounge on the lively town's buttercream beach and decide whether to push on to Cannes along the show-stopping Corniche d'Or.

Cannes (p77)

ITINERARIES

Côte d'Azur Classics

Allow: 4 days **Distance**: 97km

Tick off the classics as you journey from one end of the Côte d'Azur to the other, starting at cinematic Cannes. This itinerary arcs inland to pause at arty hilltop villages surrounded by fragranced gardens, before edging back to the coast and pastel-pretty seaside resorts near Menton on the Italian border.

① CANNES ⏱ ½ DAY

Spend the first morning soaking up the main sights in glitzy **Cannes (p77)**: walk along the palm-lined Croisette beachfront past the superyachts moored in the Vieux Port and stop for a local snack at the covered Marché Forville. Push on towards Le Suquet, Cannes' oldest neighbourhood, brimming with colourful houses with floral balconies.

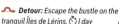 **Detour:** *Escape the bustle on the tranquil Îles de Lérins.* ⏱ *1 day*

② MOUGINS ⏱ ½ DAY

Polished stones and cascading flowers make Vieux **Mougins (p87)** an artist's dream; it's on a vast estate not far from the hilltop village where Picasso spent the last 12 years of his life. You can peek into the estate from the cypress-flanked Chapelle de Notre-Dame de Vie next door. Dine on gastronomic fare on an alfresco terrace in the heart of the old village.

③ GRASSE ⏱ 1 DAY

Synonymous with perfume, wrap yourself in the world of fragrance in **Grasse (p88)**, a town stretched across the hillside high above Cannes. Tour grand perfumeries where you can try your hand at making your own scent, linger in interactive museums inside historic houses and set foot in enchanting gardens where rose, jasmine, violet, iris and other aromatic flowers grow.

❹ VILLEFRANCHE-SUR-MER ⏱ 1 DAY

Drop back down to the coast in **Villefranche-sur-Mer (p64)**, a fishing village next to Nice whose star looks have graced the front of endless travel magazines. Practise the art of being a *flâneur*, or leisurely stroller, along alleyways shaded the colours of sunshine that lead down to a row of harbourfront restaurants. Cool down inside the imposing Citadelle Ste-Elme's sculptured gardens.

❺ ÈZE ⏱ ½ DAY

On a coastline scattered with captivating jewels, eagle's-nest **Èze Village (p64)** can claim to be the most dazzling of them all. Follow the winding lanes towards the summit where a tranquil cactus garden sprouts in the ruins of the old château. Be sure to have plenty of battery left in your phone or camera – from this height, the views across the Mediterranean Sea are out of this world.

❻ MENTON ⏱ ½ DAY

Menton (p70) defies the stereotype of unappealing border towns; just footsteps from Italy, the pastel-painted old town rising from the Mediterranean Sea is a setting that has energised artists, writers and now culinary stars like celebrated Argentinian chef Mauro Colagreco. Book a table at one of his three local restaurants (including the three-star Mirazur) or taste juicy local lemons on sunny terraced fruit groves.

WHEN **TO GO**

Most visitors come during summer holidays, but for many others, the charm lies in sunny winters and warm spring and autumn weather.

Winter – today's low season – was once the high season, particularly in the Var and on the Côte d'Azur, when everyone from aristocrats to artists flocked here for their share of New Year sun. The winter months still pack a punch, from the ski slopes of the Alpes-de-Haute-Provence to the coastal Route du Mimosa, which explodes with golden blooms come January. Visit in spring or autumn to breathe in fresh air on mountain hikes and cycling trails, or to move freely through galleries and museums. It can feel as if everyone comes to the south of France during the sweltering summer months, packing a party mood as they crowd out beaches and perched villages.

Accommodation Lowdown

As a general rule, accommodation prices are lowest in November and January. Expect a spike in rates around Christmas and New Year, as well as during February festivals. July and August command top dollar; you can find a nice price outside of these times depending on the local event schedule.

I LIVE HERE

Les Filles du Verdon know the Gorges du Verdon like the back of their hand
@lesfillesduverdon

The Verdon is hugely popular in the middle of summer, but those who live here know that every season is magical. Our favourite is spring, the moment when nature awakens. This is the best time for running, walking or cycling from site to site, far from the rest of the world. Our absolute favourite thing? A traditional game of *jeu de paume* (court tennis) in Artignosc.

LE MISTRAL

Legends swirl around the mistral, France's most famous wind. This cold, sustained wind gusts for days on end through the Rhône Valley, into Provence and out to the Mediterranean Sea. It can occur throughout the year, but it's most common in winter and early spring.

The mistral above lavender fields

Weather Through the Year

JANUARY	FEBRUARY	MARCH	APRIL	MAY	JUNE
Ave daytime max: **10°C**	Ave daytime max: **11°C**	Ave daytime max: **15°C**	Ave daytime max: **18°C**	Ave daytime max: **22°C**	Ave daytime max: **26.6°C**
Days of rainfall: **5**	Days of rainfall: **4**	Days of rainfall: **4**	Days of rainfall: **4**	Days of rainfall: **5**	Days of rainfall: **4**

SNOWFALL

Snow flurries are a rare sight on the coast, but the first dusting of snow blankets the ski resorts of the Côte d'Azur and Alpes-de-Haute-Provence in early December. Snow cover is at its most abundant in January; by March, much has melted away.

Plan in Advance Festivals & Events

Monaco goes motorsport crazy when the F1 roadshow rolls into town. The legendary **Monaco Grand Prix** (p92) is now joined on the event calendar by the **Monaco ePrix** and, every second year, the **Grand Prix Historique de Monaco**. **May**.

Classic and modern sailing yachts with a fiery competitive streak hoist their sails for over a week of racing – and the chance for serious bragging rights – during the **Voiles de St-Tropez** (p107) in the Golfe de St-Tropez. **September**.

Avignon turns 'on' and 'off' as papal courtyards, gardens and chapels transmute into stages for the annual **Festival d'Avignon** (p184) performing arts fest. **July**.

Film stars from around the world dress in their red carpet best for film screenings and press calls during the **Festival de Cannes** (p78). The atmosphere is electric. **May**

Celebrate Culture & Tradition

Mandelieu-La Napoule goes mimosa mad when the soft golden pom-poms burst into bloom. The **Fête du Mimosa** (p83) is a five-day festival of flower parades, evening animations and fireworks. **February**

The Camargue breaks out in an explosion of guitars, dancers and mounted cowboys as itinerant communities of Romanies, Manouches, Tziganes and Gitans converge for the annual **Pèlerinage des Gitans** (p172). **May**

The impromptu street corner acoustic gigs and bigger DJ parties of the **Fête de la Musique** mark midsummer across France; in Provence and the Côte d'Azur you can party till dawn in Nice and Marseille. **June**

Up to 15,000 spectators have been known to flock to Provence's iconic lavender crop at the **Corso de Lavande** (p230) in Digne-les-Bains. The dress code? Purple. **August**

Cotignac (p123)

AUTUMN STORMS

October and November are the rainiest months in the region; the changing seasons can also bring heavy storms. In 2020, Storm Alex burst river banks and washed away homes (and lives) in the mountain communities of the Côte d'Azur. The scars are still visible.

JULY	AUGUST	SEPTEMBER	OCTOBER	NOVEMBER	DECEMBER
Ave daytime max: **29°C**	Ave daytime max: **29°C**	Ave daytime max: **25°C**	Ave daytime max: **20°C**	Ave daytime max: **14°C**	Ave daytime max: **11°C**
Days of rainfall: **2**	Days of rainfall: **3**	Days of rainfall: **5**	Days of rainfall: **7**	Days of rainfall: **6**	Days of rainfall: **5**

⊛ I LIVE HERE

Jeany Cronk is a winemaker and co-founder of the Maison Mirabeau in Cotignac @MaisonMirabeau

The shoulder seasons, when it's sunny and less busy, are perfect for a visit. In early summer the vineyards are lush, the sea is warm enough for a swim and long lunches beckon. The light in September has a gorgeous intensity and everything is bathed in the soft rays. Both periods are great to embark on scenic drives and visit the towns along the Côte d'Azur.

Valensole (p240)

GET PREPARED FOR
PROVENCE &
THE CÔTE D'AZUR

Useful things to load in your bag, your ears and your brain

Clothes

Evening wear Pack a fancy frock and dress shirt for a big night out in Monaco and Cannes, but the rest of Provence and the Côte d'Azur is refreshingly relaxed about dress code.

Layers Summer nights in coastal Provence are sultry, but sunny spring and autumn days can quickly turn cold after dusk, so keep a warm jacket handy. The villages of Alpes-de-Haute-Provence are always a few degrees cooler, so layer up. even in July and August.

Shoes Flip-flops are standard uniform for beach days, but if you're planning a mountain scramble or bike ride, sneakers or hiking shoes are a must. Nice's pebbly beaches are notoriously uncomfortable;

shops facing the Promenade des Anglais sell plastic jelly shoes.

Hats In a region blessed with 300 days of sunshine, a hat is always recommended.

Manners

Covid-19 may have put a pause on *la bise* (the cheek-to-cheek air kiss), but the classic French custom is back. Just so there's no confusion, in Provence it's a peck on both cheeks.

Toast to new friendships by looking directly in the eyes of your companions as you clink glasses. *Santé!*

The **middle finger** is considered extremely offensive in France.

📖 READ

A Year in Provence
(Peter Mayle; 1989)
Mayle's humorous
account of moving to
Provence is the stuff
dreams are made of.

**The Man Who Planted
Trees** (Jean Giono; 1953)
Manosque-born Giono's
tale is a powerful
environmental allegory.

The French Riviera
(Ted Jones; 2004) The
Côte d'Azur through the
eyes of the authors and
artists who have made
it home.

**The Count of Monte
Cristo** (Alexandre
Dumas; 1844)The
Château d'If is Dantès'
island prison in this epic
tale of revenge.

Words

As the second-most-visited destination in the world's most-visited country, chances are that the local you're conversing with has better English than your French. But that doesn't mean that your effort with a few basic won't go unnoticed. The accent here can be vastly different to what you've been learning online. Closer to Marseille, see if you can make out the distinctive Provençal twang, or what sounds like an 'ng' added to the end of words ending in -ain, such as *pain* (bread) and *demain* (tomorrow).

Here's a basic vocabulary to get you started.

Bonjour (bon-zhoor) means 'good day' and is how you say hello in France.

Bonsoir (bon-swah) means 'good evening' and is how you say hello after around 6pm.

Au revoir (o-rer-vwa) means 'goodbye', but is very formal.

The increasingly universal *ciao* is more casual.

A bientôt (ah-byen-toe) means 'see you soon', even if soon is next week.

Ça va? (sa va) means 'How are you?' and is also repeated as a reply: 'I'm fine'.

S'il vous plaît (seel-voo-play) means 'please'.

Merci (mair-see) means 'thank you'.

De rien (der-ree-en) means 'you're welcome'.

Je m'appelle ... (zher ma-pel) is how to say 'My name is ...'.

Parlez-vous anglais? (par-lay voo ong-glay) is how to politely ask 'Do you speak English?'

Je ne comprends pas (zher ner kom-pron pa) means 'I don't understand'.

Excusez-moi (ek-skew-zay-mwa) means 'excuse me' when you're passing through crowded streets or if you want to stop to ask for directions.

▶️ WATCH

La Gloire de Mon Père (1990, above) Based on Marcel Pagnol's two-part coming-of-age classic.

Brice de Nice (2005) A bleached-blond surfer longing for the perfect wave in Nice's flat sea; a cult comedy.

Marseille (2016) Gérard Depardieu takes the lead role in this French Netflix political drama.

Le Gendarme de Saint-Tropez (1964) Slapstick classic that pits policeman Louis de Funès against a nudist community.

To Catch a Thief (1955) The film that brought Grace Kelly to Prince Rainier III's Monaco.

🎧 LISTEN

Riviera Radio Tune to FM 106.5 between Menton and St-Tropez for the Côte d'Azur's only English-language radio station.

Mon Paradis (Christoph Maé; 2007) Carpentras-born Maé's guitar-driven French pop is the perfect summer soundtrack.

La Solitude (Léo Ferré; 1971) Melody and melancholy in equal serves from the celebrated Monegasque singer-songwriter-poet.

13'Organisé (Jul; 2020) An album that brings together 50 rappers from Marseille; the lead single *Bande Organisée* broke French streaming records.

Cheese from Banon (p235)

THE **FOOD** SCENE

Colourful homespun ingredients rich in flavour: Provençal cuisine brings a taste of sunshine to every bite.

The cuisine of Provence reflects its snug geographic location at the intersection of two great food cultures. The ingredients that spring to mind when you think about northern French food, such as lashings of butter or thick cream, are notably absent; in their place are the olive oils and wild herbs more associated with Italy. Focaccia and chickpea-based street-food snacks also share more similarities with their neighbour. No great surprise, when you consider how fluid the modern-day borderlines have been.

Flavour-rich seasonal produce – peppers, courgettes, leafy greens and aubergines – that can thrive in dry Mediterranean soils form the base for many regional specialities, served alongside small fish caught from the shore, or, more infrequently, meat. Slow-cooked stews and soups that soften cheaper cuts of meat or bony fish have become culinary classics; something you'll agree with after your first bowl of bouillabaisse in Marseille.

In essence, this is simple, fresh, local cuisine at its best. Today, that's to everyone's tastes.

The Home Pantry

Peek inside the cupboards of a Provençal kitchen and you'll find staples such as a bottle of olive oil, most likely pressed from local olive groves and picked up at the weekly produce markets. Alongside it, other essential ingredients include coarse salt from the Camargue, to use in cooking and sprinkle over summer tomatoes cut into wedges. Some-

Best Provençal Dishes	AÏOLI	ARTICHOKES À LA BARIGOULE	DAUBE	RAVIOLIS NIÇOIS
	Garlicky mayonnaise that accompanies a variety of dishes.	Artichoke stew that can be savoured as a main or a side.	A slow-cooked beef stew, often accompanied by polenta.	Fresh pasta stuffed with *daube* and Swiss chard.

where on the shelves, you'll spot a jar or two of tapenade, a spread made of finely chopped olives, with other variations including chickpeas and anchovies. In the fridge, sheets of fresh *raviolis niçois* (beef filling) are on hand for quick and tasty lunches, while a pretty ceramic fruit bowl brims with garden lemons.

Vegetarians, Vegans and Gluten-Free

Made from little more than chickpea flour, water, olive oil and salt, Provence's two quintessential street snacks, *socca* and *panisse*, are suitable for vegetarian, vegan *and* gluten-free diets. But a lack of ingredients doesn't equate to a lack of flavour – something you'll realise the first time you bite into either, whether it's a thin and crispy slice of *socca* or a chip-like portion of *panisse*. The chickpea has taken to the coastal soil, and this cheap but nutritious legume features heavily in salads and soups – it's even pureed into spreads. Another beloved local dish, ratatouille, is a simmering delight and bursts with the flavours of the summer harvest.

Meat and Cheese

Provence's culinary traditions are notably free of two mainstays in French cuisine: beef and cow's milk cheeses. That's because this is a region where sheep and goats are the principal livestock, reared in alpine pastures. Lamb from Sisteron in the Alpes-de-Haute-Provence is a quality marker around the country, while in the Vallée de la Roya, the Brigasque is a milk-producing breed of sheep valued for its dairy products. The most famous cheese of the region hails from the small village of Banon. Known by the same name, this creamy goat cheese comes wrapped in soft chestnut leaves.

ANNABREIT/GETTY IMAGES ©

FOOD & WINE FESTIVALS

Fête du Citron (p70) Menton celebrates its juicy golden lemons during this February carnival celebration, complete with fabulous floats made out of citrus.

Oursinade (p150) Feast on fresh sea urchins by the ocean the first three Sundays in February at Carry-le-Rouet on Marseille's Côte Bleue.

Fête des Vendanges (p109) Toast to the new vintage of Provence rosé at Ste-Maxime's grape harvest festival held the first weekend of September.

Fête du Fromage (p236) Every May, the lavender-fringed village of Banon throws a huge party in honour of its eponymous goat's cheese wrapped in a chestnut leaf.

Fête de la Châtaigne (p126) Aromas of roasting chestnuts fill the air and sweet chestnut liqueur fills glasses in Provence's chestnut capital, Collobrières, the last three Sundays in October.

KIKOFOUNDIT/SHUTTERSTOCK ©

Socca (p40)

Fête du Citron (p70), Menton

BOUILLABAISSE	SOUPE AU PISTOU	LES PETITS FARCIS NIÇOIS	SÜGELI
Rust-coloured fish stew and *the* emblematic dish of Marseille.	Rustic legume and vegetable-packed soup.	Colourful market vegetables stuffed with mince and herbs.	A pleated pasta shell inscribed on France's list of intangible cultural heritage.

Local Specialities

Street Food and Snacks

Pissaladière Pizza topped with caramelised onions, olives and anchovies.
Socca Thin chickpea-flour pancake baked in woodfire ovens across Nice.
Panisse Chickpea-flour fritters: crispy on the outside, creamy on the inside.
Pizza moitié-moitié Half anchovies, half emmental cheese – a must in Marseille.
Barbajuan Small fried ravioli and Monaco's national dish.

Sweet Treats

Tarte Tropézienne A brioche sliced in two, filled with two types of cream and dusted with pearl sugar.
Tourte aux Blettes Sucrée Savoury Swiss chard in a sweet tart.
Nougat Chewy honey-and-almond confection from Sault.
Tarte des Alpes Looks like a lattice-crust pie filled with jam; tastes like childhood.
Calissons d'Aix Diamond-shaped almond-and-fruit sweet from Aix-en-Provence.

Dare to Try

Saucisson de Taureau Bull sausage; trademark of the Camargue.

Pissaladière

Pieds Paquets Slow-cooked lamb trotters and tripe stew.
Merda di Can Get past the name and you've got a plate of fresh green gnocchi in Nice.

Local Liqueurs

Genepi Fiery herbal liqueur that warms up mountain communities.
L'Orangeraie Zesty liqueur made from Monaco's very own bitter orange trees.
Pastis The aniseed drink Provence has exported to the world.
Liqueur de Lavande Provence's emblematic lavender crop in a bottle.

THE YEAR IN FOOD

SPRING

Greens from Provence include asparagus, beans and Swiss chard. Look for the telltale purple tips on *violet de Provence* artichokes, considered the cream of the crop. Families feast on Sisteron lamb at Easter.

SUMMER

Markets explode with the reds, yellows and oranges of freshly picked strawberries, tasty cantaloupes, and juicy tomatoes of all shapes and sizes. Peppers, courgettes and aubergines abound for classic ratatouille.

AUTUMN

Chestnuts crackle on open fires. Pumpkins and squashes of all colours sprout; scoop out the seeds and stuff them with cèpes from the Luberon. Olive trees are shaken down and pressed for a new vintage.

WINTER

Foodies hunt out truffles in the Luberon, sea urchins in Marseille and Menton's beloved lemons. The rich aroma of daube fills the crisp air. Christmas is celebrated with oysters, foie gras and 13 desserts!

Calissons d'Aix-en-Provence

VOLKER RAUCH/SHUTTERSTOCK ©

Hiking, Verdon Gorge (p238)

THE OUTDOORS

Hike majestic mountain ranges, cycle lavender-scented plains and stretch out by the glistening sea: in Provence and the Côte d'Azur, the good life is outdoors.

Where the Alps tumble into the Mediterranean Sea, outdoor enthusiasts are spoilt for choice no matter the experience level. Add in a mild climate and you've got hiking and cycling trails to set off on no matter the month. In winter, the low-key ski resorts of the Alpes-de-Haute-Provence come alive with the first snowfall. Spring signals the start of a new watersports season, from high-octane rafting and canyoning in the Gorges du Verdon to leisurely swimming and sailing along the Côte d'Azur.

Cycling

Home to bucket-list climbs such as the Col de la Madone de Gorbio, Col de la Bonette and, of course, the holy grail, Mont Ventoux, Provence is quite literally the training ground for the world's best road cyclists. You don't have to be an Olympic athlete to enjoy the view from the saddle, however: the quieter back roads of the Luberon and Provence Verte snake through fragranced fields and postcard-pretty villages, although you're never too far from the next incline. The TransVerdon is one of France's classic mountain bike trails. In summer, the ski runs behind Nice and in the Alpes-de-Haute-Provence turn into shaded off-road routes.

Road bikes *(vélo de route)*, mountain bikes *(VTT, vélo tout-terrain)* and e-bikes are available to hire across the region. Alongside local tourist offices for maps and

Thrills & Spills

ROCK CLIMBING
The limestone cliffs of Buoux (p210) rise high above the Luberon and are a legendary destination for climbers.

CANYONING
Jump, slide and rappel down ravines and waterfalls in the **Gorges du Verdon** (p238) and the **Gorges du Loup** (p90).

KITESURFING
For kitesurfers, the wild, windswept landscape of the lagoon beach of Beauduc (p167) is a scene of pure beauty.

FAMILY ADVENTURES

Saddle up for horse-riding adventures through the flamingo-speckled wetlands and beaches of the **Camargue** (p168).
Swim with shoals of dreamfish and skim over lazy sea cucumbers during summer's guided snorkel tours at **Domaine du Rayol** (p104).

Step into a real-life wildlife documentary at the **Parc Ornithologique du Pont de Gau** (p175) nature reserve in the Camargue.
Spot cute marmots and striking chamois as you hike into the **Parc National du Mercantour** (p73) from St-Martin-Vésubie.

Clip into the Via Ferrata du Rocher de Neuf Heures (p231) in Digne-les-Bains, a climbing route with fixed cables and ladders.
Snowshoe through enchanting snow-dusted forests in **Le Sauze** (p245) in the Ubaye Valley.

---

guides, bike cafes *(cafés vélo)* are emerging as hubs to connect with fellow cyclists, learn about local routes, sign up for group hikes and sip a seriously good coffee.

Hiking

Provence and the Côte d'Azur's postcard landscape of high hills, dizzying gorges and rocky coastlines is a delight to navigate on foot, from sweeping mountain treks across long-distance GR *(Grande Randonnée)* trails to short but steep coastal scrambles and flat island paths that weave through fragrant pine forests. Even in the bigger cities, you're never too far from a *sentier balisé* (marked path); the local tourist office hands out maps and guides, and will also point out accessible hiking trails.

Being prepared is essential; hiking shoes, water, hat and sunscreen are a must. A phone signal isn't guaranteed. The most popular trails are hot and busy in summer – high wildfire risks shutter some forested paths as well. Spring and autumn days enjoy ideal temperatures and conditions.

Skiing

In the Alpes-de-Haute-Provence, the Ubaye Valley is a sleeper of a ski hotspot where those in the know find snow even during dry winters. With 180km of runs, Pra Loup (1600m) is the largest resort in the valley and also has snowshoeing and cross-country skiing trails, as well as modern facilities. The station connects with Foux d'Allos (1800m).

The Côte d'Azur is one of the rare places where you can swim in the morning (if you dare) and be on the slopes by lunch with the closest resorts just 1½ hours from Nice. From the summit of Isola 2000 (2610m), you can see back down to the Mediterranean Sea. As unlikely as it might sound, Provence might just become your next favourite winter sports destination.

ICE BREAKERS

For more alpine activities see page 247

Isola 2000 (p75)

ALEXANDER SCHMITZ/SHUTTERSTOCK ©

RAFTING
Whether it's your first or one-hundredth time, the whitewater rapids of the Gorges du Verdon (p239) and the Ubaye (p244) promise thrills and spills.

DIVING
Wreck diving doesn't come much better than the *Grec* and *Donator* sites off the l'Île de Porquerolles (p114).

SWIMMING
Monaco's Solarium (p99) is made of concrete, but this swimming and sunning spot on the harbour breakwater is totally unique.

SAILING
Learn the ropes on a cool catamaran in the Golfe de St-Tropez (p104) and come back to crew up for the Voiles de St-Tropez in September.

ACTION AREAS

Where to find Provence & the Côte d'Azur's best outdoor activities.

Walking/Hiking

1. Calanque d'En-Vau (p146)
2. Gorges du Verdon (p238)
3. Moustiers-Ste-Marie (p242)
4. Réserve Naturelle de la Plaine des Maures (p111)
5. Île de Porquerolles (p114)
6. Sentier Nietzsche (p64)
7. Gordes (p206)

Cycling

1. Stes-Maries-de-la-Mer (p173)
2. Gorges du Verdon (p237)
3. Ubaye Valley (p246)
4. Île de Porquerolles (p114)
5. Cotignac (p123)
6. Mont Ventoux (p198, 200-1)
7. Coustellet (p216)

Boating

1. St-Jean-Cap-Ferrat (p70)
2. Parc National des Calanques (p146)
3. Vieux Port, Marseille (p141)
4. St-Tropez (p104)
5. Ubaye Valley (p244)

FRANCE

Faucon

Mont Ventoux

Vacqueyras

Orange

Châteauneuf-du-Pape

Carpentras

Gorges de la Nesque

Sault

FRANCE

Banon

Venasque

Col de Murs

Forcalquier

Avignon

Sorgue

Rhône

Viens

Coustellet

Apt

Calavon

Cereste

Durance

Cavaillon

Montagne de Luberon

Mourre Nègre

Tarascon

Parc Naturel Régional du Luberon

Eygalières

Lourmarin

Parc Naturel Régional des Alpilles

Salon-de-Provence

Durance

Arles

Meyrargues

Rians

St-Martin-de-Crau

St-Cannat

Mt Ste-Victoire

Aigues-Mortes

Parc Naturel Régional de Camargue

Le Sambuc

Aix-en-Provence

Le Tholonet

St-Maximin-la-Ste-Baume

Trets

Stes-Maries-de-la-Mer

Étang de Vaccarès

Port de Bouc

Étang de Berre

Port St-Louis du Rhône

Golfe du Lion

Châteauneuf-les-Martigues

Massif de la Ste-Baume

Carry-le-Rouet

Marseille

Mont Puget

Les Goudes

Cassis

Ollioules

Port d'Alon

Mediterranean Sea

N
0   40 km
0   20 miles

National Parks

1 Parc National de Port-Cros (p116)
2 Parc National des Calanques (p146)
3 Mont Ventoux (p196)
4 Gorges du Verdon (p237)
5 Réserve Géologique de Haute-Provence (p234)
6 Parc National du Mercantour (p243)
7 Parc Naturel Régional des Préalpes d'Azur (p90)

FRANCE

ITALY

La Mortice

Lac de Serre-Ponçon

St-Paul-sur-Ubaye

Le Lauzet-Ubaye

Barcelonnette

L'Ubaye

La Tête de la Sestrière

St-Étienne-de-Tinée

Punta Marguareis

Col de Tende

La Foux d'Allos

Barles

Mont Mounier

Parc National du Mercantour

Le Boreon

Tende

Réserve Géologique de Haute Provence

Blône

Thorame-Haute

Col de St-Michel

Guillaumes

Mont Bégo

l'Arpette

Digne-les-Bains

Annot

Var

Villars-sur-Var

Gorges de Daluis

St-Andre-les-Alpes

FRANCE

Lac de Castillon

Gorges de la Vésubie

Angoustre

Rougon

St-Martin du Var

Menton

Parc Naturel Régional du Verdon

Verdon

Collet Barris

Grand Plan de Canjuers

Bargème

Loup

La Colle Loubière

Eze

MONACO

Nice

Côte d'Azur

Montmeyan

Châteaudouble

St-Laurent-du-Var

Col de la Grange

Grasse

St-Laurent-du-Var

Lac de St-Cassien

Cotignac

Antibes

Châteauvert

Argens

Le Muy

Mt Vinaigre

Cannes

Îles de Lérins

Le Luc

Agay

St-Raphaël

Les Issambres

La Sauvette

Golfe de St-Tropez

Cuers

Collobrières

St-Tropez

Massif des Maures

Domaine du Rayol

Côte d'Azur

Hyères

Bormes-les-Mimosas

Mediterranean Sea

Port d'Hyères

Porquerolles

Parc national de Port-Cros

Snorkelling/Diving

1 Parc Marin Côte Bleue (p150)
2 Ste-Maxime (p108)
3 Île de Porquerolles (p114)
4 Îles des Lérins (p81)
5 Domaine du Rayol (p104)

PROVENCE & THE CÔTE D'AZUR

THE GUIDE

Alpes-de-Haute-Provence
p227
The Vaucluse
& Luberon
p178
Côte d'Azur
& Monaco
p48
Bouches-du-Rhône
p131
The Var
p100

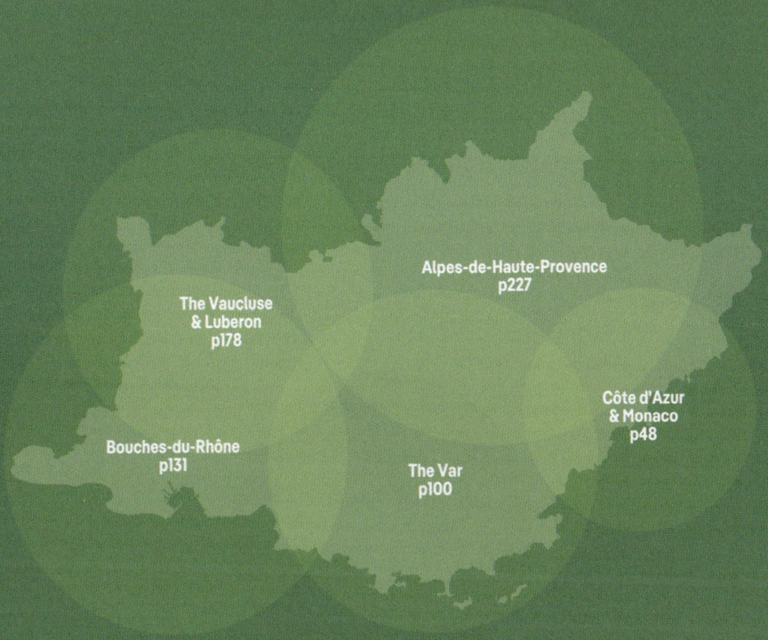

Chapters in this section are organised by hubs and their surrounding areas. We see the hub as your base in the destination, where you'll find unique experiences, local insights, insider tips and expert recommendations. It's also your gateway to the surrounding area, where you'll see what and how much you can do from there.

View of Nice from Èze Village (p67)

REMEDIOS/GETTY IMAGES ©

Côte d'Azur & Monaco

WHERE THE MOUNTAINS MEET THE MEDITERRANEAN

A world-famous coastline, entrancing hilltop villages and an emerging hinterland scene: the Côte d'Azur and Monaco is eternally chic, but there are new surprises waiting.

What's in a name? In 1887, the French writer Stéphen Liégard set off on a journey across France's eastern Mediterranean coastline, chronicling his experiences in the book *La Côte d'Azur*. Until just a few decades before, this corner of the country had acted as little more than a stopover point for intrepid travellers en route to Italy, but that was changing as a new train line unfurled from the north, bringing with it foreigners waving doctors' prescriptions for a healthy dose of the region's winter sun. Nobility, artists and royalty soon followed, ready to flaunt their best dress on waterfront promenades and in the black-tie casinos. Liégard's Côte d'Azur cast a wide net from Marseille to Genoa, but the name he coined stuck.

There's still no hard and fast starting and finishing point – you'll see the Côte d'Azur defined as stretching all the way to St-Tropez or Hyères in the Var – but what's not debated is that the sweep from Cannes to Menton, or the boundary of the Alpes-Maritimes, is France's glittering blue coast. Princely Monaco lies in its embrace. The Côte d'Azur maintains a glorious allure with its intoxicating mix of sun, sea, culture, food and wine, and the green mountain interior beckoning today's batch of adventure travellers.

MATEJ KASTELIC/SHUTTERSTOCK ©

Inset: Casino de Monte-Carlo (p96); Opposite: Villefranche-sur-Mer (p68)

THE MAIN AREAS

NICE
Beaches, architecture and a blossoming foodie scene.
p54

CANNES
Flashy festivals and refreshingly quiet spaces.
p77

MONACO
Small in size, big on glamour.
p92

Find Your Way

Tucked in the southeastern nook of France, the lively resort towns along the coast quickly give way to inland villages. Behind them, vast national parks stretch across mountain landscapes.

Greolières

Loup

Plateau de Calern

Bramafan

Courmes

Courmettes

Gourdon

Le Bar-sur-Loup

Châteauneuf de Grasse

Parc Naturel Régional du Verdon

St-Cézaire-sur-Siagne

FRANCE

Grasse

Valbonne

Peymeinade

Seillans

Tourettes

Claviers

Lac de St-Cassien

Mouans-Sartoux

Auribeau-sur-Siagne

Mougins

Le Cannet

Cannes, p77

A busy calendar of global events gives Cannes a year-round buzz, although neighbourhoods like Le Suquet and the Marché Forville add a low-key flavour.

Cannes

Mandelieu-La Napoule

Golfe de Napoule

La Napoule

Palm Beach

Île Ste-Marguerite

Île St-Honorat

△ *Mt Vinaigre*

Le Trayas

Massif de l'Estérel

△ *Pic du Cap Roux*

Le Muy

Argens

Puget-sur-Argens

Fréjus

Valescure

Agay

Anthéor

Corniche de l'Estérel

St-Raphaël

Boulouris

Cap du Dramont

Plage De L'île D'or

Golfe de Fréjus

St-Aygulf

Côte d'Azur

BUS

Cheap and comprehensive, the Zou! intercity bus network links Cannes and Nice with smaller towns both along the coast and further inland, although expect longer travel times than the train when given a choice between the two.

Les Issambres

St-Maxime

Port Grimaud

Golfe de St-Tropez

Cap de St-Tropez

St-Tropez

Mediterranean Sea

50

N 0 ___ 10 km
   0 ___ 5 miles

OPPOSITE L-R: FISHMAN64/SHUTTERSTOCK ©, SYLVAIN SONNET/GETTY IMAGES ©

ITALY

FRANCE

Nice, p54

The capital of the Côte d'Azur, Nice's richly coloured Belle Époque streetscapes are recognised by Unesco, while foodies are waking up to the city's cuisine.

Monaco, p92

With a princely palace and glitter-ball casino framing the yacht-lined harbour, Monaco is a postage-sized principality that packs a punch.

Mediterranean Sea

CAR

Driving is a hassle in Nice, Cannes and Monaco, but your own transport is the best way to see the Côte d'Azur that exists beyond these busy destinations.

TRAIN

The scenic TER Sud Provence Alpes-Côte-d'Azur train line connects the region's main seafront destinations between Cannes and Menton (including Monaco) and beats taking the car every time. A train service also links Grasse to the coast.

Plan Your Time

Get your share of both beach and culture along the coast and make easy day trips to pretty perched villages. Cool down in the mountain landscapes of the Côte d'Azur backcountry for hiking and wildlife spotting.

Vielle Ville (p57), Nice

Weekend Break

● Base yourself in **Nice** (p54) and get a taste for the city over a long brunch at **Marinette** (p61) before setting off on a walking tour of **Vieux Nice** (p57).

● Hop on the bus for the short ride around the headland to the charming fishing village of **Villefranche-sur-Mer** (p64), and wander the alleyways that lead down to a shimmering bay.

● Return to Nice for **apéro** (p59) followed by dinner at one of the new wave of restaurants reinventing **Niçoise cuisine** (p61).

● The next day, after a morning stroll along the Prom, catch the train to the world's second-smallest country, **Monaco** (p92).

Seasonal Highlights

The Côte d'Azur's winters are sunny and mild and the heat of summer is punctuated by refreshing sea breezes.

JANUARY
The **Route du Mimosa** bursts into bloom around Mandelieu-La Napoule. Ski season is in full swing just an hour from Cannes.

FEBRUARY
A frenzy of winter festivals including the **Carnaval de Nice** and **Fête du Citron** (p70) in Menton.

MAY
May is a mammoth month of public holidays, the **Cannes Film Festival** and the **Monaco Formula One Grand Prix**.

Five Days to Travel Around

● Still based in Nice, savour a local **breakfast** (p60) and learn more about its newly minted **Unesco status** (p54).

● With more nights you can extend your reach towards lemon-scented **Menton** (p70) on the Italian border, and scale the heights of **St-Agnès** (p72), Europe's highest coastal village, as well as other delightful **perched communities** (p73).

● Wake up for an early departure on the **Train des Merveilles** (p74) for a day trip to experience the Côte d'Azur's alpine side. The train also makes easy work of excursions to starstruck **Cannes** (p77) and artsy **Antibes** (p86).

Longer Than a Week

● After a few nights exploring Nice and Monaco, head west along the coast to Cannes, where the handprints of Hollywood stars are permanently cast outside the famous **Palais des Festivals et des Congrès** (p78).

● Hop on the short ferry ride to the **Île Ste-Marguerite** (p80), a pine-scented oasis off the coast, for a day looking back at the bay.

● After your fill of freshly cooked *fleurs de courgettes* from **Marché Forville** (p81), set off in the footsteps of **Picasso** (p87).

● Add on an extra night or two in perfumed **Grasse** (p88) with the **Gorges du Loup** (p90) on its doorstep.

JUNE

The summer solstice is celebrated in style: **La Fête de la Musique** is a France-wide affair but particularly rocks in Nice.

JULY

Every weekend buzzes with an outdoor event: fireworks, music, cinema. The region is packed to the rafters.

SEPTEMBER

The last days of summer are a dream for hiking and cycling in the backcountry.

DECEMBER

First flurries of snow and first mugs of mulled wine at Christmas markets, particularly in Nice, Antibes and Monaco.

Nice

Nice

GETTING AROUND

Ditch the car on your visit to Nice; driving in the centre is an increasingly frustrating and unpredictable experience. Many of the main highlights can be navigated on foot. For Ligne d'Azur's tram line and extensive bus network, tickets (€1.70 single fare) are paperless; you will have to spend an extra €2 on your first trip for the city's transport card, La Carte, available at ticket machines and booths. Near the airport, Nice St-Augustin is emerging as the main transport hub, but for the moment remains a work-in-progress, so it's worth double-checking any intercity bus departure points.

☑ TOP TIP

If you're arriving by air and travelling light, consider walking the 6km Promenade des Anglais from the airport to the city centre. The wide, beachfront pedestrian promenade is a delightful introduction to Nice's outdoor lifestyle. Similarly, there's also a bike lane – pick up a shared e-bike at the airport.

The capital of the Côte d'Azur, Nice has undergone a complete refresh in the last decade or so, with investments in a smart tram network, upgraded civic areas and new hotels – and the pace of change doesn't look like it's going to slow down anytime soon. Don't be surprised to find certain landmarks from past visits closed for renovation, or even torn down, as concrete makes way for greenery in France's fifth-largest city.

As the Unesco Winter Resort Town of the Riviera, the city has a new purpose and swagger. Nice is no longer living off its reputation for beaches, palm trees and sunshine. An exciting food scene is simmering, bringing local produce and traditional cuisine to the fore, alongside cool wine bars and independent boutiques in trendy yet local neighbourhoods such as the Port and Libération. Visit today and you'll realise that Nice is finally growing into its nickname, Nissa la Bella.

Experience Nice's Protected History

A Unesco World Heritage site

Before the Côte d'Azur became the place to sun yourself in summer, this stretch of the Mediterranean coast was the winter destination *du jour* for royalty, politicians, aristocrats and artists from Britain, northern Europe and Russia. The rich legacy of this winter high season (1760–1940) can be seen in around 800 buildings across the city. Now inscribed on the Unesco World Heritage list, Nice is known as the Winter Resort Town of the Riviera. To understand exactly what this means, the **Mission Nice Patrimoine Mondial** at the entrance to Vieux Nice is an excellent starting point, with large information boards devoted to the period. You'll visit the Mission with a guide on the Centre du Patrimoine's weekly 1½-hour English-language walking tour (When Nice Invented the Riviera), as well as several significant sights around the 19th-century **Opéra de Nice**. Your guide also holds the key to

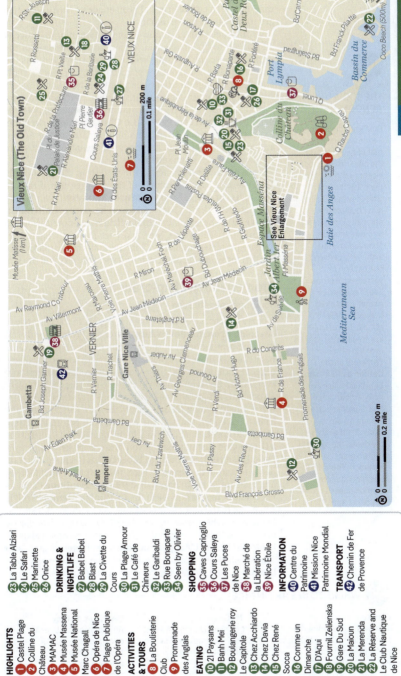

Vieux Nice (The Old Town)

HIGHLIGHTS
1 Castel Plage
2 Colline du Château
3 MAMAC
4 Musée Massena
5 Musée National Marc Chagall
6 Opéra de Nice
7 Plage Publique de l'Opéra

ACTIVITIES & TOURS
8 La Boulisterie Club
9 Promenade des Anglais

EATING
10 21 Paysans
11 Banh Mei
12 Boulangerie roy Le Capitole
13 Chez Acchiardo
14 Chez Davia
15 Chez René Socca
16 Comme un Dimanche
17 D'Aqui
18 Fournil Zelienska
19 Gare Du Sud
20 La Maïoun
21 La Merenda
22 La Réserve and Le Club Nautique de Nice
23 La Table Alziari
24 Le Safari
25 Marinette
26 Onice

DRINKING & NIGHTLIFE
27 Babel Babel
28 Blast
29 La Civette du Cours
30 La Plage Amour
31 Le Café de Chineurs
32 Le Garibaldi
33 Rue Bonaparte
34 Seen by Olivier

SHOPPING
35 Caves Caprioglio
36 Cours Saleya
37 Les Puces de Nice
38 Marché de la Libération
39 Nice Étoile

INFORMATION
40 Centre du Patrimoine
41 Mission Nice Patrimoine Mondial

TRANSPORT
42 Chemin de Fer de Provence

THE BOOM AT NOON

Nice's midday cannon – a loud boom at noon that rings out across the city – makes most visitors jump out of their skin the first time they hear it. The noisy custom was originally instigated by a wintering Brit, Thomas Coventry, in the 19th-century. The cannon of yesteryear has now been replaced by a small colourless firework that is set off rain, hail or shine in a small gated yard near the Israelite Cemetery on the **Colline du Château** by either Philippe or Kelly Arnello, a father and daughter duo and trained pyrotechnicians. For the city's residents, the sound is the signal to stop for lunch. There's only one day when the cannon doesn't go off at noon: 1 April.

Les Ponchettes, the rooftops of the traditional fishing shacks that once formed the original promenade of Nice and which are today closed to the public.

An interactive map found at patrimoinemondial.nice.fr allows you to undertake your own urban exploration of the sights (choose the heading 'sector description') and links to a complete historical outline of each listing. Art deco details and Belle Époque flourishes can be found on almost every street, but most are now private residences to admire from the outside only. Others are restaurants, including portside neighbours **La Réserve** and **Le Club Nautique de Nice**. Expect gastronomic fare with a bill to match at the former and a more casual menu and prices at the latter. Both share the same water's-edge setting.

Set in a shady garden across the road from the beach, Villa Massena is a superb example of the architecture of the era and, in its current guise as the **Musée Massena**, is a museum dedicated to the history of Nice. The entire **Colline du Château** – the city's original settlement, now a wooded outcrop between Vieux Nice and Port Lympia – is another Unesco-protected highlight. Climb the stairs to the top (or take the lift) for sweeping 360-degree views of the city and the sea.

Promenade Art Exploration

Sculptures near the sea

A curve of coast stretching from the airport to the port, Nice's sweeping **Promenade des Anglais** (or the Prom as locals call it) is the beating heart of the city. The flat pedestrian promenade directly above the beach is popular with leisurely walkers, parents with prams, kids on rollerblades, cyclists, joggers and everyone in between. The strip has also become something of an open-air art installation, with a series of statues and sculptures spread among the palm trees that are worth taking the time to consider. Start at the eastern end, before the curve around to Port Lympia, with a selfie on quai Rauba Capeu at the **#ILoveNice** installation. As you head west, keep your eyes peeled for a **replica Statue of Liberty** that is a mere 1.3m tall, just across from the Opéra de Nice. You can't miss what follows, a tall cluster of metal bars called **9 Lignes Obliques** with as many detractors as fans. Next up, **La Chaise Bleue de SAB** is a homage to the blue chairs that line the Prom. First installed in the 1950s, these wooden seats have become one of the classic symbols of the city. Further along, across from the Palais de la Méditerranée, **L'Ange de la Baie** was erected in 2022 as a sober monument in memory of the 86 people who lost their lives on 14 July 2016 in the Nice terrorist attacks.

 WHERE TO SEE ART IN NICE

Cimiez
This hillside neighbourhood is home to the Musée Matisse and Musée National Marc Chagall.

MAMAC
European and American avant-garde works from the 1950s to the present. Renovations are planned.

Les Puces de Nice
An explosion of street art decorates the walls of this small harbourside antiques market.

This colourful meander through Nice's charming old town starts outside the warm yellow façade of ❶ **Nicolas Alziari**, a local olive-oil producer whose distinctive blue tins grace the region's top restaurant tables. The flat stretch of street surrounding the grand 19th-century ❷ **Opéra de Nice** is home to some speciality shops worth browsing for a local souvenir, including the jewel box of a sweet shop ❸ **Maison Auer**, where the same family have been making chocolates for over 200 years. Continue straight ahead to the ❹ **Cours Saleya**, the city's lively restaurant-lined corso and setting for fragrant fresh produce and flower markets (Tuesday to Sunday) and an antique market (Monday). Once drawing inspiration from the scene was artist Henri Matisse, who had his studio inside ❺ **Palais Caïs de Pierlas** at the eastern end between 1921 and 1938. Take a left turn to head deeper into the busy, labyrinth-like alleyways, past the ❻ **Centre du Patrimoine**, whose tours take you deep behind the scenes of the city. On rue Doite, the wood-fired oven at ❼ **Chez Thérésa** has been baking *socca* (chickpea-flour pancakes) since 1925 (fresh platters are also cycled down to a stand on the Cours Saleya markets). The gentle rise is barely noticeable as you continue towards ❽ **Palais Lascaris**, a fresco-adorned 17th-century noble house–turned museum and wonderfully preserved example of baroque architecture. At the next corner, another history lesson awaits, if you can spot it. The heavy ❾ **cannonball** attached to the wall was fired by Turkish forces in 1543 during the Siege of Nice. The city managed to repel the forces and history has turned a local washerwoman called Catherine Ségurane into the heroine of the victory. In ❿ **place St-Augustin**, after a slight uphill stretch, you'll find a plaque in her honour.

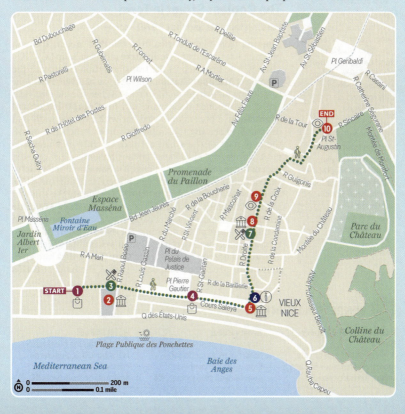

NICE: MORNING, NOON AND NIGHT

Nice-born writer and naturopath **Kalice Brun** shares her perfect day in Nice:

Morning

The best way to start the day is to jump into the sea near the **Club Nautique de Nice**, a place that recalls the Roaring Twenties with its Greek promontory and diving board looking out over the Baie des Anges.

Noon

For lunches that linger, both **La Maioun** on place Garibaldi and **La Table Alziari** in Vieux Nice cook up homemade dishes that remind me of childhood.

Night

I usually return to the old town for *apéro* at **Banh Mei**, a great address for fusion cuisine, or for an intimate dinner at **Onice**, where the next generation is interpreting Mediterranean and Nice *terroir*!

The Coolest Street in Town

Bars, restaurants and the LGBTIQ+ scene

Running from place Garibaldi to the Port, a gentrification program has turned **rue Bonaparte** into Nice's hip LGBTIQ+ district. The first step in the transformation came with the opening of **Malabar Station** (No 10), a gay bar where everyone is welcome for a drink on the terrace. When the old electrical supplies store next door made way for **Comptoir Central Electrique**, a bohemian-styled bar with exposed walls and mismatched seating that retained (almost) the same name, the cool part of town had arrived. Quickly nicknamed le petit Marais, a nod to Paris' famous bohemian gay quarter, part of the road is painted in blue, à la San Francisco's Castro District, and the strip between place Garibaldi and place du Pin is now fully pedestrianised. To celebrate the summer solstice (21 June) and France's annual **Fête de la Musique** celebrations, a massive street party erupts, only winding down in the wee hours of the morning. For the remaining 364 days, the atmosphere is always friendly and welcoming. People from all walks of life come to brunch at **Clay** (No 3), tuck into Mediterranean street food that doesn't break the bank at **Kalōs**

 WHERE TO SLEEP IN NICE

Hostel Villa St-Exupéry Beach

A mix of dorms and private rooms, an enormous bar and a bright, fun party vibe. €

Arome Hôtel

This secure, centrally located hotel run by a wonderful Franco-Italian couple is popular with solo women. €€

Hôtel St Paul

Across from the breakwater in the port, this church-run choice has the best-value seafront rooms in Nice. €€

ELENA ELISSEEVA/SHUTTERSTOCK ©

Promenade des Anglais (p56)

LGBTIQ+ NICE

Jameson Farn, who runs the LGBTIQ+ travel blog *Gay French Riviera*, has the lowdown on Nice's LGBTIQ+ scene. *gayfrenchriviera.com*

The LGBTIQ+ community in the Côte d'Azur continues to flourish, with Nice considered central to everything. Year-round, there is always something to see and do.

In summer, look out for outdoor events such as the **Dolly Parties** and **Pink Parade** (Pride). **Lou Queernaval** runs adjacent to the **Carnaval de Nice** in winter.

The Côte d'Azur covers a wide range of interests, whether it be any number of outside activities, international business networking, luxury shopping, or checking out nightclubs, saunas, cabarets and cruising bars.

(No 11), or catch up with friends over pretty plates at **Café Paulette** (No 15). Just around the corner, at 5 rue Boyer, **21 Paysans** is a delicatessen specialising in local food and flavours, such as the sunshine-filled Pastis de Nice.

A Neighbourhood to Watch

Local vibe with local finds

Gare Thiers was once an unofficial boundary for visitors, and anything further north was of little interest to travellers. But today, venture to Libé, as the cool crowd refers to the Libération neighbourhood just above Nice's main train station, and you'll immediately sense the buzz. Granted, the **Marché de la Libération** (Tuesday to Sunday) produce markets on place du Général de Gaulle has long been considered the city's best – because they serve locals day in, day out, no matter the season. **Gare du Sud**, the old train station on the square, has been recently reborn as a Mediterranean-themed food hall, while its periphery brims with an eclectic mix of fishmongers, global street food flavours and boutiques. You'll also find **l'Altra Casa**, home to the best Aperol spritzes in the city. **Kiosk Tintin** is a curbside counter that draws people north for

WHERE TO SLEEP IN NICE

Hôtel La Perouse
Clinging to the Colline du Château with a hidden pool, this delightful hotel is one of Nice's finest. **€€€**

Hôtel Amour
Uberhip Parisian hotel with an eclectic boho-chic styling and the trendiest hotel bar for miles. **€€€**

Le Negresco
The grande dame of Nice's hotels, each room here is a work of art. A spa and beach club are new additions. **€€€**

tasty *pan bagnat* (salade Niçoise in a sandwich). With over a dozen beers on tap, **Beer District** appeals to libationists, as does the chickpea-infused signature brew at urban brewer **La Brasserie Artisanale de Nice**. Behind Gare du Sud, the **Chemin de Fer de Provence** station is the departure point for the **Train de Pignes**, a charming train line that serves the communities along the River Var en route to Digne-les-Bains.

Sample the Niçoise Culinary Renaissance

Move over, salade Niçoise

Nice's street-food culture is based on the colourful vegetables and legumes that thrive in the poor, water-deprived soils of the Mediterranean coastline. It feels closer to Italy in nature and flavour than the heavier, sauce-based cuisine of northern France. You'll spot the queue at **Chez René Socca** before you see the entrance: this cheap and cheerful Vieux Nice institution is the classic Niçois street-food stop. Newcomer **D'Aqui** in the Port has made a splash as the spot for bite-sized *barbajuans* (a fried ravioli considered Monaco's national dish) to eat in or take away. If you see the Cuisine Nissarde sticker displayed proudly at a restaurant's entrance, you know their dishes respect local culinary traditions: perennial favourites include **Chez Acchiardo** and **Safari** in Vieux Nice and **Lou Balico** just outside it.

Beyond the traditional addresses, a new wave of trendy chefs are putting a fine dining twist on local dishes, elevating them to a semi-gastronomic standing. Opposite the beach on les Ponchettes, **Babel Babel** sprinkles homemade za'atar over *panisse* in a delicious twist, and dishes them up as a gluten-free alternative to chips. To nab one of 24 seats at the wonderfully rustic **La Merenda**, where a rich, slow-cooked *daube* (beef stew) is served with a half moon of crispy yet creamy *panisse*, you'll need to book in advance on its social media pages. You'll also need to book beforehand to savour chef Pierre Altobelli's classy interpretation of classics such as soupe au pistou, salade Niçoise and ratatouille at cosy bistrot **Chez Davia**.

The Best Meal of the Day

Where to breakfast and brunch

An exciting breakfast scene is simmering in Nice, as artisan bakers in unsuspecting neighbourhood bakeries bring high-quality and unusual ingredients into the bakehouse to give a new bite to the classic baguette and croissant. At

WHEN BOULES BECAME COOL

Despite its image as an old man's pastime, boules (or *pétanque* as it is also called) is anything but. Walk past a *terrain de boules* (boules court) and you'll see people of all ages playing the quintessential French afternoon sport.

To play after dark – and to see just how cool boules has become first-hand – plan an evening at **La Boulisterie Club**, a bar and indoor boules court inside an airy converted garage on rue Lascaris in the Port. Here, you'll be able to add all-important accompaniments such as chilled Provence rosé and *panisse* to your game.

The same team are behind a popular hipster boules and clothing store of the same name in the **Nice Étoile** shopping centre.

WHERE TO SHOP IN NICE

Avenue Jean Médécin
Head to Nice's main shopping strip for high-street favourites, as well as the Nice Étoile shopping centre.

Carré d'Or
Nice's fashion set makes a beeline for this chic neighbourhood where indie boutiques stock Parisian labels.

Vieux Nice
Among the tourist traps selling fridge magnets and keyrings, you'll also uncover unique handmade treasures.

ARIANA CAN/SHUTTERSTOCK ©

Sea Urchins, Babel Babel Restaurant

Boulangerie Roy le Capitole, Frederic Roy takes three days to prepare his all-butter croissants from scratch, but you won't pay a centime more than other bakeries for his handmade pastries. He is also the only baker (as far as he knows) in France to bake a delicate lavender-flavoured croissant – but get in early, as they sell out fast. In Vieux Nice, Polish historian-turned-baker Domenika Zelienska is bringing long-forgotten local flours, such as *pétanielle noire de Nice*, back to her eponymous bakehouse, **Fournil Zelienska**. Not only are her tartines ideal to takeaway for breakfast on the beach but, as she explains it, the breads are also better for both our digestion and the environment.

Not to be outdone, the brunch scene is similarly exciting. On the ubercool rue Lascaris in the Port, the owners of **Comme un Dimanche** bring culinary lessons from their three years in Australia back home, serving up favourites from down under such as smashed avo on toast and bacon and egg rolls, but with a French twist. The brunch menu recommends two to three dishes per person, but they can be filling so start with one and see how you go. If you're more sweet than savoury, it's a strictly pancakes, granola and cookies affair until 11am at **Marinette**, where dishes too pretty to tuck into are enjoyed up on a bright rooftop terrace hidden from the crowds in Vieux Nice.

A GLOSSARY OF NIÇOISE CUISINE

Socca A thin (gluten-free and vegan) chickpea-flour pancake, served fresh from a wood-fired oven.

Pan Bagnat This 'wet bread' in local dialect is a *salade Niçoise* in a sandwich.

Les Petits Farcis Typical regional vegetables – courgettes, peppers, onions – stuffed with meat.

Pissaladière Focaccia topped with caramelised onions and anchovies.

Beignets de Fleurs de Courgettes Whoever knew battered courgette flowers could taste so good?

Panisse This thicker version of *socca* is a serious challenger to the French fry.

Tourte de Blette Sucrée Sweet pastry with Swiss chard at its core.

Merda de Can Green gnocchi (also based on Swiss chard) that's surprisingly tasty.

WHERE TO SWIM IN NICE

Coco Beach
Don't tell the locals we revealed the existence of this low-key swimming spot off the rocks past the port.

Castel Plage
Nice's oldest private beach is LGBTIQ+-friendly and catches the day's last rays of sunshine.

Plage Publique de l'Opéra
Play volleyball by day or lay out a picnic with friends at night on this popular, pebbly stretch of public beach.

Happy Hour

Sunset drinks in the city

Come 5pm, under the glow of the late afternoon sun, Nice's residents flock to the nearest terrace for an *apéro*, as the pre-dinner apéritif is more colloquially known. It's an easy habit to slip into during your visit. There's a guaranteed buzz on popular squares such as place Garibaldi: smartly positioned tables alongside a beautiful vintage carousel make **Le Garibaldi** in particular a popular spot for families. Tucked around the corner, at the start of rue Bonaparte, the boho vibe and tapas plates of **Le Café de Chineurs** draw a hip after-work crowd. On the **Cours Saleya** in Vieux Nice, chilled rosé and thirst-quenching pints are served with a side of people-watching, particularly in the cluster of cafés and restaurants at the eastern end. Pull up a seat at **La Civette de Cours** for a more classic French bar experience, or hop on a stool at **Blast** if a lively American-style bar ambience is more your mood.

Many people find nothing beats a DIY *apéro* on the beach. The best place to pick up a chilled bottle is the Aladdin's cave of a wine shop, **Caves Caprioglio**. During summer, private beaches such as **La Plage Amour** are pricier and fancier options for a tipple, but also draw a party set ready to dance the night away. Rooftop bars such as **Seen by Olivier** charge top dollar for unique cocktails with panoramic mountains-meet-sea views.

BEST WINE BARS IN NICE

Rouge
This hot newbie in Port Lympia serves up stylish modern tapas plates, washed down with organic wines direct from their producers.

Cave de la Tour
A soundtrack of cool 1940s jazz, an interior that has hardly changed since then and Nice wine by the glass.

La Part des Anges
One of the earliest wine bars in the city and voted the best in France in 2020. A treasure trove of natural and organic wines.

Fanfan and Loulou
Natural wines served with cheese and charcuterie from the Auvergne in a retro 1970s setting.

La Civette de Cours

EDDY BUTTARELLI/REDA&CO/UNIVERSAL IMAGES GROUP VIA GETTY IMAGES ©

WHERE TO EAT ICE CREAM IN NICE

Fenocchio
Believe-it-or-not flavours include tomato-basil, lavender and olive in Vieux Nice's place Rossetti. €

Oui, Jelato
Stays open late for second desserts in Vieux Nice. Ice cream biscuits are a double indulgence. €

Arlequin Gelati
Neighbourhood ice creamery considered often considered the city's best. Inventive combinations rule. €

Taste Nice Wine

The city's hidden vineyards

Interspersed between the Provençal villas of Nice's western flank are nine boutique vineyards that form the Bellet AOC. Not only is this postage-stamp-sized appellation – with just 50 hectares of vines – one of France's smallest, but it's also the only one in the country to fall within city limits. Two grape varieties grown here – Folle Noire and Braquet – don't grow anywhere else in the world. These aren't the sprawling estates you'll find in major wine regions, and many still have a 'vin de garage' feel: particularly the charming **Domaine de la Source**, where brother-and-sister duo Eric and Carine Dalmasso produce wines in the backyard of their family home and pour tasting serves under the shade of olive trees. The two largest producers offer a delightful perspective of the city's history alongside a comprehensive visitor experience: **Château de Bellet** is the oldest of the Bellet vineyards, and tours start from an intimate private chapel built by the Barons of Bellet in 1873. In a towering terracotta-red, faux-medieval fortress dating from 1906, the interlocking Cs of **Château de Crémat** are said to have inspired Coco Chanel, who is known to have spent glamorous evenings on its vast terrace during the Roaring Twenties. It's up to you to decide if the logo story is fact or fiction, but the possibility does make a fascinating theme for the 1½-hour-long tour through the property, which has been freshly renovated and furnished with museum pieces from Chanel's private suite at the Ritz Paris. The visit concludes with a tasting, and includes the wines of neighbouring **Domaine de Toasc**.

Weekday Restaurants

Weekday culinary experiences

In a testament to their success, some of Nice's most beloved restaurants are open Monday to Friday only. It's something to keep in mind if you usually prefer to save the best culinary experiences for Saturday night. This includes Vieux Nice's **Chez Acchiardo** and **Chez Palmyre**, both of which are loved for their classic bistro vibe. A few streets away, **Lavomatique** is a more recent addition to the city's dining scene but has quickly won a following for tasty shared plates that turn traditional cooking codes on their head, washed down with organic wines. In the Carré d'Or neighbourhood, **Le Canon** is an unassuming favourite that brings hyperlocal to the fore.

LIVE MUSIC IN NICE

Did Kwo is a local guitarist and songwriter who has played in bars and restaurants across the city. He shares his top spots for live music in Nice.

Wayne's Bar
This fun English pub in Vieux Nice is the spot to find cover bands playing favourite party songs to get people dancing on the tables.

Shapko
A great late-night bet in Vieux Nice for jazz, soul, R&B and blues. The crowd here is all ages.

La Cave Romagnan
This wine bar near Gare Thiers is the place for early-bird jazz on Saturday night.

La Zommé
An underground venue in Libération with an eclectic lineup; keep an eye on its social media account for what's on.

WHERE TO WATCH LIVE SPORT IN NICE

Ma Nolan's
This lively Irish pub, with locations in Vieux Nice and Port Lympia, fills up fast on big match days. €

Van Diemen's
This Aussie bar with a laid-back feel on the Cours Saleya has two terraces and 11 televisions. €

Waka Bar
Fewer screens but an unbeatable location opposite the beach and a party mood once the whistle blows. €

La Brigue
St-Dalmas-de-Tende

Ste-Agnès
Menton
Villefranche- Èze Cap Martin
sur-Mer   Beaulieu-sur-Mer
Nice   St-Jean-Cap-Ferrat

Beyond Nice

GETTING AROUND

When the train runs to timetable, the TER Sud line makes small work of travel times between Nice and coastal stops and takes a supremely scenic track built right on the coast. The 607 Zou! bus sweeps along the same coastal curves at a slower pace as it serves stops between Nice and Monaco. Both can be congested during morning and afternoon commuter rush hours. A bus service connects St-Martin-Vésubie with Nice; for coastal villages such as Ste-Agnès, Menton is the base. To really dive deep into the sublime lower alpine landscapes of the Côte d'Azur, you'll need your own transport; whether car or bike is up to you.

Nice's surrounds brim with postcard-pretty resort towns, eagle's-nest villages, energising hiking trails and unexpected alpine experiences.

You don't have to travel too far from Nice to feel like you've left the big city behind; in fact, the pace turns down a few notches as soon as you arrive in Villefranche-sur-Mer, a charming fishing village joined to Nice at its eastern hip. The trio of sublime corniches, or coastal roads, layered between Nice and Monaco weave through Belle Époque coastal resorts, pass eagle's-nest villages and open onto lush hiking trails. They merge together in Italianate Menton, the last town before the border. Nice's backcountry is having a moment, too. Inspired by the dramatic pre-alpine landscapes of Parc National du Mercantour, an influx of chefs are finding space to champion locavorism.

Hike the Three Corniches
Coastal trails and supreme views

You can drive the three corniches, or you can scramble up them on foot. While there are plenty of signposted nature trails crisscrossing the hills behind Villefranche-sur-Mer, Beaulieu-sur-Mer and Èze (the excellent **Randoxygène** website and printed guide available in local tourist offices detail them in French), the **Nietzsche Trail** connecting Èze-bord-de-Mer and Èze Village is considered the definitive. Named for German philosopher Friedrich Nietzsche, who found inspiration to complete the third part of *Thus Spoke Zarathustra* while walking it, the 2.1km track can be tackled from top down, but the classic departure point is the Basse Corniche. The steep ascent from the coast on a well-defined

Èze Village (p66)

BIKE CLUB

For serious road cyclists, the mountain passes behind Nice are bucket-list rides. *Cafés vélos* – or cyclist cafés – are popping up as places not only for good coffee, but also to connect with others who are passionate about the sport and to participate in scheduled rides.

Café du Cycliste in the Port is the original bike café. Join in on a weekly group ride or set off on your own following an itinerary that starts from its doorstep into the hinterland. Road and gravel bikes are available to hire.

In Vieux Nice, **The Service Course** organises weekend group rides – view the program in advance on its website. Saturday's ride is longer than Sunday's. Participation is free with your own bike. Road bikes can be hired, too.

yet rocky path winds through Mediterranean shrub and feels far from civilisation. After about an hour, you'll emerge at the base of medieval Èze Village on the Moyenne Corniche. Most people pause to enjoy this jewel of the Riviera before turning around, but if you're in a particularly sporty mood you can push on even higher to **Fort de la Revère**. Dating from 1870, this fort perched above the Grande Corniche is now a glorious picnic area and nature reserve. Signposted as **Fuont Roussa**, the path starts on av de la Marne, 200m past the entrance to the Fragonard perfumery. The ascent is similarly steep through scented pines and wildflowers, but some of the best views on the Côte d'Azur are your reward. Count on about 30 minutes to reach the Grand Corniche and a further 15 minutes for the fort, depending on how many stops you make for photos. Dozens of trails cut across this plateau if you're energised to push on further; otherwise, follow the marked path back down.

TOP TIP

Keep your eye on the time: restaurants keep to strict lunch hours, usually between noon and 2.30pm.

WHERE TO PICNIC ALONG THE THREE CORNICHES

Jardin de l'Olivaie
Even in the height of summer, this shady olive grove in Beaulieu-sur-Mer can feel like your own private garden.

Plateau de St-Michel
Arrive early to nab a picnic table with sweeping views in this high-altitude neighbourhood of Villefranche-sur-Mer.

La Pinède
A quiet, pine-dusted picnic area just before the Tête du Chien in La Turbie, with gorgeous views over Monaco.

Driving the Three Corniches

The three corniches (coastal roads) cling to the cliffs between Nice and Monaco. With a new favourite vista around every bend, the views of the Mediterranean can be a distraction, but thankfully there are plenty of lookout points. You could drive this route without stopping in under an hour, but that would mean skipping many of the Côte d'Azur's crown jewels.

❶ Mont Boron

Begin at Nice's wooded eastern fringe, the Parc Forestier de Mont Boron. This urban forest is a hiker's favourite, but you can park close to the 16th-century Fort du Mont Alban for scene-stealing views across the bay of Villefranche-sur-Mer – a taster for the road ahead.

The Drive: This fairly flat 5km stretch of the Basse Corniche clings to the coast. Stop for photos at the Mémorial Princesse Grace viewpoint at the entrance to Villefranche-sur-Mer.

❷ Villefranche-sur-Mer

Villefranche-sur-Mer's Citadelle Ste-Elme looms tall at the entrance to the small harbour, but don't let the immense walls scare you off: inside, a charming sculpture garden blooms under the nurturing touch of the Mediterranean sea breeze.

The Drive: Continue along the low road for a further kilometre, before turning left onto av Léopold II, a narrow road that winds up to the Moyenne Corniche. Settle in for a scenic 5km stretch to Èze.

EQROY/SHUTTERSTOCK ©

Roquebrune-Cap-Martin

❸ Èze Village

Parking can sometimes be tough but this isn't a stop to miss: snuggled into a rocky nest nearly 500m above the sea, Èze is a Côte d'Azur sparkler where the narrow medieval streets all lead to one place, the Jardin Exotique d'Èze, a serene multi-level garden where cacti grow among the ruins of the old château.

The Drive: Not long after leaving the village, turn left onto the route de la Turbie to head even higher above the sea. At the top, merge onto the Grande Corniche and La Turbie will appear around the first bend.

❹ La Turbie

So high is La Turbie that the village often sits in a soft cloud. When it clears, you can clearly make out three countries from the Tête du Chien viewpoint: France, Monaco

and Italy. You can't miss the Trophée d'Auguste, a victory monument raised for Roman emperor Augustus. Even better: the buttery croissants at Ma Première Boulangerie, some of the best in the region.

The Drive: Staying on the Grande Corniche, the road twists and turns for 5km as you sweep around Monaco.

❺ Roquebrune-Cap-Martin

Prepare to be dazzled by the all-glass Maybourne Riviera as it comes into view. On the top floor of this swanky luxury hotel just before the turnoff to Roquebrune village, celebrated chef Mauro Colagreco's Mediterranean-inspired temple, Ceto, awaits. Feast on fish matured inside a rock salt chamber with underwater-aged wines poured to match. From the terrace, you feel you'll drop into the sea below.

La Flânerie in Villefranche-sur-Mer
Pretty streets and slow living

Irresistibly photogenic **Villefranche-sur-Mer** starts at Nice's eastern edge but is a world away from the buzz of the big city. This is small village life, where locals catch up on gossip at the Wednesday and Saturday morning produce markets or play *pétanque* in the shadow of the high-walled 16th-century **Citadelle Ste-Elme**. The pedestrian streets of Villefranche's old town are ideal to awaken your inner *flâneur* – one who strolls in a leisurely manner. Start by admiring the green thumbs of residents along rue Volti and rue Baron de Brès, who have turned their pastel-palette façades into delightful street gardens that have become impromptu settings for social media shoots. Staircases down to the water frame views of the glistening sea. Just before the waterfront, rue de Poilu is a hub of activity with restaurants and small lavender-fragranced boutiques selling floaty dresses and wide-brimmed straw hats. One street down, **rue Obscure** is a 130m-long vaulted alley that offers a shadowy glimpse into the village's medieval past. Pause for lunch along the quay: the crisp, white tablecloths of **La Mère Germaine** signal the classic fine dining experience (with prices to match). Locals prefer **Lou Bantry** for Niçoise cuisine. The whimsical brushstrokes of Jean Cocteau cover the walls and ceilings of the must-see **Chapelle St-Pierre**, telling the story of Villefranche's fishing traditions. Next door, the rooftop bar of **Achill's** is a nocturnal draw for a hip crowd.

Who Wants to Be a Billionaire?
A fairy-tale villa and enchanted garden

Jutting out into the Mediterranean with the bays of Ville-franche-sur-Mer and Beaulieu-sur-Mer on either side, **St-Jean-Cap-Ferrat**'s leafy streets provide the perfect cover for their grand private residences. High walls and locked gates obscure most of the multi-million-euro mansions from view. However, the peninsula's greatest architectural treasure, the **Villa Ephrussi de Rothschild**, is one of the finest attractions on the entire coast. As soon as you set foot inside the ornate pink-and-white Belle Époque villa, commissioned by Baroness Béatrice Ephrussi de Rothschild and completed in 1912, you'll be swept back to a time when Louis XVI furniture and Fragonard paintings were the height of fashion. Save plenty of time for the nine themed gardens that fan out from the villa, an enchanting landscape of sweeping stone staircases,

WHY I LOVE VILLEFRANCHE-SUR-MER

When the hit Netflix show *Emily in Paris* came to the Côte d'Azur in season 2, many of the scenes passed off as St-Tropez were actually filmed in Villefranche-sur-Mer.

For residents like me, it affirmed what we already knew: our colourful seaside village outshines its more glamorous coastal neighbours.

There's the obvious natural beauty of the deep bay; add in the pastel-hued buildings cascading into the sea and you have one of the classic Côte d'Azur scenes. Yet the feel here is more low-key than jet-set; there's no blingy nightlife or designer boutiques, just local faces behind bars and in shops, who have now become friends.

WHERE TO EAT AND SLEEP IN VILLEFRANCHE-SUR-MER

La Regence
Top-value find in the centre of town with charming, Provençal-styled rooms and a family feel. €

Hôtel de la Darse
Basic but smart two-star choice across from the water in the quiet port neighbourhood. Sea-view rooms. €€

Le Serre
Tucked under vaulted archways back from the tourist trail in the old town, this restaurant has great pizzas. €

rose-covered pergolas and even a theatrical musical fountain. The sea views from all angles are sublime.

Belle Époque Beaulieu-sur-Mer
Step inside an aristocrat's mansion

With splendid turn-of-the-century residences complete with rosy cherubs and other ornate details, **Beaulieu-sur-Mer** is just as popular with wealthy foreigners as it was during the late 19th-century when aristocratic Russians and Brits passed the winter months under the mild Riviera sun. You'll spot them sipping coffee or coupes of Champagne in the cafés around **place du Général de Gaulle**. At the nearby **Office du Tourisme**, you can pick up a map of Belle Époque Beaulieu for a self-guided walking tour of the architecture of the era. A guided tour is also planned for the near future. There are over a dozen stops; some, like the **Résidence Eiffel** (built in the 1880s, it was owned by Gustave Eiffel's family until 1977), are sumptuous private residences to admire from the outside. Others are national treasures open to the public. You'll feel like you've been given a glimpse of antiquity just next door

ANASTASIA KRUTIKOVA/SHUTTERSTOCK ©

Villa Ephrussi de Rothschild

FOOD TRUCKS AND BEACH SHACKS

Tuck into some of the most memorable dining experiences on the coast in these casual open-air food spots with superb views and reasonable prices. Open summer only.

La Voile Bleue
A simple shack on the beach at Villefranche-sur-Mer, they serve some of the best *pan bagnat* on the coast and chilled glasses of rosé. €

Le Cabanon
Amid all the mansions is this no-frills kiosk with a feet-in-the-sand setting, directly on the coastal path in St-Jean-Cap-Ferrat. €

Food'eze
Parked high on the Moyenne Corniche before Èze, the speciality at this food truck is hamburgers, served with a side of sensational sea-blue views. Park next door. €

WHERE TO EAT IN BEAULIEU-SUR-MER

Rotisserie Sandwicherie
Tiny snack bar where rotisserie chicken is carved and packed into a baguette with roasted potatoes. €

La Maison de la Sauce by Pignatelle
The accent here is on fresh ingredients and flavoursome sauces. Lovely terrace. €€

Tennis Club
This courtside restaurant is open to non-members. Ace salads, pasta and meat dishes at great prices. €

GIANCARLO LIGUORI/SHUTTERSTOCK ©

Fête du Citron, Menton

SEE THE SEA

There is no shortage of boat rental and excursion providers to get you out on the water beyond Nice, but only one offers the opportunity to sail up to 35km off the coast on board a replica 16th-century wooden Mediterranean trading boat – and you can help safeguard the ocean along the way.

For over three decades, local association **SOS Grand Bleu** has fought for the protection of dolphins and whales in the Mediterranean. In 2005, they took possession of the 23m *Santo Sospir* sailing yacht. For €65 per person, you can jump on board this beautiful vessel for a full-day group outing (maximum 20 passengers) in search of these majestic marine animals.

Pack your own picnic lunch, sunglasses, hat, sunscreen and swimming costume. April to November.

at **Villa Kérylos**, a faithful mosaic-sprinkled replication of a 2nd-century BCE ancient Greek residence built on the Baie des Fourmis. Nearby, both **La Rotonde** and the **Casino de Beaulieu** overflow with period detail shaded in buttermilk. Finish up submersed in the theatre of the gilded Gordon Bennett Bar inside the five-star **La Réserve de Beaulieu**, where guests like Walt Disney and Clark Gable arrived by seaplane.

Menton's Precious Lemons
Celebrate citrus

There's something about the mountains-meets-sea microclimate of **Menton**: this last curve of France before the Italian border is the most northerly place in the world that lemons can grow. Historically a mainstay of the town's economy, a combination of factors saw the decline of production in recent years. Happily, the crop is undergoing a renaissance and today the *citron de Menton* is feted anew for its sweet taste and impressive size. During February's annual **Fête du Citron** celebrations, the streets around the waterfront light up in every shade of yellow and orange. Tickets are required for the lively street parades of floats built out of citrus fruits

WHERE TO LOUNGE ON THE BEACH BEYOND NICE

Baia Bella
France's first carbon-neutral private beach, in Beaulieu-sur-Mer. Solar panels and recycled water.

Plage Paloma
This iconic private beach in St-Jean-Cap-Ferrat has silver screen cred, and is a favourite filming location.

La Réserve de Mala
Tucked below sheer cliffs, the hidden beach here is far from the crowds but a privilege you'll need to pay for.

and flamboyantly dressed dancers, but you won't need to pay a cent to admire the gigantic citrus displays sculpted to a different theme every year in **Jardins Biovès**. The two weeks of the festival is also the only time that the **Casetta**, Menton's municipal garden, throws open its gates to the public for guided visits. Reserve your place at the **Office du Tourisme**.

For a more perennial experience, look for local lemon producers proposing farm visits. High up behind the cemetery, **Maison Gannac** opens its doors to early risers for a 9am tour through its nursery and orchard. You'll learn about different varieties of citrus, from thin finger limes to puckered bergamot, and even take home some tips to ensure your plants thrive at home. The visit, which lasts around an hour, finishes with a tasting of its products. Booking in advance (either on Instagram or in-store at Au Pays du Citron, 22 rue St-Michel) is necessary for a visit to **La Ferme des Citrons**. The excursion starts at a central meeting point in Menton where a 4x4 awaits you for a short yet steep drive to the farm. After an hour-long guided tour through avocado trees, olive groves and, of course, lots of lemon trees, you are allowed ample time to relax on a sunny terrace with a shaded children's play area and nature's best views. A tasty picnic lunch is included in the price of the visit, although you'll have to pay extra for a bottle of locally brewed lemon-infused beer (La Mentounasc) and other thirst-quenching beverages. Request an English-speaking guide when booking.

Le Corbusier's Château

A remarkable seaside home

Le Corbusier called it his Château on the Côte d'Azur: a small 14-sq-metre pinewood cabin at the water's edge in **Cap Martin**. Now a Unesco World Heritage site, **Le Cabanon**, as it's known, remains the only structure that the Swiss-born architect designed for himself. It was built as his summer residence in 1952 on a strip of land adjacent to **Villa E-1027**; the latter was designed by his friends, Irish interior decorator Eileen Gray and Romanian-born architect Jean Badovici. An early example of modernist architecture, the villa dates from 1929. Badovici's death in 1956 signalled the start of a turbulent chapter in the property's history, including a period when many of Gray's custom furnishings and fixtures were stripped and sold at auction, only to appear in museum collections around the world. Now a protected monument, the villa has been meticulously restored to Gray's original vision, down to a faithful replica of the door handles. The ensemble of the site – including the **Étoile de Mer**, the neighbour-

EATING IN MAURO'S MENTON

After opening **Mirazur**, a Michelin three-star address just footsteps from the Italian border, celebrated Argentinian chef Mauro Colagreco's Menton empire has been steadily expanding. And the good news is you don't have to fork out fine-dining prices for the experience.

Across the road from Mirazur is **Casa Fuego**, his sexy Argentinian grill and the Riviera's best date-night destination. Along the newly refreshed beachfront, Les Sablettes, you'll find **Pecora Negra**, his casual family-friendly pizzeria. And on the central pedestrian shopping street that runs parallel to the waterfront is his organic **Mitron Bakery**, which is bringing France's rare and forgotten flours back to the bakehouse.

WHERE TO DRINK AND EAT IN MENTON

Ferdinand
Tasty rum cocktails, live music and an all-round great atmosphere just across from Les Sablettes. €

L'Endroit
Locals swear this is the place for casual drinks that turn into long dinners and live music on weekends. €

Les Enfants Terribles
Despite the name, children are more than welcome at this family-friendly seafood restaurant in Menton. €€

ing bar shack owned by Thomas Rebutat, and its five holiday cabins designed by Le Corbusier – now goes by the name of **Cap Moderne**. A detailed two-hour guided tour of the four buildings departs on foot daily at 10am and 2pm from a hangar at the Gare Cap-Martin-Roquebrune train station. Arrive 15 minutes early to have a chance to browse the informative exhibition inside. Booking well in advance is encouraged; make sure you select the English-language visit. Le Corbusier had a heart attack swimming off the rocks outside his cabin in 1965 and is buried in the cemetery in medieval **Roquebrune** village, 300m high above his beloved 'castle' on the coast.

Strategic Ste-Agnès
Medieval garden in the sky

Clinging to a rock face 800m above Menton, **Ste-Agnès** claims to be the highest coastal village in Europe and is classified as one of *Les Plus Beaux Villages*. All roads leading here share tight bends and narrow lanes, particularly if coming from La Turbie over **La Col de La Madone de Gorbio** mountain pass, one of the legendary bicycle rides on the coast. From the pretty paved alleyways of the quaint village, a 10-minute climb up stairs will lead you to the original settlement at an even dizzier altitude. The 10th-century château lies in ruins, but the site is passionately maintained by a volunteer association who have planted a small but colourful medieval garden behind the ramparts. Handwritten signs lead the way through vines, herbs and wildflowers. The panorama is showstopping – the semi-trailers that plough the busy A8 motorway are mere specks below – but those wary of heights-may feel a little squeamish, particularly atop the rickety ruined fort with a 360-degree view. Think Èze, but without the gloss or crowds – and therein lies the real charm. Also of note here is the stark Maginot Line concrete military fortification dug into the rock. Equivalent to a four-storey building built deep below the village, guided visits to **Le Fort de la Ligne Maginot** are in French only.

Escape to the Peaks
Wildlife and hinterland communities

The coastline and the sea's blues might steal the limelight, yet the interior's dramatic mountain terrain covers over 80% of the Alpes-Maritimes, the French *département* which lies in the Côte d'Azur's embrace. An hour inland from Nice

MENTON'S GARDENS

Considered the green lung of the Côte d'Azur, Menton dazzles with its remarkable gardens.

Jardin Botanique et Exotique du Val Rahmeh
Just back from the beach, over 1700 different species bloom in this 120-year-old terraced garden, originally designed for British general Sir Percy Radcliffe.

Jardin Serre de la Madone
Ponds, pergolas and plenty of statues decorate this charming garden on the road to Gorbio. It dates to 1924, when Anglo-American Laurence Johnston started planting flora here collected from his world travels.

Jardin Fontana Rosa
Colourful tilework adds an additional flourish to this Spanish-flavoured garden, once owned by Vincente Blasco-Ibañez. Open for guided visits only.

WHERE TO WALK THE COAST BEYOND NICE

Promenade Maurice Rouvier
This flat, paved 1.3km path links Beaulieu-sur-Mer with St-Jean-Cap-Ferrat and is accessible for all.

Sentier de Cap d'Ail
A popular 5km track leading from Plage Marquet at the western edge of Monaco to the hidden bay of Plage Mala.

Le Tour du Cap-Ferrat
This rocky 4.8km trail around the Cap-Ferrat headland passes a lighthouse, hidden coves and the Grand-Hôtel.

Gorbio

BEST OF THE REST: PERCHED VILLAGES

Gorbio
Shaded by a 300-year-old elm tree that dominates the main square, Gorbio is a classically beautiful Provençal hilltop village without the tourist buses.

Castillon
Quirky artists' village completely rebuilt on a new site in the 1950s after it was destroyed first by an earthquake and then war. A rock-climbing paradise.

Castellar
This Italianate hilltop village behind Menton brims with local flavours on Sunday mornings for the weekly produce market. *Barbajuans* are a speciality.

Peillon
Half the adventure is getting to Peillon on a twisty mountain road. Book ahead for lunch at the Auberge de la Madone.

and 1000m above sea level, **St-Martin-Vésubie** has been nicknamed La Suisse Niçoise for its green setting and pretty wooden chalets. In 2020, lives were lost and buildings and bridges washed away when Storm Alex struck the **Vallée de la Vésubie** and the **Vallée de la Roya**. The scars are still evident, but the community is showing its mountain spirit as it rebuilds after the devastation. Your support is an enormous boost to their efforts – but you'll get something back, too. In the centre of the village itself, **Vésubia Mountain Park** is a multi-million-euro indoor adventure sports centre where kids and adults scale climbing walls, kit up for canyoning or tackle the rooftop adventure course. When the time comes for a pause, you can decide for yourself if the spring water from the River Vésubie is what makes the local brew, **Brasserie du Comté**, so refreshing: the taphouse has been completely rebuilt on a new site just outside the village after the storm washed away the original one. Guided tours and tastings run in the summer months and can be booked either direct or through the **Office de Tourisme de St-Martin-Vésubie**. Outside of that, an on-site boutique sells beers and other merchandise and has a couple of the most popular brews on tap. The village is also a jumping-off

WHERE TO EAT BEHIND MENTON

Le Righi
The terrace views from this St-Agnès institution might be the best of any restaurant on the Côte d'Azur. €

L'HarTmonie
This bistrot de pays in Castillon supports employment for people with disabilities and emphasises regional cuisine. €

Le Beauséjour
A dining room straight out of a French country magazine, overlooking Gorbio's beloved elm tree. €€

THE VÉSUBIE VALLEYS

Which Vésubie hike should you choose? **Guillaume Mathurin** from the Bureau des Guides Vésubie Mercantour (bureau-guides-vesubie-mercantour.fr) recommends several of his favourites.

Salèse
For gentle strolls under larch trees that invite contemplation, this region is a place to unwind.

Boréon
More family-friendly, the majestic Cougourde summit has everything, from refreshment on the edge of a torrent or alpine lake to the craziest of climbs.

Madone de Fenestre
A stone's throw from Italy, this hike will take you to meet the rulers of the territory: the chamois, ibex and marmots.

Gordolasque
The alpine atmosphere is the drawcard here, with its many glacial lakes. This is the gateway to the **Vallée des Merveilles** and its Bronze Age petroglyphs.

point for numerous hiking trails in the **Parc National de Mercantour**, a magnificent national park that encompasses 679 sq km, stretching from the Côte d'Azur into Haute Provence. In the company of friendly English-speaking guides from the **Bureau des Guides Vésubie Mercantour**, you'll uncover the best mountain paths to get up close to majestic chamois and whistling marmots.

Ride the Train of Wonders

A magical alpine rail journey

The regular commuter train that connects Nice with the mountain communities of the Vallée de Roya is known as the **Train des Merveilles**, and for good reason. Stretching to the Italian border, it carves a dazzling course through the deep gorges, pine forests and rushing cascades of the Côte d'Azur backcountry. Completed in 1928, the track once connected Nice with Italy but now French trains can only go as far as **Tende**, a village 800m above sea level in France's most easterly nook

 WHERE TO EAT AND SLEEP IN THE VÉSUBIE

Le St Mart'
This wine bar and bistro tucked away from the main square serves up all the classics, executed to perfection. €

Relais de Merveilles
Cosy hikers' inn with dorms and doubles at the entrance to the Gordolasque. Open from late April to October. €

Pure Montagne
This swanky new resort brings a touch of alpine glam to St-Martin-Vésubie and is a top choice for families. €€€

(you can jump on Trenitalia trains from here). Feats of engineering to make such a route possible include dizzying viaducts, plenty of tunnels (including the second longest in the country) and spiral loops. From June to September on the daily 9.08am service, a dedicated guide provides live commentary on the route and its construction in both French and English at no extra cost (in April and October, it's weekends only). You'll arrive at Tende at 11.30am, with two return services to Nice in the afternoon. That's enough time to meander through the amphitheatre-shaped village clinging to the mountainside. The ornate baroque façade of the **Collégiale Notre-Dame de l'Assomption** can be spotted from most angles and is accessed through a warren of pedestrian streets with a distinct Italian flavour. Don't miss the **Musée des Merveilles** just across from the station, with its large visual displays and artefacts that trace the history of the prehistoric carvings of the **Vallée des Merveilles**. Other stops along the line include **Breil-sur-Roya** (with a wonderful transport museum), the **Ecomusée du Train des**

LA VALLÉE DES MERVEILLES

Thibaud Duffey (carambaam@yahoo. fr) is a qualified mountain guide based in Saorge who regularly leads hikes into the Vallées des Merveilles and de Fontanalba.

High up in the **Parc National de Mercantour**, you'll find two mysterious valleys shaped by the glaciers, with numerous crystalline lakes and more than 40,000 engravings from the Neolithic and Bronze Ages. Reach the carvings after two to four hours of walking from the car parks in Les Mesches or Casterino, from the end of May to the beginning of October. It's best to sleep on-site at the nearby *refuges* **Merveilles** and **Fontanalbe**. Take the Train des Merveilles (from Nice) or bus 25 (from Menton) to reach St-Dalmas-de-Tende, from where bus 23 leads to Les Mesches and Casterino (four per day).

TIMSAXON/GETTY IMAGES ©

Tende

WHERE TO SKI IN THE BACKCOUNTRY

Auron
Bucketloads of alpine charm and a lively après-ski scene just an hour and a half from Nice.

Isola 2000
The good: great slopes with Mediterranean views from the summit. The bad: uninspiring 1970s architecture.

Valberg
The first ski resort on the Côte d'Azur and a firm favourite with weekend skiers from Nice.

Merveilles, **St-Dalmas-de-Tende** (the jumping-off point for **Casterino** and the Vallée des Merveilles) and **La Brigue**.

A Forgotten Cuisine, Refound

Returning traditions

Centuries ago, the pastoral communities of the high **Vallée de Roya** herded their flocks of Brigasque sheep from the mountains to the coast in autumn, returning to the mountain meadows again the next spring. Along this transhumance route, a particular cuisine developed. Named for the colourless aspect of the main ingredients, such as flour, potatoes, leeks and dairy products, **cucina bianca** grew out of the need for simple meals that could fuel shepherds and their families en route. While the practice of transhumance has since died out, at **Auberge St-Martin** in **La Brigue**, owner and chef Patrick Teisseire is bringing *cucina bianca* back to the kitchen. Come for lunch – or stay overnight in one of the nine simple but good value rooms – and sample specialities such as *sügeli*, a shell-shaped pasta inscribed on France's list of *patrimoine culturel immatériel* (intangible cultural heritage), and *brousse*, a pungent cream cheese from the Brigasque sheep. Teisseire also organises cooking classes by prior reservation. Be sure to make time to visit the **Sanctuaire Notre-Dame-des-Fontaines**, a 15th-century church dubbed the Sistine Chapel of the Southern Alps for the detailed frescoes that cover every centimetre of the interior. The church is 4km from La Brigue. When taking the Train des Merveilles, note that La Brigue is the stop five minutes before Tende.

CHRISTOPHE BOISVIEUX/ALAMY STOCK PHOTO ©

Sanctuaire Notre-Dame-des-Fontaines

Cannes

Cannes

Cannes is the host with the most; not content to hold just one world-leading industry affair a year – yes, Cannes Film Festival, we're looking at you – the conference and event schedule is so busy that dates spill out from the calendar most months. It's a place that always feels on and dressed in its global party best, pushing local traditions and experiences into the wings as a consequence.

Yet, despite first impressions, usually superyachts crowding the bay and luxury cars double parked outside the designer boutiques of La Croisette, Cannes is an old Provençal soul, as the brightly coloured wooden fishing boats bobbing in the harbour or the battered courgette flowers cooked fresh in the Marché de Forville bear witness to. And, in a world now celebrating what makes each destination unique, this understudy is starting to shine.

Festival Fever
Roll out the red carpet

For two weeks every May, Cannes rolls out the red carpet for a galaxy of stars during the annual **Festival de Cannes** (Cannes Film Festival). The harbourfront **Palais des Festivals et des Congrès** is the epicentre. Months ahead of the event, film buffs submit an application at festival-cannes.com to be one of the lucky few selected for a pass to access screenings – those who demonstrate a verified interest in cinema have a better chance of success. If you're prepared to stand for hours in smart dress outside the Palais, you may find someone willing to offload a ticket for a screening they can no longer attend. A makeshift sign stating what you want to see will increase your chances. After sunset, everyone is invited to **Cinéma de la Plage**, the free open-air cinema that runs for the duration of the festival on Plage Macé. Mostly showing classics, with the occasional world premiere, you may rub shoulders with a member of the cast or crew. Arrive early for the best seats.

For the remainder of the year, the gloss barely fades. Handprints of over 400 stars are cast in stainless steel outside the Palais des Festivals et des Congrès along the **Chemin des Étoiles**. Dates for tours inside the Palais are only scheduled six weeks in advance by the **Office du Tourisme** (conveniently

GETTING AROUND

Palm Bus A connects Cannes and Mandelieu-La Napoule, with multiple departures every hour; for Vallauris, hop on bus 9. Both Zou! intercity bus lines 663 and 664 leave from Square Stephan Vahanian in Cannes and pass through Mougins, although you'll need to be prepared to walk 1km from the Qui Vend Bon bus stop to the hilltop village.
  The train ride between Cannes and Grasse takes just half an hour. Heading west from Cannes, the train is also the best option for Antibes. For the Gorges du Loup and beyond, your own wheels are recommended.

TOP TIP
Keep your eye on the time: restaurants keep to strict lunch hours, usually between noon and 2.30pm.

HIGHLIGHTS
1 Chemin des Étoiles
2 Église Notre-Dame de l'Esperance
3 Le Suquet des Artistes
4 Musée des Explorations du Monde

ACTIVITIES & TOURS
5 La Croisette (Private Beaches)

SLEEPING
6 Carlton Cannes

EATING
7 L'Ardoise
8 Le Pompom
9 Pizza Cresci

10 Restaurant Bella

DRINKING & NIGHTLIFE
11 Charly's Wine Bar
12 Le Hive
13 Le Roof at Five Seas Hotel
14 Ma Nolan's
15 Morrison's Pub
16 The Quays

SHOPPING
17 Marché de Forville

INFORMATION
18 Palais des Festivals et des Congrès

TRANSPORT
19 Quai Des Iles

housed in the building), depending on the upcoming event schedule. When visits do run, you're given a 1½-hour behind-the-scenes insight into one of cinema's most mythical venues.

A Village in a Town

Art and viewpoints

Meaning summit in Provençal, **Le Suquet** is Cannes' oldest neighbourhood and relaxes with its sleepy charm. Feel the crowds and the big-name bling of La Croisette fade into the distance as you wander the quiet streets stretching up from the western edge of the Vieux Port. Loops of colourful village houses with floral balconies are crowned by a cluster of historic attractions, including the medieval castle of the monks of the Lérins Islands that now, as the **Musée des Explorations du Monde**, harbours treasures from all four corners of the world. Outside the entrance, the Cannes selfie sign is deliberately angled to capture a stunning view of the bay, although go one better by scaling what's left of the castle

 WHERE TO SLEEP IN CANNES

Hôtel de Provence
The early bird gets the worm at this leafy oasis in central Cannes. Opt for rooms 12, 14 or 15. €€

Hôtel Le Mistral
The friendliness of owner Jean-Michel and the nightly price make up for some dated decor. €€

Centre International de Séjour Îles de Lérins
The dorms are simple but what a setting, inside Fort Royal on Île Ste-Marguerite. €

Looking right from the Gare de Cannes, the first painted wall is easy to spot, atop the rise on place du 18 Juin. Named **① Le 7ème Art**, it's an appropriate starting point for a tour of murals grouped around what the French consider the seventh art: cinema. Look at the figures closely. Do any look familiar? The next artwork is harder to spot, on the left wall at 3 bd Victor Tuby. The stretch of road between the two, bd de la Ferrage, isn't the most attractive and runs alongside one of Cannes' busiest arteries, but there's a pedestrian footpath that descends just as quickly as it rises. What you're looking for here is an image of the swashbuckling **② Gérard Philipe**, a French actor born in Cannes. At number 29 on the same road, 250m further along, **③ Buster Keaton** bursts from the wall. Just next door, at 7 rue des

Suisses, **④ L'Envers du Décor** shows a behind-the-scenes view of a director's set – the panorama across to the Massif de l'Esterel from here is also spectacular. Leave the traffic behind as you enter Le Suquet, Cannes' calm, pedestrianised old quarter. On place du Suquet, the neighbourhood's central square, you'll quickly spot **⑤ Hôtel de la Plage**, painted in memory of French director Jacques Tati, who directed beloved films such as *Les Vacances de Monsieur Hulot*. The *trompe l'oeil* **⑥ Le Barbarella** is actually facing west on the side wall of the building opposite. From there, it's a quick drop down along the restaurant-lined rue du Suquet and rue St-Antoine to the most photographed mural of all at place Cornut-Gentille: **⑦ Cinéma Cannes**, depicting some of Hollywood's most iconic characters.

CLAY COURT LEGENDS

Legend has it that clay court tennis was born in Cannes in the 1880s when two-time British Wimbledon winners, the Renshaw brothers, found that grass courts couldn't handle the heat of the Côte d'Azur. Turning to ground-up terracotta pottery from nearby Vallauris, the duo covered their courts with this inventive material.

Just like that, tennis had a new surface. While arguably no more than a great story, what isn't debated is that the **Carlton Cannes**, the iconic Belle Époque hotel on La Croisette, hosted the match of the century between France's Suzanne Lenglen and America's Helen Wills on this surface in 1926 (Lenglen won, if you're wondering). You'll find fine terracotta powder encased under the glass reception desk, among other nods to this sporting history.

ramparts in front of the 17th-century **Église Notre-Dame de l'Espérance** around the corner. At the base of the hill, in a low-lying hall that once housed the city morgue, **Le Suquet des Artistes** is a small but avant-garde exhibition space that brings local artists to the fore, with four of the most prominent based in workshops on-site.

ART IN ACTION

You can also see the street engravings of Olivia Paroldi, one of the artists based in Le Suquet des Artistes, in the back alleys of **Antibes** (p79).

Escape to the Islands

History, nature and holy wine

When you're shoulder-to-shoulder with crowds on **La Croisette**, it's hard to believe that a pocket of Cannes exists where the buzz of doing business is replaced by the sweet smell of pine and the gentle sound of waves. But look up and out to sea and you'll spot two islands off the mainland: the Îles de Lérins. The larger of the two, **Île Ste-Marguerite**, is closest to the shore, with the smaller **Île St-Honorat** tucked behind it. Ferries to both islands take approximately 20 minutes and leave from **quai des Îles** at the western edge of the harbour. Unfortunately, there's no inter-island ferry, so to visit the pair of them you have to return to Cannes first. Swimsuits and suncream are essential items, no matter which island you choose.

Both are covered in numerous walking trails with hidden coves for refreshing dips, although they each have distinct characters. Serene Île St-Honorat is privately owned by a community of monks. A group of 25 work and pray away from prying eyes and, although much of the 19th-century **Abbaye Notre-Dame de Lérins** is closed to the public, visitors are allowed into the church and to participate in mass. You'll need about an hour to complete the shady, eucalyptus-fringed loop that skims the circumference of the island. Unlike its bigger neighbour, vines also thrive in St-Honorat's soil. Once a month, you'll learn why during a short vineyard tour and tasting of two wines. Tickets for this **Journée Vignes-Vins** must be booked in advance (cannes-ilesdelerins.com) and the price includes the return ferry. You can also taste this holy wine at La Tonnelle, the island's only restaurant. Be prepared: the feet-in-the-sand setting comes with fine-dining prices and you'll need to reserve in advance (there's also a snack bar in-

WHERE TO EAT IN CANNES

Le Pompom
A menu of creative small plates that changes daily with the season. Colourful ingredients and beautiful presentation. €€

Pizza Cresci
This legendary address is beloved for half-moon pizzas that overhang the plate, hot from the wood-fired oven. €

L'Ardoise
Weekday workers flock to this unpretentious restaurant serving regional fare at knock-out prices. €

St-Honarat, Îles de Lerins

side for takeaway paninis and drinks).

By contrast, Île Ste-Marguerite feels more action-packed, and that's not only because it's inside the 17th-century **Fort Royal**, where the mysterious man in the iron mask was incarcerated under the orders of King Louis XIV. You can stand inside the exact cell – and learn about the island's strategic importance – when you visit the **Musée du Masque de Fer et du Fort Royal**. Weekends are particularly popular with families and groups of friends making the crossing from Cannes to picnic and swim in shallow waters. The cedar-framed trails that crisscross the 3.2km-long island are much less trodden. You'll also find a duo of overpriced restaurants, as well as two shacks selling sandwiches and cool drinks and the jumping-in point for the **Écomusée Sous-Marin de Cannes**.

Shop Like a Local

Cannes' covered market

Skip the supermarket and make your way instead to **Marché Forville**, behind Le Vieux Port. Open Tuesday to Sunday from 7.30am to 1pm, Cannes' covered produce markets are an explosion of juicy fruit, plump vegetables and food stalls serving up cuisine from around the world. Seasonality rules, so depending on the time of year, fill your basket to the brim with ruby-red strawberries from nearby Carros or pungent black truffles snuffled out from the neighbouring Var. Between

UNDERWATER MUSEUM

At depths of 3m to 5m below sea level, an underwater gallery of seafloor sculptures by Jason deCaires Taylor sits off the southern coastline of the Île Ste-Marguerite.

The six submerged statues of the **Écomusée Sous-Marin de Cannes** stand 2m high and depict the faces of residents of the city. The renowned British underwater sculptor has chiselled their profiles out of pH-neutral marine-grade cement, a textured material where marine life can set up home.

Located between 84m and 132m away from the shore, access to the site is free from the island. BYO mask and snorkel.

WHERE TO DRINK IN CANNES

Ma Nolan's
Nice's most popular Irish pub brings the same winning recipe to Cannes. The place for good craic and pub grub.

The Quays
This friendly harbourside Irish pub is a Cannes institution with cold beer, happy hours and live sports.

Morrison's Pub
Rock out the weekend with live bands till late, or take the stage on open mic Tuesdays.

MY PERFECT DAY IN CANNES

Carolyn Paul
@Ablacarolyn is a Cannes blogger. Here are her top spots in Cannes.

Breakfast at Le Duplex
Opposite the Plage du Mouré Rouge, this local favourite has a laid-back Californian vibe. Sip a coffee in the morning while enjoying a bowl of granola or a croissant and contemplating the Mediterranean.

Lunch on Île St-Honorat
A haven of peace where you can get drunk on wild beauty. Right next to the boarding quay is the only restaurant on the island, La Tonnelle, a real Cannes institution.

Dinner at Restaurant Bella by Eyal Shani
This rooftop is one of the most beautiful in Cannes. At sunset, you can sip a cocktail and share Mediterranean dishes where local vegetables shine.

March and late October, the **Rotisserie du Marché** batters and deep-fries crispy *beignets des fleurs de courgettes* (fried courgette flowers) in front of your eyes – grab a half-dozen fresh as they are best savoured warm and crunchy. At **Soupe Poisson Forville**, Alexandre Serre has swapped fine-dining kitchens (including Monaco's five-star Hôtel Hermitage) for a stand near the *carré des pêcheurs* and starts cooking big pots of *soupe de poissons* (fish stew) before sunrise to be ready for the morning trade (his *bouillabaisse* needs to be pre-ordered). Crisp on the outside, creamy on the inside *panisse* – either *au nature* (plain) or infused with flavours such as truffle, *herbes de provence* and green olives – is the speciality at **Socca'nnes**. On Mondays, the space brims with curios for the weekly **Marché de Brocante** flea markets.

Meet and Greet

Neighbourhood walks and new friends

A 20-minute walk east from the centre of Cannes, the hillside neighbourhood of Californie has been one of the city's most exclusive addresses since the first lavish villas went up in the mid-19th-century. You'll break out into a sweat on the climb up from the waterfront along av de la Favorite. 'That's why *les Cannois* don't come here,' jokes Simone Revel, a Cannes Greeter. You can pound the footpaths of Californie yourself, but a local guide like Revel will regale you with the anecdotes a quick Google search won't. Like how the stately **Villa Wenden** (now Villa Le Rouve), built for Grand Duchess Anastasia Mecklembourg Schwerin, the granddaughter of Tsar Nicolas I of Russia, was the first in Cannes to connect to electricity. Or how Queen Victoria built the **Chapelle St-Georges** in memory of her son, the Duke of Albany, who died in Cannes in 1884 at age 30, using materials imported from England. 'There is not a speck of anything French inside,' Revel laughs. Greeters networks – locals who volunteer their time to show others their city through their eyes – exist across France and Revel is one of 10 in Cannes who propose, for free, a variety of experiences in the city. From little-trodden nature trails at its outer edges to the Croisette, but seen through the lens of a Cannes native, the two to three hours you spend with your Greeter will gift you a whole new perspective of the city. See cannesgreeters.com.

 WHERE TO GO OUT IN CANNES

Charly's Wine Bar
Dress to impress at this wine bar in Le Suquet, where it's not uncommon for the dancing to spill onto the bar.

Le Hive
It's about drinking, eating and geeking out at this bohemian neighbourhood bar with a busy program of gaming nights.

Le Roof at Five Seas Hotel
Only have time for one Cannes rooftop? Make it this beachy restaurant and lounge bar perched high above the centre.

Gréolières
Réserve
Biologique
des Monts d'Azur   Le Bar-sur-Loup
Grasse   St-Paul-de-Vence
Mandelieu-   Antibes
La Napoule
                Cannes

Beyond Cannes

Let Cannes be your springboard into perfumed villages bathed in a light that has inspired generations of artists.

The coastal roads out of Cannes lead either towards the Mimosa-scented Mandelieu-La Napoule, which once exported these floaty yellow flowers to the furthest corners of Europe, or Antibes and Juan-les-Pins, neighbouring resort towns that groove to the smooth beats of jazz come summer. The pine-shaded landscapes of this coastal stretch have long been a magnet for artistic types, and this heritage can still be felt in irresistibly pretty inland villages such as Mougins, where Picasso saw out the last years of his life. Rising up behind them, Grasse's flowers scent fragrances sold around the world, while the landscape of the Gorges du Loup and Préalps that neighbour it are simply out of this world.

A Festival of Winter Flowers

Celebrate mimosas in bloom

Between January to March, a perfumed curve from Bormes-les-Mimosas in the Var to Grasse explodes in a thick yellow brushstroke of mimosa (wattle) bloom, a plant that is said to have arrived on the Côte d'Azur from Australia via the suitcases of wintering Brits. The Route du Mimosa is a fragrant 130km tourist route connecting the two, following coastal roads and inland trails. **Mandelieu-La Napoule**, the resort town at the western end of the Baie de Cannes, is considered the mimosa capital. The main events to note in your calendar during flowering season include February's **Fête du Mimosa**, a five-day celebration with flower parades,

CYCLING THE COL DE VENCE

Former Olympic sprinter and personal trainer **Marc Raquil** takes us to the top of the Col de Vence.

This is one of the Côte d'Azur's classic and most beautiful cycling routes. The wide road crisscrosses the mountain that rises high behind Vence.

The views en route are magnificent; you can see cars from far away. A lot of champions use the climb for training, the rest of us time ourselves just for fun.

From the fountain in the middle of Vence, which acts as the unofficial starting point, to the sign at the top of the summit is 10km. The fastest finish is 25 minutes; my own best time is 37 minutes.

TOP TIP

Local tourist offices (*offices de tourisme*) are worth a detour as they offer an increasingly dynamic range of activities.

DRIVING THE ESTEREL

This drive along the Corniche d'Or, or the Gold Coast, is a Côte d'Azur classic. Start at ❶ **Château de la Napoule**, a waterfront medieval fortress turned magnificent villa set in 6 hectares of manicured gardens in Mandelieu-La Napoule. In its current life as an art foundation, the property is open for visitors. Plan on an hour-long visit before jumping in the car to continue west; from here, the road lights up in gold in winter as part of the Route du Mimosa (p119). Depending on traffic, you'll reach the pretty beachfront of Théoule-sur-Mer in a handful of minutes. The soft sand of the public ❷ **Plage du Suveret** beckons for a refreshing swim. You could also continue around the hairpin bend to ❸ **Pointe de l'Aguille**, a castaway cove with shallow waters and a wide panorama back towards the Iles de Lérins (p80) and Cap d'Antibes beyond. Pushing on, the landscape starts to transform as you enter deep into the Massif de l'Esterel, the dramatic red-ochre mountain range that frames the eastern edge of the Alpes-Maritimes. For the next 20km, the road mimics the twists and turns of the craggy coastline, cutting through the rich red rocks that cascade into the translucent sea below, with the train line running alongside you. See if you agree that the scattered neighbourhood of ❹ **Le Trayas** is the Côte d'Azur's most beautiful, with waterfront homes overlooking sparkling *calanques* (small coves). Many are only accessible by boat, although some can be accessed from land, including the sheltered ❺ **Calanque de Maubois** with its steep staircase. The route continues all the way to St-Raphaël (p112), but most people can't drive on past the ❻ **Agay** beachfront strip with its cafés and watersports.

Massif de Tanneron

**TENDER IS
THE NIGHT**

A century ago, before it became the postcode of choice for the world's elite, verdant Cap d'Antibes – with its multi-million-euro villas and fabulous 5km coastal footpath, the **Sentier de Tirepoil** – was a playground for the Lost Generation: American writers like Ernest Hemingway and F Scott Fitzgerald.

They whittled away days at **Plage de la Garoupe**, today a half-private, half-public beach. The Cap's legendary five-star **Hôtel du Cap Eden Roc**, immortalised as the Hôtel des Étrangers in Fitzgerald's *Tender Is the Night*, was another favourite hang. Fitzgerald's tome was actually written in a waterfront villa at the other edge of the peninsula in Juan-les-Pins, which would become another five-star lodging: **Hôtel Belles Rives**. Inside the art deco stunner, the street-level Bar Fitzgerald is still furnished with some original pieces.

eveninganimations, fireworks and a party mood. You can also join in on daily hikes deep into the Massif de Tanneron, considered Europe's largest mimosa forest, with qualified local guides such as Maddy Poloméni (maddypolomeni.com). In the historic neighbourhood of **Le Capitou**, growers carefully packed cut mimosa flowers inside baskets woven from cane and willow for export by trail to flower markets in London and Moscow at the start of the 20th-century. Dive deep into the history of mimosa as a crop in **Parc Emmanuelle de Marande**, where over 100 varieties from around the world are planted among informative exhibition boards and a children's playground. Today, the handful of remaining *mimosistes*, as the growers are known, are based at the foothills of the Massif de Tanneron in Pégomas, directly north of Mandelieu-La Napoule. At **Colline des Mimosas**, you're welcome to drop in for big bunches of freshly cut flowers or to learn more about the tried-and-tested technique of forcing flower buds to open in hot, humid rooms called *forceries*.

WHERE TO SLEEP AND SNACK IN MANDELIEU-LA NAPOULE

Hôtel Casarose
This fun hotel brings a funky California vibe and bright decor to the Côte d'Azur. An Instagram favourite. **€€**

La Boutique de l'Oasis
The pâtisserie counter of this refined restaurant is the easy way to taste the chef's creations on the cheap. **€**

**Louise Glaces
Mandelieu-La Napoule**
During the winter flowering season, scoops of mimosa ice cream are a speciality. **€**

Vallauris

A ST-PAUL-DE-VENCE CIRCUIT

A 40-minute drive northeast from Cannes, St-Paul-de-Vence is another ridiculously pretty hilltop village that is a particular magnet for tourist buses in summer. Beat the crowds by following the **Sentier des Fortifications Henri Layet**, a discovery walk around the base of the ramparts that tells of the village's history as both a military stronghold and an agricultural heartland.

Cast your gaze down the flanks and you'll notice neat rows of vines. This municipal parcel is cultivated by **Domaine des Claus**, a biodynamic vineyard in nearby Tourrettes-sur-Loup. The path ends at the southern part of the thick medieval walls.

From there, you can head back into the village – but before you do, pay your respects to **Marc Chagall**, who is buried in the local cemetery.

Street Art in Antibes
Bringing new life to an old town

The annual Coul'Heures d'Automne Festival in **Antibes**, a 20-minute drive east from Cannes, transforms bare walls and garage doors into expressive canvases for street artists from around the world that then remain as permanent installations. A cluster can be viewed on foot as you stroll through **Vieil Antibes**, the lovely cobblestone old town, bringing a modern touch to this seaside resort so beloved by artists and writers, including Pablo Picasso and Graham Greene. Facing the Grande Roue, Antibes' answer to the London Eye, the figures in WilliaNN's *Le Jazz des Cigales* feel ready to jump out of the scene. Two blocks further north, on the corner of bd d'Aguillon and rue Lacan, Monkeybird's stunning *Le Jardin d'Eden* covers the entire rear wall of Cineplanet cinema complex and will mesmerise with its bold, geometric detail. Continue straight along rue Lacan; above the Utile supermarket Nice artist Wanjah depicts a baby being fed words of love. The trail to local artist Olivia Paroldi's urban prints will lead you deep into Antibes' back streets and a delicate engraving on a wooden garage door on rue Paul Bourgarel. Opposite the

WHERE TO DRINK IN ANTIBES

Absinthe Bar
Put on a funny hat and sip the green fairy in this dimly lit cellar bar, an Antibes institution. Live music. €

Le Bam Éphémère
Set around the landmark Le Nomade statue, this summer pop-up bar has a showstopping setting. €

Drinker's Club
Where the yachtie crowd flock for cool cocktails and chilled beer near the ramparts in Vieil Antibes. €

Office du Tourisme, Astro has turned the wall of the Chez Victoire restaurant into a modern trompe l'oeil. You can ask inside the tourist office for a map, although be aware that some locations aren't always plotted in the exact places.

On the Trail of Picasso

War and peace in Antibes

Pablo Picasso settled on the Côte d'Azur in his 60s, yet his life here was anything but a quiet retirement, as the numerous works he produced during this time attest. Start your trail at the **Musée Picasso** in Antibes, set inside the imposing 14th-century Château Grimaldi where Picasso set up studio in 1946. The Spanish artist famously quipped, 'If you want to see the Picassos from Antibes, you must come to Antibes to see them', so do as he instructed.

Heading 20 minutes inland, you'll arrive at **Vallauris**, a name so intertwined with ceramics that many of the street name signs are petit works of art. Picasso settled here between 1948 and 1955 and enjoyed a purple patch; he fired around 4000 ceramic pieces as he played with different techniques. It's the medium most celebrated inside the **Château-Musée** with three museums in one: Musée National Picasso 'La Guerre et la Paix'; Musée Magnelli; and Musée de la Céramique. Standing surrounded by his colourful, distinctive brushstrokes covering the small 12th-century chapel that tell the story of war and peace is the undisputed highlight. On place Paul Isnad outside, *L'Homme au Mouton*, a bronze statue of a man with a sheep that he gifted the town, has pride of place. There are prettier spots on the Côte d'Azur, but Vallauris is a worthwhile stop to browse local ceramic studios, especially along av Georges Clemenceau.

After a brief stint in Vauvenargues near Aix-en-Provence (where he is buried), Picasso returned to the Côte d'Azur, settling in **Mougins**, a 15-minute drive from Vallauris, in 1961. The hilltop *vieux village* is a photographer's delight for snapping dreamy Provençal scenes. At its entrance, the imposing **Tête de Picasso** sculpture is there to greet you. This sunny spot is still the place for art (and gastronomy). Picasso spent the last 12 years of his life here and passed away in 1973 at his home, a sprawling 800-sq-metre farmhouse called **Notre Dame de Vie**. Now privately owned, you can still peek into the estate from the **Chapelle de Notre-Dame de Vie** next door. Flanked by tall Tuscan cypresses and an olive grove, this peaceful 12th-century chapel houses a small collection of black-and-white photographs of Picasso at home. Road access

BEST DIVING SPOTS

Alex Diamond, PADI course director and freelance instructor operating in the south of France since 2005, shares his favourite spots to dive on the Côte d'Azur.

Beginner
La Lauve off the Cap d'Antibes is a magical place to first experience scuba diving. The rock formations are beautiful and just beneath the surface awaits a shallow plateau teeming with life.

Intermediate
The Dromadaire and L'Enfer de Dante off La Fourmigue in Golfe Juan. Spectacular rock formations and underwater cliff faces with grouper, barracuda, dentex and gardens of gorgonian coral.

Advanced
The wrecks of *The Grec* and *Donator* off Île de Porquerolles are something else. The decks are 40m deep and the sea bed is simply awesome – it's so rich in marine life!

WHERE TO SLEEP AND EAT IN MOUGINS

La Lune de Mougins
With a pool, spa, tennis court, restaurant and kids' play area, this spacious three-star is recommended. €€

Brasserie de la Méditerranée
Stylish food in a stylish setting. The snack bar serves up tasty omelettes and salads at lunch. €€

La Cave de Mougins
Chic wine bar with a sunny terrace at the entrance to the village; tasting boards to nibble on. €€

PERFUMED GARDENS

Jardins du Musée International de la Parfumerie
It's worth the 20-minute detour to nearby Mouans-Sartoux to visit the enchanting gardens of the Musée International de la Parfumerie. In this tactile garden, the world's greatest perfume flowers grow: it's particularly lovely in spring when the Rose de Mai is in full bloom.

Domaine du Mas de l'Olivine
Audrey and Thierry Bortolini have transformed the terraced grounds of the family *bastide* in Peymeinade into an explosion of rose and lavender bushes, violet plants, fragrant mint and other perfume flowers. This precious crop is then transformed into a variety of fragranced sweet treats, from lollies to jams. Book the visits and confectionary workshops well in advance.

for the last few hundred metres is paved but narrow. In July, the scene is an atmospheric stage for the annual **Mougins Festival de Musique**.

Follow Your Nose in Grasse

Perfume houses and museums

Grasse's status as the world capital of perfume was cemented with the awarding of Unesco's Intangible Cultural Heritage status in 2018. A trio of local fragrance houses dominate this sprawling town stretched out high in the hills above Cannes, a 40-minute drive to the south. With its historic factory at the entrance to the pedestrianised old quarter, **Fragonard** is the most visible. See original extraction and distilling equipment up close during the free 20-minute guided visits of the factory floor, while the two upper levels of the building are given over to a gorgeous boutique and small self-guided perfume museum. An easy 10-minute walk away on bd Victor Hugo, the cherry-red **Molinard** *bastide* (country house) features a glass roof constructed by Gustave Eiffel. Heading out of town, the **Gallimard** factory along the route de Cannes proposes similar guided visits for free.

PHILIP LEE HARVEY/LONELY PLANET ©

Bottle of custom perfume, Galimard

WHERE TO EAT AND DRINK IN ST-PAUL DE VENCE

La Cave de St-Paul
An atmospheric multi-level medieval cellar with local wines, including the vineyard just below the ramparts. €€

Café de la Place
The service may be slack, but this French bistro overlooking the boules courts is the place to people-watch. €€

Le Tilleul
A shady terrace and a menu of fresh flavours beckon you to settle in for a long lunch on the ramparts of the village. €€

Hands-on experiences are the real highlight when in Grasse, allowing you the chance to play perfumer for anywhere between 20 minutes to an hour. You can reserve workshops at all three perfume houses online, but with its city-centre location, Molinard is the easiest to reach on foot. In a high-ceiling, monochrome-tiled room, you'll mix and match dozens of top, middle and base notes to create a custom scent to take home. A short *Petit Parfumer* experience offers children aged four to eight an introduction to the wonder of scent.

Don't miss the wonderful museums here, either. The **Musée International de la Parfumerie** is a must, even if you're not a perfume lover, presenting three millennia of perfume history in a variety of ways: sight, sound, smell and even touch. The interactive elements are especially a hit with children. Fragonard's stand-alone museums are also worthwhile detours. In a former *hôtel particulier* (private residence) at the start of the umbrella-festooned rue Jean Ossola, the **Musée Provençal du Costume et du Bijou** showcases traditional Provençal clothing and jewellery. A few metres further down, inside another magnificent former private residence, the **Musée Jean-Honoré Fragonard** celebrates Grassois painter Fragonard (1732–1806), even if, during his lifetime, the subject of his work shocked French society.

Scenic Villages along the Loup River
Stunning scenery meets gastronomic delights

From the mountain plains high above Cannes, the Loup River runs all the way down to the Mediterranean and is at its most dramatic northeast of Grasse, snaking through a landscape of plunging cliffs, perched villages, refreshing waterfalls and thick forest, an area known as the **Gorges du Loup**. Meaning wolf in English, the Loup has given its name to a cluster of delightful villages, starting with sun-kissed **Le Bar-sur-Loup**, which has a rich tradition of cultivating bitter oranges (a heritage celebrated every Easter Monday with the annual **Fête de l'Oranger**). The village is also the departure point for the **Chemin du Paradis**, a sporty 1½-hour hiking trail along an old mule track that winds up in Gourdon. The next wolf along, **Le Pont du Loup**, is more hamlet than village, but the craft beer brewed at **Bacho Brewery** attracts a crowd from Nice and beyond. Set among a terrace of orange trees lit by fairy lights, this atmospheric microbrewery is the place for a quiet drink or a party night, depending on your mood. **Tourrettes-sur-Loup**, the village of violets, is emerging as the foodie destination of the Côte d'Azur hinterland. Word is spreading about chef Raphaël Grima's gastronomic cuisine, so

CANYONING IN THE GORGES DU LOUP

Lionel Richard is a climbing and canyoning guide with Bureau des Guides LesGeckos (lesgeckos.eu) in Courmes. Here's why he says the Gorges du Loup is paradise for outdoor sports.

Le Pont du Loup is the launching pad for incredible hiking, swimming, rock-climbing and canyoning adventures. Most of the rock-climbing sites are for experienced climbers, although close to Gourdon the **Belvédère** site is suitable for beginners. Canyoning is our most popular activity during summer. On a half-day excursion, we begin at the bottom of the **Courmes waterfall** and abseil into the gorge, followed by plenty of jumps and slides – at one point, you get to plunge 8m into the water below! Our half-day tours take about three hours and are for ages eight and up.

WHERE TO EAT IN GRASSE

L'Arrosoir
A creative family-run restaurant in Grasse that's won a following with its tasty home cooking. €

Café des Musées
Daily menu of quiches, salads, croque monsieur and a *plat du jour* at this popular and well-located café. €

Les Delicatesses de Grasse
Part-restaurant, part-deli on place aux Aires with tasting boards of cheese, charcuterie and tapenade. €

you need to reserve to get a table at **Spelt**. Signature dishes include a divine spelt risotto with lobster, served in hand-made olive-wood bowls. Save space for a scoop of violet ice cream for dessert at **Tom's Glacier**.

Panoramic Préalpes

Drive the Côte d'Azur's wild side

Push on past **Le Pont du Loup** on the D6 and before too long the windy road gives way to the first glimpse of the moody mountain faces of the **Parc Naturel Régional des Préalpes d'Azur** staring back at you. A veritable natural terrace over-looking the coast, the national park extends across a vast inland territory almost 900 sq km in size. This 50km loop is a delightful two- or four-wheel route through many of the highlights. The first village of note is **Gréolières** (800m), with a buzzy Saturday morning market that attracts local market gardeners and honey producers. Continue the ascent along the route Gréolières, at times a sheer, cliff-edge road, until the wildflower-covered plains of the plateau open out in front of you. You'll share the flat stretch of road, the RD2, with packs of cyclists and motorbikers, as well as the odd supercar at speed. **Gréolières les Neiges** is a small family-friendly ski resort that is particularly popular with locals come snow season.

At the roundabout just after the entrance to the **Réserve Biologique des Monts d'Azur**, head south back on the D5 towards Caussols, over the **Col de Castellaras** mountain pass (1248m) where views plummet into the deep valley below. The road skims the ridge for more dramatic views before another blissfully flat expanse around **Caussols**, a mountain commune that, according to local folklore, possesses the ideal terrain for UFO landings. The Mediterranean comes back into view before you start the winding descent towards **Gourdon**, a fortified village dangling high above the Gorges du Loup. Just before you arrive, a gravel car park to your left denotes the start of the **Plateau de Cavillore** hike, a short trail that ap-pears steep to look at, but the switchbacks that lead towards the summit are fairly gentle, making it a popular family out-ing. With superb panoramas from all angles, the walk is the ideal pre-lunch scramble before dropping into Gourdon itself. It's a minimum one-hour drive to Gréolières from Cannes.

THE FLORA OF THE PRÉALPES

Beth-Jane Marshall is creating a small botanical garden in the heart of the Préalpes: the **Jardin Botanique de la Flore des Alpes-Maritimes**. *jbam.fr*

The flora of the Alpes-Maritimes is truly incredible. This is a biodiversity hotspot, situated at the transition zone between the Alps and the Mediterranean Basin, and contains over 60% of the entire flora of France. Approximately 3300 species can be found in this area alone. Due to its unique geographical position, range of altitude, geology and climate, the region harbours many species that are found nowhere else. *Erodium rodiei* and *Campanula albicans,* for example, are two beautiful plant species which can only be found growing in the Préalpes d'Azur.

WHERE TO SLEEP IN THE GORGES DU LOUP

Hôtel Particulier des Jasmins
Rustic yet romantic rooms inside an old perfumers house with deep valley views. **€€**

Auberge Les Gorges du Loup
This great-value find in Pont du Loup has oodles of Provençal charm. Pet friendly and hugely popular with motorbikers. **€**

Auberge de Tourrettes
Classy boutique hotel with a pool and 10 stylish rooms, some with sea views, straight out of a design magazine. **€€€**

Into the Wild

Bison, boars and nature

In 1993, Dr Patrice Longour, a French veterinarian, established the **Réserve Biologique des Monts d'Azur** in order to achieve his long-held vision: rewilding mammals at risk of extinction, such as the European bison, Przewalski's horse and elk (moose). The 700-hectare reserve is located just past the turnoff to Greolières-les-Neiges in Thorenc, a little over an hour's drive north of Cannes. Visit and you'll quickly get the sense that the fences are more to keep people from going in rather than the animals from coming out. Access to the sprawling reserve is either on foot (two hours) or on a horse-drawn cart (75 minutes). Both tours are led and narrated by a qualified guide well-versed in tracking the park's resident three-legged wild boar and judging just how close visitors can get to the majestic herd of 50 bison. The cluster of buildings at the entrance once formed part of a small hamlet and now functions as a variety of visitor services, including a snack bar serving up hot drinks and crêpes, a children's play area, a small open-air museum and a restaurant where organic ingredients shine. Linger by booking one of the prairie-facing glamping tents (May to October only) and sleep under the stars, or reserve a room in one of two well-appointed eco-lodges that are open year-round and are particularly cosy when dusted in winter snow. Starting in September, the *brame du cerf* (rutting season) is a particularly memorable time to pay a visit.

ROUTE NAPOLÉON HIGHLIGHTS

Pascal Brochiero, general manager of the Pays de Grasse Tourist Office, shares his Route Napoléon highlights.

On 1 March 1815, Napoléon escaped the island of Elba and landed in Golfe-Juan with the intention of marching to Paris and reclaiming France – which he briefly did.

The mythical Route Napoléon follows his journey from the Côte d'Azur through the Alps. Passing through **Cannes**, Napoléon headed towards **Grasse**, and stopped at **St-Vallier de Thiey**, site of the the Napoléon Column. He then pushed onwards to **Escragnolles** to admire its grandiose mountain setting. At **Séranon**, the **Bastide du Broundet**, where he spent a night, still stands today.

BILL CINI/SHUTTERSTOCK ©

Gourdon

WHERE TO EAT IN THE PRÉALPES

La Vieille Auberge
Delightful restaurant inside the village of Gréolières, serving up family favourites on a shady tree-lined square. €

Les 3 Vallées
Friendly roadside lunch spot on the Route Napoléon in Seranon. Easy parking and generous bistro favourites. €

Restaurant Les Chasseurs
Pizzas and a sunny outdoor terrace with a wide-angled view get a big thumbs up at this family restaurant in Andon. €

GETTING AROUND

On foot is the best way to get around Monaco with no distances longer than an hour's walk apart, but the terrain can be very steep. Swap the stairs – and catch your breath – in one of the principality's 79 public lifts or 35 escalators. The Compagnie Autobus de Monaco operates six bus lines that serve all corners of the principality; tickets can be purchased on board the bus. MonaBike is Monaco's excellent electric bike-sharing scheme; register in advance on the Monapass app. If driving, avoid commuter hours as traffic is bumper to bumper. Public parking fills up fast and can be pricey during daytime hours, although the hourly rate drops significantly come evening.

TOP TIP

Download the Monapass app before you arrive to reserve tickets for local buses and main attractions, including the Oceanographic Museum and Prince's Palace State Apartments, as well as to unlock the principality's MonaBike shared electric bicycle scheme and pay for street parking.

Monaco

Monaco

Monaco is constantly evolving. Towering cranes are as ubiquitous as superyachts and sports cars as the principality stretches up and out to sea to maximise every centimetre of its limited space. Nowhere else on the Côte d'Azur feels so built up, but in fact over 20% of Monaco's territory is made up of gardens. Spearheaded by HSH Prince Albert II, the principality harbours even greater green ambitions with a goal of carbon neutrality by 2050.

'Green is glam', as Monaco's sustainable push with a luxury twist is known, is the latest chapter in the Hollywood history of the world's second-smallest country, whose reputation was built on a lavish Belle Époque casino and sealed with the marriage of a Grimaldi prince to a silver-screen princess. The glitz is as pervasive as ever, but is now balanced out by local experiences – and flavours – that add another side to Monaco's real identity and culture.

Motorsports in May

Fast cars, three ways

In May, you either love Monaco or hate it, and which way you lean depends on how you feel about cars racing around in circles. Most residents get out of town, but if you're a car-racing fan, there's no place better to be once the **Formula One** roadshow rolls into town. Tickets for the four days of racing go on sale on the **Automobile Club de Monaco**'s online portal around six months ahead of the race. You can nab a seat at Thursday's practice sessions for €30 but expect to pay three figures for even the cheapest seats for Sunday's race day. Even if you don't have a ticket, it's still worth coming to Monaco on the weekend. The echoes of engines reverberate off every building and the excitement builds with every driver appearance at the fan zone on place d'Armes. Many restaurants stream the race live so you don't miss any of the action. Unfortunately, it's almost impossible to find anywhere to view the circuit for free anymore, unless you head up onto the Moyenne Corniche in **Beausoleil**, the French town that seeps into Monaco, with some powerful binoculars. An abridged

HIGHLIGHT
1 Casino de Monte Carlo

SIGHTS
2 Automobile Club de Monaco
3 Cathédrale de Monaco
4 Jardin aux Canards
5 Jardin Exotique
6 Jardins St-Martin
7 Musée d'Anthropologie Préhistorique de Monaco
8 Musée Océanographique de Monaco
9 Palais Princier de Monaco
10 Parc Princesse Antoinette
11 Plage des Pêcheurs
12 Plage du Larvotto
13 Princess Grace Irish Library
14 Roseraie Princesse Grace
15 Villa Paloma
16 Villa Sauber

ACTIVITIES, COURSES & TOURS
17 Académie Monégasque de la Mer
18 Solarium
19 Stade Nautique Rainier III

EATING
20 Beef Bar
21 Cantinetta Antinori
22 Marché de la Condamine
23 Pecherie U Luvassu
24 U Luvassu

DRINKING & NIGHTLIFE
25 Bar Américain
26 Brasserie de Monaco
27 Coya

ENTERTAINMENT
28 Stade Louis II

SHOPPING
29 La Distillerie de Monaco
30 La Maison du Limoncello

FOR THE REMAINING 11 MONTHS...

Visiting Monaco outside of May? The starting grid and pole positions are marked on the road outside 17 bd Albert Ier on Port Hercules.

At number 23 is the member-only **Automobile Club de Monaco**; browse the memorabilia that dresses the window. On the street behind it (rue Grimaldi) is a sleek souvenir boutique.

Now safely tucked up in their new display on route de la Piscine on Port Hercules, Prince Rainier III's magnificent car stockpile, the **Collection de Voitures de SAS le Prince de Monaco**, includes the horse-drawn carriage he used to court Grace Kelly with, as well as a whole floor of rally cars.

A plaque marks the famous hairpin bend outside the **Fairmont Monte-Carlo** near pl du Casino. It's the slowest corner of any F1 circuit.

CRISTIANO BARNI/SHUTTERSTOCK ©

Monaco Grand Prix, Monte Carlo

version of the famous street circuit has become an annual May fixture on the ePrix calendar as well. Tickets for the **Monaco ePrix** cost €30, no matter which stand you sit in. If you prefer vintage classics over modern iterations, the **Grand Prix Historique de Monaco** is held two weeks before the Formula One race every second year (2024 and 2026 are the next dates). Watch champions from yesteryear compete for a variety of trophies – and bragging rights. Tickets start from €50, also via the Automobile Club de Monaco.

Uncovering a Palace's Past

Hidden Renaissance frescoes

From the **Palais Princier de Monaco** high up in Monaco Ville, or Le Rocher as locals refer to Monaco's oldest neighbourhood, the Grimaldi family has ruled over the principality since the late 13th-century. Still the official residence of the sovereign family, only the **Grands Appartements**, or staterooms, are open to public eyes – and only between April and October for self-guided visits with an audio guide (except for the Formula One Grand Prix weekend in late May). These formal rooms, which still have a ceremonial function, display

WHERE TO SLEEP IN MONACO

Hôtel de France
Cheapest hotel in Monaco itself with 26 well-appointed rooms and airy high ceilings; there's no lift. **€€**

Columbus Hôtel
This stylish three-star hotel in Fontvieille punches above its weight with a pool and great views. **€€€**

Hôtel Miramar
Boutique hotel on Port Hercules with a chic nautical theme and a cool rooftop bar. **€€€**

a princely penchant for heavy drapery, extensive gold-leaf panelling and fine art.

The entire experience has been elevated with the uncovering of over 600 sq metres (and counting) of captivating Renaissance frescoes that depict three heroes from antiquity – Hercules, Odysseus and Europa – hidden for centuries under layers of paint. The work is ongoing, as the metres of scaffolding attest, using natural solvents and environmentally friendly solutions to gradually restore walls and ceilings to their original decoration. It's a project those at the palace believe will last the lifetime of the current sovereign, His Serene Highness, Prince Albert II. Time your visit around the changing of the guards, daily at 11.55am.

In the Footsteps of Princess Grace

A princess in her principality

When Grace Kelly met Monaco's Prince Rainier III during a photocall in the Palais Princier de Monaco in 1955, the first chapter was written in a fairy tale that enchanted the world. Four decades after her death, the legacy of the golden girl from Philadelphia turned Mediterranean princess still lingers strong. With the **Palais Princier de Monaco** behind you, head into the charming warren of narrow alleyways of **Monaco-Ville**. You can browse the spines of her personal book collection in the **Princess Grace Irish Library**, now the guardian of her precious tomes of Irish literature and Irish-American sheet music. On rainy days, the extensive kids' corner is a welcome shelter. Perhaps the most important pilgrimage spot is just around the corner: in the choir of the **Cathédrale de Monaco**, the grave of the princess lies alongside that of her prince.

In the Fontvieille neighbourhood below, a statue of Grace watches over the **Roseraie Princesse Grace**, a serene, English-style garden where 6000 rose bushes burst into bloom in spring. The princess also designed the famous red-and-white jersey of the AS Monaco Football club in 1960; the team's home ground, **Stade Louis II**, is looking a little tired, but between June and October you can step beyond the pitch for stadium tours. On the other side of Monaco, av Princesse Grace is one of the principality's most exclusive addresses, where luxurious apartment blocks overlook the Larvotto beachfront. About half way down on place Josephine Baker, you'll find the **Hommage à la Princesse Grace** sculpture fountain. The location is no mere coincidence. The two women were firm friends; Grace was instrumental in helping Baker, an American dancer and civil rights activist, set up home in the principality.

WHERE I GO OUT IN MONACO

Philip Culazzo founded Monaco's first distillery, La Distillerie de Monaco, in 2017. He shares his favourite drinking spots. @distillerie-demonaco

The absolute grande dame of Monaco bars has to be the **Bar Américain** in the Hôtel de Paris, with its old-school charm, great live music and amazingly talented barstaff, who will literally whip up any cocktail you can name. We have a signature drink on the menu called La Condamine, named after the location of our distillery in Monaco.

For the nightowls, **Coya** and the newly opened **Maona** are lively spots with really good mixologists, but I'm just as happy sitting on **place d'Armes** under a carob tree sipping on a refreshing sundowner.

WHERE TO EAT IN MONACO

Les Perles de Monte-Carlo
Tuck into oysters reared on-site at this marine research centre-turned-seafood counter in Fontvieille. €€

Le Petit Bar de Monaco
A French bistro run by an Australian chef in Monaco's oldest neighbourhood. Have the lunch *plat du jour*. €

Sexy Tacos
Fiery Mexican cuisine and zesty margaritas make this the hottest address on the Larvotto beach strip. €€

BEST MONACO MUSEUMS

Musée Océanographique de Monaco
This world-class multi-level marine museum includes an aquarium and floor-to-ceiling multimedia shows. A fabulous excursion for children.

Nouveau Musée National de Monaco – Villa Sauber
Two thought-provoking temporary exhibitions a year light up one of the few stand-alone Belle Époque villas still standing in the principality.

Nouveau Musée National de Monaco – Villa Paloma
Same idea as the Villa Sauber, high up in the Jardin Exotique neighbourhood.

Musée d'Anthropologie Préhistorique de Monaco
Connected to the Jardin Exotique gardens, this small but informative museum showcases prehistoric treasures unearthed in digs around the principality.

The Jewel in the Crown

A casino and a work of art

Fun fact: Monaco nationals are not allowed to gamble at the **Casino de Monte-Carlo**, the Belle Époque marvel that put the principality on the map when it first opened in the 1860s. For all other nationalities, gaming starts at 2pm. You must be at least 18 years and have a photo ID. There's a strict dress code: think smart attire rather than shorts, sportswear and flip-flops. In the mornings (10am to 1pm; last entrance at 12.15pm) you can ogle the ornate marble and gold-leaf clad *salons privés* without risking a cent on a self-guided tour through the venue. Take your time and admire the intricate detailing of each of the 10 rooms you pass through. Even the fittings and fixtures are works of art. In Salle Europe, the oldest gaming room, roulette wheels spin underneath eight dazzling Bohemian crystal chandeliers, weighing 150kg each. Salle Blanche, a private den, sparkles with mosaic detailing and caryatids. The Empire-style Salle Médecin, where the casino's original high rollers played away from prying eyes, is also a silver-screen star with two Bond movies, *Golden Eye* and *Never Say Never Again*, shot here. The casino is also home to one of Monaco's classic dining experiences. Deep inside the gaming area, **Le Train Bleu** is a narrow alcove dressed up as a railway dining wagon from the golden age of train travel, complete with crisp white tablecloths and rich wood panelling. Open Thursday to Sunday for dinner only, you'll quickly spend the €40-plus required on the delicate high-end Italian dishes to be reimbursed the €18 casino entrance fee.

Made in Monaco Drinks

Taste the local spirit

Agriculture was the lifeblood of Monaco's economy until the mid-19th-century when the Grimaldi family ceded 95% of its territory to France. Today, if you look closely enough, there are still clues to this heritage, such as the 600 bitter orange trees that line some of the principality's main boulevards (particularly rue Grimaldi behind Port Hercules). Rather than confining the fruit to waste, **La Distillerie de Monaco** transforms this tangy citrus into a punchy orange liqueur, called L'Orangeraie. Since opening in 2020 on rue de la Turbie behind La Marché de La Condamine, two more distinctly Monégasque drinks have been added to the made-in-Monaco spirit cabinet: Carruba, a rich, velvety chocolate liqueur made from Monaco's national tree, the carob, and a

WHERE TO FIND A COLD BEER IN MONACO

La Rascasse
Legendary harbourside bar on the F1 corner of the same name. Chilled happy hours, loud late-night parties.

Slammers Monaco
Small pub with big sports screens and a reputation for atmosphere, especially on Grand Prix weekend.

Gerhard's Café
This friendly, long-running pub on Fontvieille's bar and restaurant strip shouldn't be overlooked.

seven-citrus Gin aux Agrumes. Book ahead to organise a visit of its compact premises – there's also a bar pouring taster measures to people who stop by.

Up on Le Rocher, you may get to see luminescent limoncello being bottled at **La Maison du Limoncello**. For a variation on the theme, there's also lime, mandarin, grapefruit and bitter orange versions – you're welcome to taste them all to decide your favourite. Beer drinkers should bookmark the **Brasserie de Monaco**. This boisterous microbrewery on the harbourfront bar and restaurant strip pours organic pale ales and wheat beers brewed in a shiny on-site brewhouse, along-side a typical pub grub menu. Happy hour runs from 6pm to 8pm, a time when the venue buzzes with the after-work crowd.

Where the Locals Lunch

A small square and big market

Despite its glitzy image, the good news is that you don't have to take out a loan to eat well in Monaco. The hub of cheap and cheerful eats is the bustling **Marché de la Condamine** on place d'Armes. This lively square just back from Port Hercules

BEST MONACO GARDENS

Parc Princesse Antoinette
An all-around family favourite with table tennis, a mini-golf course, a petting farm and plenty of shade.

Jardin Exotique
After closing for renovation, this magical succulent and cactus garden that clings to a cliff face is finally set to reopen in 2024.

Jardins St-Martin
Skirting the southern rim of Le Rocher, Monaco's first public garden is shaded by its national tree, the carob.

Jardin aux Canards
Ducks love the centrepiece fountain of this leafy green space adjacent to the Roseraie Princesse Grace. Pram and wheelchair friendly.

HORIZON IMAGES/MOTION/ALAMY STOCK PHOTO ©

Casino de Monte-Carlo

WHERE TO TASTE WINE IN MONACO

Supernature
This trendy wine bar in La Condamine is a welcome addition to the sometimes stuffy Monaco scene.

Les Grands Chais Monégasques
On a side street near the port, a magical shop for wine lovers to lose themselves for a while.

Lounge Solaire
This sparkling seasonal pop-up Champagne truck in Monte Carlo oozes only-in-Monaco glamour.

THE LAST FISHER

There used to be a dozen or so fishing families in Monaco, their wooden boats sharing the harbour with early pleasure yachts. Today, only Eric Rinaldi continues the tradition. Around here, Rinaldi is known as the last fisherman of Monaco and his two fibreglass workboats, moored on quai Hirondelle, are a stark contrast to the gleaming yachts alongside. Like his father, grandfather and great-grandfather before him, Rinaldi heads out to sea most mornings, netting smaller species such as red mullet, sea bream and scorpion fish close to shore and bigger fish such as swordfish and tuna further out. Rinaldi's daily catch is sold fresh or cooked before your eyes at **Pêcherie U Luvassu**, the harbourside fishmonger and restaurant behind his berth, which he co-owns.

in the Condamine neighbourhood bursts with fresh flowers and colourful fruit and vegetables in the morning. The food hall inside starts to buzz as workers from nearby offices flow in for lunch, but shutters start to rise much earlier for the breakfast trade. If you need a shot of caffeine to get going in the morning, you can't go past **Le Comptoir** for seriously good Italian coffee (the focaccia is also tasty, especially if it's just out of the oven). If you're more a sweet tooth first thing in the morning, then the local outpost of celebrated Argentinian chef Mauro Colagreco's organic bakehouse, **Mitron Bakery**, is your chance to sample his signature *tarte au citron* (lemon tart) without venturing to Menton. The lunch crowd flock with good reason to **La Maison des Pâtes** for strings of fresh tagliatelle or pouches of ravioli – don't let the queue put you off, it's worth the wait. Regional street food is also represented: so renowned is the *socca* and *pissaladière* at **Chez Roger** that there's little need to sell anything else, while **A Roca** is the spot for *barbajuans*, a tasty fried ravioli considered the principality's national dish. Many of the stands close after lunch but some have a second wind come evening, such as **Bar Le Zinc**, which pours what must be Monaco's cheapest glass of wine (€2).

CHRISPICTURES/SHUTTERSTOCK ©

Stade Nautique Rainier III

 ## WHERE TO SIP COFFEE AND TEA IN MONACO

Costadora Social Coffee Monaco
Espresso, Chemex, V60, Plunger: find your preference at this Italian café.

Mada One
Sipping a latte macchiato on this posh terrace near the casino is Monaco glitz at an affordable price.

Le Teashop
Cute neighbourhood café on bd des Moulins, with 100-plus teas plus plenty of tea-adjacent finds.

Urban Beach Days

The Grimaldi cannonball

You might not think of Monaco as a beach destination, but the principality has a knack for sculpting space into whatever use it needs, so pack your swimsuit, even if you're just coming for the day. You'll sunbathe with locals at **Plage du Larvotto**, the beachfront strip east of Port Hercules that has recently benefited from serious upgrades. The sunloungers at **La Note Bleue** private beach and restaurant are perennial favourites (as are the weekend live-music sessions in summer), but there's also plenty of public beach to lay down your towel for free. Between May and October, you can hire stand-up paddleboards at **Académie Monégasque de la Mer**. Generations of Monégasque children have learnt to swim at **Stade Nautique Rainier III** on route de la Piscine. This open-air Olympic-size pool with diving board and slide is set among the luxury yachts of Port Hercules, but it's small change to enter for the day (€12 for non-residents) by comparison – the extra €6 for a sunlounger and parasol is a worthwhile investment as there's little shade. An unlikely swim spot has emerged on the concrete outer wall on the western side of the harbour, behind the cruise terminal. Known simply as the **Solarium**, the wide steps are an ideal jumping-off point to cool down on a hot day, although the arrival of **Maliza Mar** restaurant and bar with sunloungers has made it now the kind of place to stay the day. Just be aware that the water here is deep and unpatrolled. Close by, on the **Promenade des Pêcheurs** path at the base of the rock, you'll find the steps down to **Plage des Pêcheurs**, a hidden half-moon of pebbly beach snuggled into the cliff face that's bliss at low tide and calm seas – but not when the sea is up.

LEMON LOVE

Mauro Colagreco first conquered Menton with **Mirazur**, the restaurant that went on to earn him three Michelin stars. But the Argentine chef continues to expand his Menton empire with **Casa Fuego** and **Les Sablettes** (p71), where you don't have to fork out Michelin prices.

LUNCHTIME SPECIALS

Although still considered pricey in most other destinations, Monaco's high-end restaurant menus that veer towards exorbitant for the dinner service are often more wallet-friendly for weekday lunch. Here's what a budget of around €30 will get you.

Song Qi
Cool Shanghai art deco design with a set menu of two starters, a dish of the day, rice and a glass of wine. **€€**

Beef Bar
Legendary carnivore emporium in Fontvieille serving a starter, beef tartare with chips and a glass of wine. **€€**

Cantinetta Antinori
Antipasti, a main course and a glass of Tuscan wine at this Larvotto outpost of the classic Florentine restaurant. **€€**

WHERE TO SHOP IN MONACO

One Monte-Carlo
Uber-designer brands flock to the glossy retail space around the casino.

Metropole Shopping Monte-Carlo
With polished marble and fancy chandeliers, the Metropole is great for window shopping.

La Condamine
Independent boutiques share rue Grimaldi with high-street names and souvenir shops.

The Var

BEACHES, HILLTOP VILLAGES & THE SEA

From the waters and coastal beaches of the Mediterranean to the forests and perched villages of the inner Var, southern Provence lives vibrantly here.

Glamour and sophistication along the Gulf of St-Tropez, family-friendly beach access near Hyères, medieval cities stretching from the coast to the northern edge of the region – the Var is more than the coast. But it is that, too.

Want to get in on the glitz? Head to St-Tropez and experience the finest beaches, cocktails and hotels – luxury yachts included. The village streets are home not just to high-end shopping, but also to some of the finest artisanal boutiques on the coast. Don't get caught up on labels, but look instead for craftsmanship. Get some air in the breezy Mediterranean gardens and come in winter to revel in the mimosa flowering season.

Looking for a more laid-back scene? Try the Presqu'île de Giens or one of the Golden Isles – Porquerolles, the Levant and Port-Cros – by bicycle, snorkel or foot. A day spent in the underrated city of Hyères will certainly please those who've done it all on the Côte d'Azur. Villages like Cotignac – with its cliffs, caves and time-worn main street bustling with restaurants – quickly anchor themselves in the heart.

Foodies, the coast is your hotspot for seafood and cocktails. Inland, dine on heartier Provençal meals like stews and stuffed vegetables. But leave room for a scoop of local chestnut ice cream, and then raise a glass of rosé to toast the sunset. From the hills to the coast, the Var is yours.

NEWPHOTOSERVICE/SHUTTERSTOCK ©

Inset: Cycling, Hyères (p113); Opposite: St-Tropez (P104)

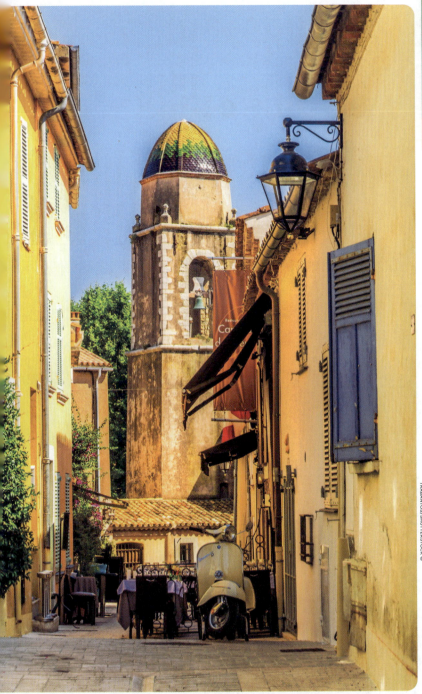

Find Your Way

In the coastal cities it's best to get around without a car. Inland, in contrast, is easier with a car. The main train station is Hyères; smaller stations are in St-Tropez and Ste-Maxime.

CAR

The pros: get around the inner Var easily. The cons: the coastal road is a traffic-clogged driving nightmare, and parking in coastal towns comes with a gold-plated price tag.

BOAT

On the Gulf of St-Tropez, grab a boat ferry to cross from Ste-Maxime, Grimaud or St-Tropez. Les Bateaux Verts (bateauxverts.com) is the main provider.

St-Tropez, p104

The capital of hot summer nights. Come here to live out your French Riviera dreams.

Provence Verte, p121

Escape the crowds and heat in the shrubby winegrowing plains and hilltop villages.

Hyères, p113

All the elements of a classic Côte d'Azur town, without the rush or bling. Islands, too.

TOP: NITO/SHUTTERSTOCK ©, BOTTOM: BEARFOTOS/SHUTTERSTOCK ©

0   10 km
0   5 miles

St-Tropez from the citadel (p106)

Plan Your Time

Can't move to the south of France? Don't try to get it all in at once. Here are some ideas on planning your time without stretching it too tight.

Weekend in St-Tropez

● Spend the morning on a catamaran touring the gulf (p104) and return for lunch at a club on **Pampelonne beach** (p107).

● Stay out till dawn, ending the night at one of St-Tropez' **dance halls** (p108).

● Sleep off last night on a lounger at another beach club, then hit the boutiques for some high-class **souvenirs** (p106) before heading home.

Four Days Inland

● Connect with nature by sleeping at **Montrieux-le-Vieux** (p125), where you can hike through nearby pristine forests.

● Go **wine tasting** (p122) to find your favourite rosé before sleeping below the cliffs of Cotignac.

● In the morning, cycle along gravel tracks through to **Barjols** (p123) and back.

● The next day, explore the troglodyte caves of nearby **Villecroze** (p121) before driving down to the coast.

Seasonal Highlights

SPRING

The mimosas bloom in late winter and early spring – rendezvous for the **Mimosa Festival** (p120) in Bormes-les-Mimosas.

SUMMER

In early summer, go snorkelling along the Porquerolles' coast. In high season, reserve early and join the throngs of beachgoers.

AUTUMN

Les Voiles de St-Tropez (p107) takes over the gulf and port for 10 days; visit to see the world's finest yachts in action.

WINTER

The days are short, but this is the best time to cycle through the inner Var – calm roads, friendly people and mild temperatures.

St-Tropez

St-Tropez

St-Tropez is the most desired destination on the French Riviera. Sail the gulf, dine in the glitzy restaurants, sunbathe on the loungers and dance till dawn. But dig deeper and you'll get your art, shopping, festival and design fix too. Across the gulf is laid-back Ste-Maxime, which is perfect for families and those not wanting to spend the bling-bling budget on a single cocktail. Or escape to Grimaud, niched between the two – it's small, but with just enough narrow streets, beautiful flowers and accessible art to make for a great day away from the beach. St-Tropez is busy, it's flashy, and in the summer months it's also jam packed. But that shouldn't discourage you from enjoying yourself and filling your days with satisfying activities, in addition to meeting kind strangers, locals and world travellers. The French Riviera is what you make of it, so make it fabulous.

Hit the Open Seas

Hire a captain and set sail

Skip the speed boats and opt for a water-skimming catamaran on the Gulf of St-Tropez. Sailors start their day early in the morning to embark on a journey towards the breathtaking *calanques* (inlets) of Cap Taillât.

More than just a leisurely boat trip, **Gael and Bruno's crew** (sport-decouverte.com; French only) provides an engaging adventure: try your hand at sailing by assisting with maneuvers, or enjoy kayaking, paddleboarding or snorkelling. You might even spot some sea creatures such as wrasse fish, sea bream, starfish and occasionally seahorses or groupers. Not in the mood for adventure? Spend the boat ride relaxing on the suspended nets of the catamaran, sandwiched between the blues of the sea and the sky. Tours run for a half (€55 per person) or full day (€95 per person).

GETTING AROUND

The coastal road that links St-Tropez to Grimaud and Ste-Maxime gets congested early in the day and is frustratingly busy during high season. Boat shuttles take just as long as driving but with a more soothing atmosphere.

Sunset Spots on the Coast

Watch the day melt into night

Back on land, sunset is the moment when St-Tropez transitions from lazy beach days to wild beach nights. Plan the sunset moment in advance so you'll have the best seat in the house. Watching the sunset at the **Plage de Gigaro** in La Croix Valmer (17km south of St-Tropez) is hands down the best sunset spot.

In town, **Plage de la Bouillabaisse** is a convenient spot to have a sunset drink while soaking up the ambience of the port before heading home to change before dinner. The beach bars here are usually packed, so unless you've been at one all day, don't count on waltzing in for a drink.

For the more adventurous sunset spotters, bring your own snack or bottle to the **Cap Camarat lighthouse,** perched on the edge of the peninsula.

St-Tropez Shopping Spree

Elegance and style

Most global luxury brands have a boutique in the narrow streets of St-Tropez. But look past the flashy names and you'll discover some unmissable shopping spots. Like in Capri and Minorca, St-Tropez has its own signature sandal: **Rondini**. For over 80 years, the Rondini family has been crafting high-quality leather sandals emblematic of St-Tropez. Their flagship model,

> ☑ **TOP TIP**
>
> Not planning to party till dawn? Then late May and June are good times to visit the region as most of the beach clubs will be open for day-lounging, but with a chiller vibe. Avoid driving if you can – parking costs a fortune and the traffic jams into town are legendary.

SIGHTS
1 Bel-Air Fine Art Gallery
2 Fondation Linda et Guy Pieters
3 La Citadelle
4 La Vielle Mer
5 Plage de la Bouillabaisse

DRINKING & NIGHTLIFE
6 Hôtel Cheval Blanc
7 Pearl Beach St-Tropez

SHOPPING
8 Be-Store

9 La Cabane d'Anoé
10 Les Galeries Tropéziennes
11 Marinette Décoration
12 Rondini Sandals

LINE HOLTERMANN-JUGE/SHUTTERSTOCK ©

Classic sailboat, St-Tropez

the gladiator, is available in both low-cut and ankle-wrap versions and is exclusively made-to-measure.

Want your kids looking dapper too? Exquisite **La Cabane d'Anoé** provides a unique shopping experience for parents and children alike, with a wide selection of items from top brands, including the ever-popular Louis Louise. If you're searching for ways to elevate your home decor, **Marinette Décoration** is the perfect place choice. This company specialises in chic and inspiring decorating ideas that seamlessly blend modern and authentic elements.

Men in particular can stop by **Be-Store**, a mono-product boutique specialising in all things shorts. Going beyond cargos or golf shorts, Loïc Berthet's cotton shorts come in a vast choice of colours and styles and are size-inclusive.

Bargain hunters should visit **Les Galeries Tropéziennes**. No sacrifice on quality, this bazaar-style shop has been a mainstay in St-Tropez shopping life since 1903. On one side, a practical space brings together everyday accessories (haberdashery, metre fabrics, brushes, household linen) while the other side is an emblem of St-Tropez elegance (swimsuits, espadrilles, cashmere sweaters, straw hats and tableware).

 WHERE TO DINE WITH THE IN-CROWD

La Petite Plage St-Tropez
Cool, refreshing appetisers, an oyster bar and caviar. And that's just the starter menu. €€€

La Sauvageonne
Relaxed jungle chic bar and restaurant, with an additional piano bar. Locally run. €€€

Zetta
Easy-chic Italian, expect pizzas, big salads and gourmet desserts. A bargain in St-Tropez. €€

Gallery Day in St-Tropez

Culture fix

Looking to do more than lounge about during your stay? Art lovers will certainly find pieces that inspire in the village. Visit the **Fondation Linda et Guy Pieters** (free), one of the most prestigious contemporary art collections on the Côte d'Azur; it's just off the place des Lices in the centre of town. Keep on the contemporary trend by popping into the **Bel-Air Fine Art Gallery** next. Part of the largest fine art gallery groups in Europe, the pieces are curated to meet the tastes of St-Tropez while still highlighting trends in the international art world.

If marine nostalgia is more your vibe, wander the small streets until you reach the villa that houses **La Vieille Mer**, a cavern of treasures from the sea. Ships' lanterns, wheels, telescopes, clocks and all forms of marine memorabilia are on display.

The **Musée de l'Annonciade** showcases an impressive collection of modern art in a gracefully converted 16th-century chapel, with a focus on pointillist Paul Signac.

The Yachts Sail In

The finest vessels on the Med

The end of summer sees the winds turn on the Mediterranean, and with it comes the return of the largest yacht and sailing festival on the coast: **Les Vioiles de St-Tropez**, which takes over the gulf and the port for 10 days at the end of September. Watch races from the water on one of **Les Bateaux Verts** boats or spy the grand departure from the St-Tropez port in the mornings. If you have a few sailing skills, find a captain on **Vogavecmoi** (vogavecmoi.com) to take you on board to watch the racers up close.

A Guide to the Beach Clubs

Toes in the sand

Beach clubs first took root in St-Tropez in the 1950s, when a 22-year-old Brigitte Bardot turned the town into a popular destination for the rich and famous. Since then, there has been no turning back.

The **Plage de Pampelonne** is the most famous of the beaches here and has the largest selection of clubs. It's a must-do for first-time and returning visitors to St-Tropez. There are public areas for most beaches here, Pampelonne included, but this beach is the place to see and be seen – you'll want to reserve a lounger and lunch. Lined with clubs, it's about as 'hot European summer' as you can get, with neat rows of

WHY I LOVE ST-TROPEZ

Ashley Parsons, Lonely Planet writer

Not everyone loves the bling-bling of St-Tropez, but if you give the place a chance, you'll find that the year-round community here is one of friendliness, timeless style and refined taste.

I love to visit St-Tropez in spring or autumn and chat with the barstaff at Café de Paris.

During the slower season, when the sun is less insistent that a spot on the beach is the only way to survive the day, I love to wander cafe to cafe, peeking into the shops or stopping to eat a famous *tarte Tropézienne*.

🏪 WEEKEND MARKET DAYS AROUND THE GULF

Friday
Ste-Maxime year-round; Le Rayol (west along the coast) April to September.

Saturday
St-Tropez and Cogolin (inland village) year-round.

Sunday
Port Grimaud, La Garde-Freinet (inland village) and Ramatuelle (south of St-Tropez), all year-round.

picture-perfect parasols and chairs lining the coast. Atmosphere? Indulgence, glitz and relaxation.

A glass of rosé is just the starting point of the offerings. Book a lounge chair and lunch at **La Réservie à la Plage**, a bohemian chic club on the peninsula, which has artfully curated cocktails, a boutique and a bar, to discover the real Pampelonne experience.

To catch the sun early, **Cabane Bambou** is the best club for early birds, offering a breakfast service and loungers from €29.

Looking for a quieter beach experience without sacrificing luxury? Book ahead for **La Cabane Méditerrane**, on the edge of La Plage d'Héraclée (loungers from €24). A bit further from St-Tropez, the beach is wilder than Pampelonne, and the club is tucked up into the edge of a rock.

If you're not staying in Pampelonne, it's best to taxi in and out of this exclusive area. There is, however, a local bus service, line three, that connects the main bus station of St-Tropez with Pampelonne.

Plages, Promenades and Ports

Discover Ste-Maxime in style

Ste-Maxime lies just across the gulf from St-Tropez. This town is home to long white-sand beaches that are perfect for a day out with family and friends. Unlike the beach clubs of St-Tropez, Ste-Maxime has a more egalitarian atmosphere, making it the destination for those who want to escape the hustle and bustle of the coast and enjoy a more laid-back experience.

The private **Barco Beach** has a special kid's corner and runs family activities all summer long – perfect for parents who enjoy organised fun with the kids. For nature enthusiasts, **Plage de la Madrague** is a must-visit. This beach is home to a variety of marine life, and visitors can don a snorkelling mask and gaze at the rock fish that flit around the coves.

The proximity to the long coast gives visitors to Ste-Maxime the opportunity for long promenades or walks through the area. Before or after dinner, walk underneath the pine trees of the **Promenade Aymeric Simon Lorière** near the port. Essential to the village's soul, you'll find an antique market here on Wednesdays, and on summer evenings there's usually free live music.

Docked in the **port of Ste-Maxime** are more than 800 boats – from sailboats and fishing boats to motorboats and

---

FAMILY-FRIENDLY BEACHES

St-Tropez is notorious for being a partygoer and luxury vacation spot. For family beach clubs, try **Ste-Maxime**, the **Presqu'île de Giens** (p115) or **Nice** (p61) instead.

THE ST-TROPEZ PRICE TAG

As the jet-set destination of the Côte d'Azur, visiting St-Tropez on a budget can still take a chunk out of your vacation fund: the glamour dust sprinkled on fish and chips doesn't come cheap! Hotels in the city start around €200 a night, while beach-club loungers run from €50 to €150 (and some require you to eat lunch or dinner at the establishment). To keep your budget balanced, skip the beach lounger at Pampelonne by arriving early to claim a space on one of the stretches of public beach. And to eat on a budget, reserve a table at **Le Sporting** bistro – pizzas start at a wallet-friendly €11.

CLUBS AFTER THE BEACH CLUB

Le Piaf St-Tropez
Dinner, cocktails and dancing, the red booths of the Piaf are part of the upscale A Table Paris family.

L'Esquinade
The gay club in St-Tropez, just off the port, is the last stop for clubbers. It goes hard till dawn.

Club le Gaïo
Since 1958, the stars have come here to hit the dancefloor. Nikkei cuisine from the kitchen; open till 6am.

mega yachts, and even the occasional dinghy – the port is constantly alive with movement and marine activity. Nearly every evening during the summer, the **Théâtre de la Mer** at the port's edge stages musical or theatrical entertainment, and it's free to the public.

To get between Ste-Maxime and St-Tropez, take a Les Bateaux Verts shuttle boat (bateauxverts.com; 15 minutes).

Photography in Grimaud and the Port

Venice on the Côte d'Azur

If you're looking to post some likeable photos and get out of town, here's the short list of where you should stop to snap a pic. **Port Grimaud** lies between St-Tropez and Ste-Maxime and is a modern pleasure port barricaded from the busy N98 by high walls, with photogenic pointed footbridges and cute motorboats.

Up the hill 7km is **Grimaud** itself – a medieval hilltop village surrounded by vineyards, olive trees and the oak-and-beech-clad foothills of the Massif des Maures. Track down **rue de la Treille** in spring to snap a photo of the exploding blooms, and capture **Pont des Fées** (Fairies Bridge) from below to make this tiny and well-preserved footbridge seem larger than life.

JUERGEN WACKENHUT/SHUTTERSTOCK ©

Ste-Maxime

BEST WALLET-FRIENDLY EATS IN STE-MAXIME

La Maison Bleue
The celebrated restaurant is under new ownership but still upholds the same family values. Enjoy the comfy seating arrangements and the inspired cuisine, like octopus with chorizo or Provençal aïoli. €€

Le Carillon
Come to Le Carillon for typical Italian-French coastal fare. More than a safe bet, it's a good quality-to-price ratio for the pizzas, grilled dishes and daily specials. It's close to the church. €€

La Casa Mia
Unpretentious family restaurant with homemade brasserie food: big salads, daily specials like mussels and fries, stuffed squid and beef tartar, all at unbeatable prices. €

 SEASONAL EVENTS IN ST-TROPEZ

Fête des Vendanges
Each September at the beginning of the month, join the party honouring the grape harvest.

Fête de la Libération
15 August marks the day Ste-Maxime was liberated in WWII; enjoy fireworks over the gulf.

Fête du Vélo
This new cycling festival, launched in 2022, takes place in early April.

MEET THE HERMANN'S TORTOISE

The western Hermann's tortoise *(Testudo hermanni hermanni)* is an endangered species found in small pockets of the Mediterranean coast: it mainly lives in Italy, Sardinia and Corsica, but you can still find a number of them living in the Var – notably in Grimaud.

Outside the village, near the Pont des Fées, is one good place to look. The tortoise is fairly small – they only grow 7cm to 18cm long – but the distinct black-and-yellow pattern on its shell makes them easy to recognise (assuming they're not camouflaged in the underbrush).

To get to know them better, visit the tortoise sanctuary, the **Village des Tortues** in Carnoules, about a half-hour drive inland.

You could take your photos and leave, but why not stay a while and savour the village's rich culture? A leisurely stroll will allow you to fully immerse yourself in the sights, sounds and smells of the ocean and the blooming flowers. For a true culinary adventure, head to the historic centre and dine at **Chez Jeff et Ju**, a cosy tapas restaurant that offers a unique and flavourful menu. If you're in the mood for something sweet and refreshing, be sure to grab an ice cream from **J'aime les Glaces**.

Grimaud comes alive during the summer months, when street artists from around the world are invited to participate in an outdoor art festival. You may even spot a few well-known names. And the offbeat vibe continues into August with **Les Grimaldines**, an annual world music and street performance festival.

Bus 887 connects St-Tropez to Grimaud village. To get to Port Grimaud, it's easiest to take a ferry.

Pont des Fées, Grimaud (P109)

WHERE TO STAY IN ST-TROPEZ

Lily of the Valley
Renowned five-star hotel with a new beach club that's exclusive and intimate. €€€

Lou Pinet
Laid-back vintage chic hotel; some rooms have private gardens. Visit the secret spa inside a cave. €€€

La Bastide d'Antoine
Slightly cheaper hotel in St-Tropez with stylish rooms, suites and villas. €€€

Fréjus
St-Raphaël
Reserve Naturelle
de la Plaine des Maures
St-Tropez

Beyond St-Tropez

Venture inland to explore a nature reserve or try the less expensive cities of Fréjus or St-Raphaël for a beach day.

North of St-Tropez is the inland Réserve Naturelle de la Plaine des Maures. Here, visitors will get some fresh air away from the coast. There are endless hikes in the reserve, and it's a window into the countryside life of the inner Var.

To the east of St-Tropez stretch long swaths of coast that lead towards Antibes and Nice. Adventurous travellers can strike out on the hunt for the perfect rocky cove for a dip. St-Raphaël and Fréjus are a good match for families or laid-back travellers, and both are a little easier on the wallet. Don't get hung up on St-Tropez – there are plenty of other places along the French Riviera awaiting your visit.

Maures Nature Reserve

A wild refuge at your doorstep

Looking for a fun and easy outdoor activity to do with the family? Try hiking the 12.6km loop trail in the **Réserve Naturelle de la Plaine des Maures**.

As you hike through the reserve, passing parasol pines, cork oaks and maquis scrub, try to spot the animals that call the area home: wild boars, foxes, deer and many bird species, both sedentary and migratory.

Along the way, you'll also have the chance to see migratory birds nesting near the beautiful **Lake Escarcets**, which is a highlight of the trail. The lake is surrounded by reeds and rushes, providing a habitat for various water fowl, such as ducks and coots.

GETTING AROUND

There is no real limit between Fréjus and St-Raphaël; if you're sticking to the centre of either then getting around on foot is fine. For excursions further away, the simplest option is a car, but be prepared to spend time and money finding a parking spot.

☑ **TOP TIP**

Fréjus and St-Raphaël both have good overnight options to break up a travel day between Nice and St-Tropez.

Coastal City Vibes

Urban beach access

Fréjus and St-Raphaël are two beach towns further east along the French Riviera. While they may not have the same level of fame and glamour as St-Tropez, both have their own unique charms and attractions.

Founded by Julius Caesar in 49 BCE, **Fréjus** has many ancient Roman ruins, including an amphitheatre and aqueduct. Visitors can also explore the town's medieval quarter, which features narrow streets and picturesque buildings, including the Gothic **Cloître de la Cathédrale de Fréjus**.

Plage de St-Aygulf is a popular spot for swimming and sunbathing, while **Plage de Port-Fréjus** offers a more tranquil setting with calm waters and sandy shores.

St-Raphaël, in contrast, is a more modern town with a vibrant beach scene. The town features a long stretch of sandy beach, perfect for swimming, sunbathing and watersports. Take a break in the town's lively marina area, where you'll find plenty of restaurants and shops.

BREEZY RESTAURANTS

Le Baïa
Spend an evening at the port of St-Raphaël at Le Baïa's three levels: bar, restaurant and rooftop summer club. The Asian fusion and Mediterranean dishes are delightful and not too heavy. €€

Le Touring
Le Touring is the glittering French Riviera at its finest. With its chic atmosphere, the rooftop restaurant is a corner of peace in the busy centre of St-Raphaël. €€€

Seventh Heaven
Fourth-floor rooftop restaurant and bar, Seventh Heaven is located in Fréjus, with a view over the Port St-Raphaël that stretches all the way to St-Tropez. Dining service, bar and music till 2am. €€

A. FREUND/SHUTTERSTOCK ©

Cloître de la Cathédrale de Fréjus

Hyères

West of St-Tropez, Hyères is a coastal city that has a rich history and a sparkling beach scene. Be sure to check out the medieval castle; the once strategic viewpoints are now superb panoramic spots. Visit historic homes and contemporary galleries to get your culture fix.

Just a short ferry ride from Hyères is the Île de Porquerolles, a paradise for outdoor enthusiasts. Visitors can rent a bike and explore the island's many beaches, coves and hiking trails. And for those looking for a more adventurous experience, the nearby Île de Port-Cros offers some of the best hiking trails in the region, with stunning views of the Mediterranean and the surrounding islands.

For families, Hyères and its surrounding areas offer a range of camping options, with many old-fashioned campsites located just steps from the sea. Kids will love spending their days on the beach and exploring the stunning natural beauty of the region.

Hyères by Foot

A day in the city

Over 2400 years of fascinating history, and you've only got time for a day in Hyères? Here's how to hit the highlights.

Begin your day by exploring the **vieille ville** (old centre), which is full of picturesque streets, colourful façades and monuments and historical sites that have been preserved for centuries. Begin on the western side of place Georges Clemenceau at the 13th-century **Porte Massillon**. West along cobbled rue Massillon is rue des Porches, with its polished flagstones and shady arcades. You can spend hours exploring the narrow streets and alleys and admiring the beautiful architecture.

Follow up a tour of the centre with a climb to the **Château d'Hyères**, located on the heights of the Castéou Hill. The original structure dates back to the 10th-century. Walk back to **Castel Ste-Claire**, a superb neo-Romanesque mansion built on the foundations of an old convent. The adjoining park of the same name is classified as a remarkable garden with 6500 sq metres of flowers and tropical vegetation.

If you're a foodie, eat lunch at **L'Enoteca**, an upscale restaurant in the old town run by a passionate couple. The cuisine is modern, authentic and generous.

GETTING AROUND

For travel around Hyères and between the town centre and the beaches, use the Mistral bus system. Line 67 connects the town centre with the Presqu'île de Giens. Between coastal cities, transport options are the Zou! bus system or the train.

☑ TOP TIP

To fully enjoy your trip to the Île de Porquerolles, it's recommended you reserve a spot early; the island limits visitors to 6000 per day. The same goes for lodging during the high season.

HYÈRES

Col de Caguo-Ven

Aiguebelle

La Londe-les-Maures
Bormes-les-Mimosas
Le Lavandou

Hyères Vieille Ville

D98

Port Miramar

Cap de Brégançon
Cabasson

L'Almanarre
Port d'Hyères
Cap Bénat
Cap Blanc

Plage de l'Almanerre
La Capte

Presqu'île de Giens

Giens

La Tour Fondue

Îles d'Hyères

Port-Cros

Parc National de Port-Cros

Porquerolles
Île de Porquerolles

Parc National de Port-Cros

Île de Port-Cros

Mediterranean Sea

0   4 km
0   2 miles

ARTISTIC INSPIRATION

Hyères has all the elements of a decadent holiday in the south of France, and best of all, it remains a relatively unsung destination. For some travellers, the fact that the distractions of the hipper cities are out of reach will make it that much more appealing. For generations, writers and artists have come here to work.

Joseph Conrad mentions the peninsula in his final work, *The Rover;* F Scott Fitzgerald corrected the manuscript of *The Great Gatsby* here too. Robert Louis Stevenson, for his part, wrote several of his novels, including *Prince Otto,* at the Grand Hôtel des Îles d'Or in 1884. Could this be the writer's retreat you've been looking for?

Move on to the **Villa Noailles**, a national art centre that houses the Museum of Modern Art. The modern architecture and cubist garden were designed by Gabriel Guévrékian. In this atypical place, modern art exhibitions rotate throughout the year; there's also a permanent collection of artwork and furniture. End the day at **Vinoteer Happy**, a local wine bar with light tapas, natural wine and good energy.

Find Paradise on the Île de Porquerolles

Bikes and bathing suits only

Close to the mainland but fostering its own unique personality, the **Île de Porquerolles** is a haven for families and nature lovers. The island can be visited only by foot or bicycle; reserve your bike rental with the ferry ticket. This mode of transportation makes it easier for visitors to reach the furthest beaches on the island without having to walk for hours. Get the most out of the bike rental by pedalling across the island to the **Calanque de l'Oustaou-de-Diou**. Hang out for a few hours, and then pedal back, making a detour to the black beaches on the far east side of the island.

Looking for a souvenir? Pick up a bottle of rosé from the **Domaine d'Île**, one of the island's three vineyards.

WHERE TO EAT AND DRINK IN HYÈRES

Vola Cafe
Longstanding mainstay in the centre of town, with cute blue shutters and a leafy *terrasse.*

Vinoterre Happy
Wine bar with a good selection of natural wines, local wines and tapas to munch on.

Au Fil de L'eau
Refined seafood restaurant with good catch-of-the-day selections like sea bass, bream or flatfish. Reserve.

The French art of naming things strikes again with their word for snorkelling: *randonnée palmée,* or hiking with flippers. Off the coast of Porquerolles, spend a few hours in the water on one of these underwater hikes. The **Calanque de Brégançonnet** is an easily accessible spot for those who decide to go without a guide. Otherwise, book a boat and a guide with **Ileo Porquerolles** (ileo-porquerolles.fr) for €65 and spend several hours discovering the vibrant and delicate underwater ecosystem off the coast. Most frequently spotted fish include tiny Blenny fish, shiny mendoles and the large black-headed sea bass.

Year-round ferries (20 minutes) here are operated by **TLV** (tlv-tvm.com), leaving from **La Tour Fondue** at the southern end of Presqu'île de Giens. Note that some trails may be closed in high season due to risk of fire.

Beach Days on the Presqu'île de Giens
From windsurfing to wading

Presqu'île de Giens is due south of Hyères, facing the Île de Porquerolles. The peninsula is home to stunning beaches and historic salt pans that were once used to harvest sea salt. Although the flats are no longer productive, walking along the salt road is still a popular activity and a great spot for birdwatching. You can see various bird species, including pink flamingos, feeding in the saltwater pools.

If you love to windsurf or kitesurf, **Plage de l'Almanerre** – the western shore of the 'leg' connecting to the peninsula's foot – is for you. With its white sand and shallow water, this beach is not only safe for swimming but also a haven for practising your favourite watersports. Visitors do need to swim in designated areas.

Plage du Pradeau, near the peninsula's heel,is another beach not to be skipped. Only accessible by foot or boat, the beach is sheltered from the wind, and in summer motor boats are forbidden. Is this the world's best beach?

Handiplage Plage de la Bergerie, along the eastern shore of the 'leg' connecting to the peninsula's foot, is an excellent example of how tourism can be made inclusive for people with disabilities. The accessible beach is equipped with special installations, such as amphibious wheelchairs, assistance for entering the water and adapted restroom facilities. The beach also has a team of trained volunteers available to assist visitors with disabilities, ensuring that everyone can enjoy the beauty of the Presqu'île.

CAMPING ON THE COAST

Camping à la Ferme le Pradeau
This small campground has direct access to the beach and reasonable prices. Restaurants are within walking distance. Central location for beach-hopping across the Presqu'île de Giens. €

Camping Bernard
Shaded by eucalyptus trees, this small campground also has direct access to the beach and a boules terrain where you can befriend French vacationers. There's a restaurant on-site. €

Camping les Moulières
A four-star campground near the coast that has resisted the temptation to pack in mobile homes like sardines. There are a few glamping tents that have kitchen corners and shaded living room spaces. €€

BEST BEACHES ON THE ÎLE DE PORQUEROLLES

Calanque de l'Oustaou-de-Diou
Small rocky cove on the south side of the island, great for short snorkelling excursions.

Plage d'Argent
Close to the port, the Plage d'Argent is a favourite for families with young children.

La Plage Notre-Dame
This is the largest beach on the island. It's on the northwest coast, a 30-minute walk from the port.

HIKE THE PRISTINE ÎLE DE PORT-CROS

Discover France's smallest national park, Parc National de Port-Cros. This 14km hike circles the island clockwise, starting at the Fort du Moulin and ending at the Port-Cros port. To get here, take a one-hour TLV ferry (tlv-tvm.com) from the Port d'Hyères or La Tour Fondue.

The hike starts with a visit to **❶ Fort du Moulin**, a fortification from the 18th-century that overlooks the harbour and offers stunning views of the sea and surrounding cliffs. At **❷ Plage de la Palud**, you can choose to switch to an underwater hike that follows a marked snorkelling path with six stops, each tied to weights, that educate divers on different species and biodiversity points of interest under the waves. Rent equipment from portside outfit Sun Plongée.

Continuing on foot, the trail runs alongside the rocky cliffs of the north side of the island, providing hikers with a refreshing sea breeze and fresh views of the Mediterranean. Around 5km into the hike, you'll reach the **❸ Plage de Port Man**, a quiet bay where you can take a break and have a dip in the sea. A short detour can also be made to visit **❹ Fort de Port Man**, which was built to keep an eye on marine passages between Port-Cros and Île du Levant.

The trail then turns south. Here you'll pass **❺ Fortin de la Vigie**, built on the highest point of the island. The hike finishes at the Port-Cros port, but before heading back, spend a few hours at **❻ Plage du Sud**, the most popular beach on the island. The wide sandy shores and shallow waters are an oasis for beachgoers. Bring picnic supplies and drinking water from the mainland.

Bormes-les-Mimosas
Domaine
du Rayol
Hyères

Beyond Hyères

Let the mimosas be your guide to discovering new corners of the Côte d'Azur.

The French Riviera is famous for its stunning coastline and luxurious resorts. But what if you let flower power guide your vacation? The region's gardens and winter mimosa blooms are unrivalled.

Start with the Domaine du Rayol, a protected natural site that showcases the landscapes of the world with a similar climate to the Mediterranean. Visitors can admire a variety of different species, from Chilean mimosa trees to bamboo and cycas in the subtropical Asian garden.

Artists will be inspired when visiting Bormes-les-Mimosas during the flowering season. Embark on a road trip, driving a section of the Route du Mimosa, from Bormes-les-Mimosas to St-Raphaël, for a glimpse into the region's rich cultural heritage.

Mediterranean Gardens of the World

A botanical world tour

Growing continuously since its conception in 1910, **Domaine du Rayol** is a protected natural site that is home to a unique botanical garden. It features plants from around the globe that thrive in Mediterranean-like climates. The dense flora cascades down the hillside to the sea, and while the flowers are at their best in April and May, it's always worth a visit. What makes a Mediterranean garden special is its ability to thrive in a hot and dry climate, and these gardens often feature drought-resistant plants, such as succulents and cacti, as well as fragrant herbs and flowering shrubs. Admire mimosa trees in the Chilean Mediterranean area or eucalyptus trees in the Australian garden. The garden is also home to a marine snorkelling garden that is open during summer for visitors ages eight and up.

GETTING AROUND

Zou! buses run to St-Tropez, Hyères and Toulon. There is also a TGV station in Hyères and Toulon. A car can be useful, but if you're staying along the coast, e-bikes will do the job.

☑ **TOP TIP**

This part of the coast is a winter getaway waiting to happen. With the mimosas in bloom, you'll forget it's February.

Rayol-Canadel-Sur-Mer

LOCAL PRODUCE TO SAMPLE

Marion Laperche is the creator of Lemon Story. She cultivates rare citrus fruits in the south of France and transforms them into divine jams, pickles and spirits. *@lemonstory*

Personally, I love summer for its warmth, the sea, bouillabaisse (fish stew) and tomatoes. Winter, when the citrus fruits ripen, is my busy season. In spring, I love how the trees come back to life with buds on each branch and the fragrant aroma of all the blossoms.

While in the region, don't miss my favourite local produce: Solliès figs (available in September and October), fish from the Niel port, olive oil from the Domaine du Moulin, and wine made with Tibouren grapes from the Clos Cibonne in Pradet.

Reserve ahead for any of the numerous activities held here, including children's programs, yoga classes, exhibits and open-air concerts. The gardeners not only care for the plants and landscapes, but also provide educational tours and workshops.

Located 37km east along the Corniche des Maures, expect to take an hour to reach the gardens by car. In July and August, a free shuttle runs from the nearby town of Rayol-Canadel-Sur-Mer.

In addition to the Domaine du Rayol, there are other gardens worth exploring in the region. The **Parc Gonzalez** in Bormes-les-Mimosas is an elegant example that features a variety of plants, including olive trees, cypress trees and lavender. The **Jardin Emmanuel Lopez**, located in Porquerolles, is another stunning garden that showcases the unique flora of the region, including citrus trees, palm trees and exotic plants from around the world.

 WHERE TO DINE IN PARADISE

Le Café des Jardiniers
Inside the Domaine du Rayol, this cafe is reason alone to visit the gardens. Housemade thyme lemonade. **€€**

L'Estagnol
Built in the *guinguette* (dance hall) style it serves wood-grilled dishes and local fish from the market. In Bormes. **€**

Le Jardin Restaurant
Hidden in a cool garden at the top of Bormes-les-Mimosas, with a special accent on edible flowers. **€€€**

DRIVING THE ROUTE DU MIMOSA IN AN EV

The Route du Mimosa is a fragrant journey along the Côte d'Azur, showcasing all the beauty of the coast in the winter. Embark on this scenic 60km route from Bormes-les-Mimosas to St-Raphaël in an electric car.

You can hire an electric Fiat from Carrefour (location.carrefour.fr) in Bormes-les-Mimosas. Villages usually have one or two public charging stations.

Start your journey in **❶ Bormes-les-Mimosas**. The nursery here has 90 varieties of mimosas and is the largest in the region. Before setting off on the route west, detour by **❷ Fort de Brégançon**, an official French presidential residence on the cape south of the village.

As you continue along the route, you'll reach the **❸ Col du Canadel** overlooking the sea. Take a stroll along the beach and enjoy the scenery; the panorama stretches all the way back to Hyères' three islands. About 42km into the journey, stop at **❹ Ste-Maxime** for a snack break. Try a madeleine with mimosa at Chez Taste Gourmet, a local bakery that specialises in delicious pastries and baked goods. The delicate flavour of the mimosa flower adds a unique twist to this classic French treat.

Your last destination in the Var is **❺ St-Raphaël**, which is 59km from your starting point. Here, you can hike the **❻ Calanque d'Anthéor** on the edge of the Estérel. The trail winds down the sinuous route de la Corniche d'Or on the cliffside to reach the water's edge.

If time permits, continue driving the rest of the route, with stops are in Mandelieu-la-Napoule (108km), Tanneron (112km), Pégomas (115km) and Grasse (130km).

COMFORTABLE STAYS NEAR BORMES-LES-MIMOSAS

Hôtel le Bailli de Suffren
Exceptionally elegant hotel right on Rayol Beach. Vintage charm, spacious rooms, a private pool and upscale service. €€€

La Villa Thalassa
Comfortable and calm B&B with three bedrooms, plus a very cute wooden caravan. There's a pool with a view and a patio for watching the sunset. €€

Hostellerie du Cigalou
Occupying an unimprovable central location in Bormes-les-Mimosas, the Cigalou has 20 plush rooms and is convenient, comfortable and good value. €€€

Hôtel California
Located in nearby Le Lavendou, this vintage hotel has clean rooms and all the essentials for travellers on a budget. €

Land of Mimosas

The 12th-century floral village

Bormes-les-Mimosas, 20km east of Hyères, is named after the numerous mimosas that grow here, an iconic symbol of the region. In fact, Bormes-les-Mimosas is home to over 100 different species of mimosa, which bloom between January and March, filling the town and surrounding countryside with a burst of vibrant yellow colour.

The town's love affair with the mimosa began in the 19th-century when the flower was introduced from Australia, where it's known as the yellow wattle. The plant quickly became popular among locals and was cultivated extensively throughout the region. Today, many local businesses use the flower in products such as perfumes, soaps and candles.

Maybe it's the floral history of the region, or the airy breeze that sweeps away stagnating ideas, but the artists and creators of Bormes-les-Mimosas always seem to be on the cutting edge of creativity. Got the shopping itch for a special souvenir from the south of France?

Darling and dapper hats can be found at **Les Bibis du Midi**, where hatmaker Clémence Grisot crafts bespoke and semi-bespoke hats for all occasions. Glassmaker Stéphane Marchioni runs the glass jewellery shop **A l'En Verre**. Pick up handmade soaps, candles and other natural products at the **Savonnerie de Bormes** on the main pedestrian street.

Every February, Bormes les Mimosas hosts a **Mimosa Festival** to celebrate the flower's beauty and significance to the town. Visitors can also take guided tours of the town's mimosa groves and learn about the history and cultivation of the flower.

MARINA VN/SHUTTERSTOCK ©

Bormes-les-Mimosas

Provence Verte

Provence Verte

The Provence Verte is known for its lush green hills and rocky hilltop villages. Inland from Hyères, this region is a paradise for nature lovers, with its rolling hills, dense forests and sparkling rivers that provide a tranquil retreat from the busy coast. Glean hints of what daily life was once like by visiting the narrow streets, stone houses and ancient castles in the villages of Bargème, Tourtour Châteaudouble, Cotignac, and Barjols. Dirt tracks link up these communities, and cyclists, especially those with young children, will appreciate pedalling away from the main road.

After a less demanding holiday? Rosé is the word of the day in Provence Verte. Spend the evening in one of the vineyards that produce the finest rosé in France. With a mild Mediterranean climate – hot summers and softer winters – Provence Verte can, and should, be enjoyed all year long.

Villages de Caractère
Castles, churches and caves

Fifteen Varois villages bear the label *village de caractère:* can you discover their personalities in a visit? If it's your first journey into the inner Var, consider stopping at these standouts.

Bargème, founded in the 9th-century, is the highest village in the Var region. Its winding medieval streets and stone houses make it a charming destination. Be sure to visit the 13th-century castle ruins, which offer stunning views of the surrounding countryside. If it's understated views you're after, **Fayence** is built on the flank of a hill overlooking the plain. It may not be the Gorges du Verdon or Tourtour, but the landscape evokes a sense of calm.

Overlooking the Nartuby River is **Châteaudouble**. Feel free to take a dip in the natural rock pools at the foot of the

GETTING AROUND

Renting a car is the simplest way to get around, but if you're staying in a village for a few days, renting an e-bike is a great ecofriendly option. Expect to pay from €35 per day for an e-bike rental.

☑ **TOP TIP**

If you're thinking of reserving a villa inland and driving down to the coast every day, think again – you'll hit the dreadful littoral traffic jam. Best to spend half your stay beachside, and then book a few days inland to explore.

SIGHTS

1. Bargème
2. Château Nestuby
3. Châteaudouble
4. Commanderie de Peyrassol
5. Cotignac
6. Domaine Rabiega
7. Entrecasteaux
8. Fayence
9. Tourtour

ACTIVITIES, COURSES & TOURS

10. Villecroze

SUNSETS IN TOURTOUR

The best sunset in the inner Var is found from the centre square of **Tourtour**. Known as the village in the sky, the amber-stoned village is perched on a hilltop overlooking the surrounding countryside. The centre of this medieval town is pedestrian-only, and its cobbled lanes filled with galleries and shops make it a peaceful and relaxing destination for visitors with or without children.

If you're visiting Tourtour, be sure to stop by **La Table**, a quaint cafe located in the heart of the village. The barista makes a fluffy cappuccino for a steal and refreshing drinks.

village. Hikers will love visiting the **Gorges de la Nartuby**. In town, visit the 12th-century church and the castle ruins. If you're into châteaux, you'll love **Entrecasteaux**. The 16th-century castle is the imposing watchdog of the town, but a visit to its lovely French gardens isn't the only reason to stop by. Over the centuries, the residents and architects of the village managed to create a functional and aesthetically pleasing irrigation system of aqueducts, canals, fountains and wells – see how many surviving fountains you can spot today.

Legends swirl about the caves in **Villecroze**, which formed 700,000 years ago. Explore the caves and learn about their history or take a walk through the gardens and admire the waterfalls and sculptures.

Rosé All Day

Châteaux, domaines and vineyards

Leave the coast behind and head inland to hunt down Provence's finest rosés. Choosing from more than 300 regional vineyards may leave you feeling overwhelmed, but here's where to start.

History, art, hospitality and fine wine come together at the **Commanderie de Peyrassol**. Founded by the Knights Templar in the 12th-century, the estate today is a sought-out destination. Our choice? A bottle of Le Clos Peyrassol Rosé from 2022, the year the vineyard officially became organic. Book a vineyard visit and stay for a light lunch at **Le Bistrot de Lou**, or, on Thursdays in summer, visit the vineyard in the afternoon and stay for a musical cocktail hour in the evening.

A staple at lunch tables across Provence, a rosé from the Var tastes of the rocky clay soil and the two winds that sweep

CYCLING FROM COTIGNAC TO BARJOLS AND BACK

This 41km cycling trip through the inner Var by bicycle is accessible to all types of cyclists. Start the day beneath the cliffs of ❶ **Cotignac**; there have been settlements here since the Bronze Age. Bobby at Coti's Bike rents both e-bikes and classic bikes. Climb up the big hill to start and admire the cliffs the town is famous for. Turn left on route de Sillans to head out of town. Within minutes, cyclists will pass briefly onto the D13 before turning left onto Clos de Meya.

The gravel path runs along a hillside and through a shrubby forest: *voilà*, the landscape here is where the region gets its name. In 9km, riders will be just below the ❷ **Gros Bessillon** rock formation. The next 10km will fly by; it's all downhill to ❸ **Barjols**. In the 19th-century, Barjols was known for its leather tanning and fountains. Take a lunch break in the centre at Popote et Tambouille Bistrot.

Continuing the bike ride, follow the Route Brignoles. After the village of ❹ **Châteauvert**, the path enters into the beautiful ❺ **Gorges du Vallon Sourn**. Here you might take a dip in the Argens River.

The next destination is ❻ **Correns**, a small village that prides itself on being the first organic village in France. Visitors can stop at the central square for a refreshing lemonade or if it's early evening, a drink at Le Petit Corrensois.

Save some energy for the ride home; the next section follows the gravel track through the forest, scrub and vineyards along the Vieux Chemin de Cotignac.

If you're staying the night in Cotignac, grab a shower and then rendezvous for dinner at the Jardin Secret – the ultimate comfort after the day's adventure.

VINEYARD DINING

Chez Gavoty
Each Thursday in summer, visit the Domaine Gavoty for cocktail hour: music, tapas and wine tasting. It's conveniently located just off the A8, south of Cotignac. €

La Table de St-Roux
The chef prepares dishes from what's available at the market and serves the creations at the chic indoor dining room or the shaded terrace of the Château St-Roux. Find it close to where the A57 and A8 merge. €€

Le Patriarche
At the Château Ste-Croix, dine by the vines on mille-feuille of foie gras, truffle and asparagus ravioli or desserts centred around strawberries and vervain (verbena). It's south of Cotignac. €€

Troglodyte caves, Villecroze (p122)

the landscape: the bit of sea breeze that sneaks up from the coast and the mistral that slams down from the north. Try the wine at **Domaine Rabiega** in a hamlet outside of Draginuan, and pair it with the local beer-marinated pigeon – a bucket-list meal that's surprisingly refined.

If you are travelling in a group or as a family, reserve a *visite ludique*, or 'fun visit', at **Château Nestuby** for an easy-on-the-wallet price of €17. Travellers awaken their five senses through different activities as they get to know the vineyard and its wines.

Long embedded in the agricultural tradition of the region, wine cooperatives also dot the Var. Here, grape growers must adhere to strict cultivation standards for the cooperative's wine production.

WHERE TO STAY IN PROVENCE VERTE

Hotel La Falaise
A bright, clean and spacious hotel in Cotignac, in a yellow building. €€

La Petite Nice
Old-fashioned luxury decor, a charming garden and a nice price in Barjols. €€

Camping de Correns Le Grand Jardin
Just outside of Correns, this family-friendly campground has access to the river. €

Provence Verte

Montrieux-le-Vieux   Collobrières

Beyond
Provence Verte

Chestnut forests, Chartreuse monks and
Provençal markets: wander deeper into
Provence Verte and be surprised by the heart of
the Var.

Acting as natural borders between the coastal sea breezes and the sundrenched inner Var, the Massif des Maures and the Massif de la Ste-Baume ranges are incredibly well-preserved patches of green landscape, nearly free from villas and modern development. Discover the chestnut forests, cork groves and Massif de la Ste-Baume nature reserve, laced with sparkling rivers and dotted with flowering shrubs. The latter contains the mythical last resting place of Mary Magdalene. The humans here are just as resilient as the plants: from the ancient Chartreuse monks who first preserved these forests to the eco-community in the Ste-Baume that's giving new life to the region, resilience is the word of the day in the heart of the Var.

Spend the Night in an Eco-Village

A renaissance in the Ste-Baume

The region around **Montrieux-le-Vieux**, roughly 30 minutes south of Brignoles and a similar distance north of Hyères, has been inhabited by religious communities for centuries. Recently, a group of socio-democratic investors bought one of the monks' old dwellings, Montrieux-le-Vieux, in order to undertake a massive restoration project within this forested region.

GETTING AROUND

It's likely you'll need a car for this region. If you're planning to drive around the Massif des Maures, consider getting a medium-sized vehicle over anything 'mini' as the roads can be rough.

☑ TOP TIP

Come to this region to relax and wander. Most restaurants and bars have high standards, though they're few in number.

125

WESTERN VAR

A less-crowded corner of the coast, the stretch of land between La Ciotat and Toulon is often passed over in favour of more famous destinations – all the more reason to visit.

For beach lovers, **Bandol** is a nice surprise compared to the crowded beaches further east. And inland, travellers can explore the hiking trails and nature in the **Parc Naturel Régional de la Ste-Baume**.

Le Castellet, founded in the 12th-century, is known for its beautiful Romanesque church and, outside of town, the Paul Ricard (yes, like the pastis) speedway.

Stop by **L'Insolite le Castellet** to pick up one-of-a-kind curiosities spanning the region's rich natural history.

The *eco-lieu* (eco-village) is set to become an example of resilience in an ecologically changing world. It's possible to book a night in one of the pastel bed-and-breakfasts or at the small hotel (montrieux.org/le-hameau). In an airy open dining room with olive-green decor, you can enjoy mornings while overlooking the garden. An ethno-agricultural specialist has been brought in to help plant and maintain a native garden – chickpeas planted at the base of olive trees are not surprising here.

In the summer, a patio close to the river serves as a small *guinguette* (dance hall), an outdoor bar and restaurant. Local beers, lemonade and sodas are popular, and the chefs try to use as much produce from their garden as possible. In the monk's former chapel, lovers can become bride and groom, and impromptu concerts take place on the spur of the moment – the acoustics that the chanting monks sought are great for today's love ballads. It's a great place to stay as a family, with surprises and projects everywhere you look. Take a break from the coast to discover what the future of eco-resilience and strong social fabric might look like.

MONASTERY VISITS

If you're interested in visiting a working monastery, try the Abbaye Notre-Dame de Sénanque near **Gordes** (p206), famous for its lavender fields, or the **Monastère Notre-Dame de Clémence de La Verne** (p128) in the nearby Maures range.

Chestnut Tasting in the Maures

Where time ceases to exist

The dense red village of **Collobrières** occupies a central location, halfway between the inner Var and the beach. It's roughly an hour with a change from everywhere: St-Tropez, Hyères and Brignoles in the Provence Verte.

One of the best Provençal markets of the region takes place in the centre of town on Thursday and Sunday mornings. Awaken your taste buds with one of the local chestnut specialities: chestnut ice cream. For three weekends in October, the French specialities of *marrons glacés* (candied chestnuts) and *crème de marron* (sweet chestnut spread) are in the spotlight here – can your sweet tooth handle it?

Wander onwards and outwards. Nearby, visit a ridge-top monastery that seems to reach for the clouds. Originally

Opposite: Abbaye Notre-Dame de Sénanque

WHERE TO HIKE IN THE MASSIF DE LA STE-BAUME

The Gorges du Caramy
An 8km hike along the Caramy River, flanked by the cliffs. Especially great in autumn.

L'Abîme de Maramoye
Easy 5km hike to a ravine, with an unobstructed view and non-technical path for all hikers.

Trou Zéro
From Bastide Blanche to the gaping rock at Trou Zéro, this 11km hike explores several old ruins.

BEST MAURES TABLES

La Petite Fontaine
Come here for wild boar stew and lamb with candied vegetables beneath the shady plane trees of Collobrières. For dessert, it's the famed chestnut ice cream. €€

La Ferme de Peigros
Lost in the greenery of the Maures range, new owners Carole and Zete have poured their hearts into this restaurant with a view. Try the homemade pasta with rabbit ragu; it's ultra-local, in the sense that they raised the rabbits themselves. €€

L'Auberge du Lac
Fresh trout and homemade seasonal dishes with a hearty kick, outside Carnoules. €€

ANDRZEJ65/GETTY IMAGES ©

Monastère Notre-Dame de Clémence de la Verne

dedicated to the goddess Laverna, the protectress of forest bandits, the **Monastère Notre-Dame de Clémence de la Verne** has a long and tumultuous history. Founded in 1170 and maintained by the Chartreuse monks, the monastery was ruined and rebuilt on several occasions throughout the centuries.

The cloisters and chapels all date from the 15th- to 18th-centuries. Muse on the tales while wandering through the chestnut forests, pastures and trails that connect the village of Collobrières and the monastery. Entry is €7 per person. The stables, cellars, oils press and bakery are all open to visitors. The interior of the monastery will remain a mystery for visitors – the cloisters and lateral chapels are off-limits. The nuns live partially off sales from the shop (closed Sundays), which sells products like local chestnuts or honey.

HIKING THE AIGUILLES DE VALBELLE

The hike starts 1km south of Méounes-les-Montrieux, near the new monastery, and ambles through the forest. A 14km loop with trail signs, it passes below the striking limestone formations of the Aiguilles de Valbelle, some of which are more than 15m high. To begin, park off the D202. If you pass Domaine de Montrieux le Vieux, don't worry, just turn around and you'll find the right spot.

As you begin walking towards ❶ **Chartreuse de Montrieux**, you'll soon realise that this is a special place, although the monks received more visitors than they could handle and chose to close the monastery to the public. As you pass the monastery, stay right and start climbing up the hillside. From the 12th-century until the French Revolution, the ❷ **forest of Morières-Montrieux** was owned by different religious communities. Imagine how people lived and used the forest

back in earlier times, and managed to leave so much of the stands intact today.

To stay on the loop, turn left after about 4.3km (look for the yellow hiking signs). The tree treasure hunt begins: how many species can you identify? The most common trees here are oaks and maples. The forest is also home to the Eurasian eagle-owl, but it's unlikely you'll spot one during the day.

The trail curves around, and on the south side, the towering ❸ **Aiguilles de Valbelle** are unveiled. Bursting forth from the ground, this natural monument is a sight to behold. Take a moment to admire the view and snap some pictures.

Then, continue walking along below the Aiguilles de Valbelle until the trail curves back to the monastery. As you return to the parking lot, take in the beauty of the forest one last time.

Bouches-du-Rhône

FOLLOWING THE RIVER TO THE OCEAN

This is a region that veers from enthralling city life to the gentle murmuring of the Mediterranean.

When you find yourself awash in the region's famous light, it will make sense that so many artists were magnetically drawn here for centuries to unlock something bigger than themselves. This is a land that is the epitome of springtime, where the great post-impressionist painters Cézanne and Van Gogh created their seminal works.

As the mistral wind howls its way down the Rhône Valley to the sea, slamming the wooden shutters of homes throughout the night and clearing the skies for what feels like endless amounts of glorious sunshine, it creates a climate that is not only inviting for travellers but one that is ideal for farming. Sampling all that is nurtured and grown here will be part of your journey, especially in the bustling markets and endless stretches of vineyards.

The region's palpitating heart is Marseille, France's second-largest city and a place of real cultural energy. Spreading out from the concrete margins are pine-swaddled coastal uplands cut by ravishingly beautiful *calanques* (coves), while inland are the still-thriving Roman towns of Aix-en-Provence and Arles. At the mouth *(bouche)* of the River Rhône is the timeless beauty of the Camargue wetlands, home to tens of thousands of migratory birds. Whether lost within nature, driving the countryside roads or sprawled on the sand, absorbing the rhythm of the cicadas' cries, the Bouches-du-Rhône is a sensuous Mediterranean wave for you to discover, sparkling gloriously beneath the sun.

ALLA KHANANASHVILI/SHUTTERSTOCK ©

Inset: Great blue heron, Parc Ornithologique de Pont de Gau (p175)
Opposite: Calanque de Port-Miou (p148)

THE MAIN AREAS

Find Your Way

The Bouches-du-Rhône *département* is well-connected by air, road, rail and sea to the rest of France and the Mediterranean beyond. In the countryside a car is best, though you can generally get around without one.

Sauveterre
Sorgues
Sorgue
Avignon
Durance
Châteaurenard
Nîmes
Caveirac
Beaucaire
Tarascon
St-Rémy de Provence
Eyragues
Maillane
Bellegarde
Canal du Rhône à Sète
Eygalière
Parc Naturel Régional des Alpilles
Fontvieille
Maussane-les-Alpilles
Mouriès

Arles, p161

A slow-paced Roman town with a preserved grandness that goes back centuries. Food, drink and nightlife reflect the untamed soul of Camargue life.

Arles
Gimeaux
Raphèle-les-Arles
St-Martin-de-Crau
Mas du Pont de Rousty
Gageron
Albaron
Villeneuve
Aigues-Mortes
Montcalm
Méjanes
Domaine de Beaujeu
Étang de Vaccarès
Église des Stes-Maries
Le Sambuc
Canal d'Arles
Ploch Bedet
Port-Camargue
Canal de Sylvéréal
Étang de l'Impérial
Grand Rhône
Parc Naturel Régional de Camargue
Port de Fos
Fos-sur-Mer
Stes-Maries-de-la-Mer
Golfe de Beauduc
Étang du Fangassier
Salin de Giraud
Port St-Louis du Rhône
Gol du Lio
Beauduc
Étang de Vaccarès
Grand Rhône

Mediterranean Sea

Stes-Maries-de-la-Mer, p173

A tiny fishing village in the Mediterranean backwaters that comes alive in spring and summer and is home to a spectacular parade every May.

0   10 km
0   5 miles

TRAIN

Both Marseille and Aix connect to Paris, Lyon and Avignon via TGV, while slower services head west (to Montpellier) and east (to Nice and Italy). The regional train west along the Côte Bleue has spectacular views.

CAR

Driving in this region is a joy, though parking can be a pain – especially in Marseille and Aix. If you plan on exploring tiny villages, far-flung vineyards or the Camargue, however, plan on renting a car.

BUS

The local bus network, lepilote. com, is inexpensive and has regular and extensive services across the region, including multiple connections from the Marseille airport.

Aix-en Provence, p151

The heart of Provence is a place of refined elegance: fountains, narrow streets, high-end shopping and plenty of green spaces.

Marseille, p136

A cutting-edge city transforming itself for a new generation. As historic as it is fun, and home to some of the most unspoilt coastline in France.

CLOCKWISE FROM LEFT: ALEXEY FEDORENKO/SHUTTERSTOCK ©, ROSSHELEN/SHUTTERSTOCK ©, LAURENT FIGHIERA/SHUTTERSTOCK ©

Plan Your Time

This region is easiest to navigate if you base yourself in one place: Marseille for city life and the *calanques*, Aix for classic rural Provence or Arles for art, Roman ruins and the Camargue.

Cycling, Camargue (p173)

Pressed for Time

● With only a day or two, stick to just one place: **Marseille** (p136) makes sense if you want to explore this dynamic cultural melting pot, which presents a unique take on modern French life, with easy escapes along the coast.

● Well-heeled **Aix-en-Provence** (p151), meanwhile, is the opposite experience: think elegant architecture and highbrow culture, surrounded by prosperous farms, independent vineyards and charismatic stone villages perched on hillsides.

● For more art, plus the region's best Roman ruins, riverside **Arles** (p161) is a lovely base, with direct access to the wild and wonderous wetlands of the **Camargue** (p173) beyond.

Seasonal Highlights

Winters are usually mild, but a mistral wind can change that in a second. Spring and autumn are blissful, summers hot and crowded.

MARCH
On the third weekend in March, the raucous **Carnaval de La Plaine** (p138) brings joy and protest to Marseille.

APRIL
Early spring harvests make their way to stalls around the region, with local produce on display on market days.

MAY
Gypsies (Romanies, Manouches, Tziganes and Gitans) pour into Stes-Maries-de-la-Mer on 24 May, ending their annual **pilgrimage** (p172).

A Long Weekend in Marseille

● Breakfast at the **Hôtel Bellevue** (p139) on the port before a ferry to the **Château d'If** or the **Îles du Frioul** (p143).

● Spend the evening in **Cours Julien** (p136), the epicentre of social life, before dinner at **Bambino** (p144) in the Camas neighbourhood.

● Next morning, embark on a walking tour of the old **Panier neighbourhood** (p139), then lunch at the **Chalet du Pharo** (p140) before an afternoon winding your way along the **Corniche Kennedy coastline** (p140).

● Day three sail out to **Les Goudes** (p141), kayak to the **Calanques** (p147) or take the train along the **Côte Bleue** (p149).

More Than a Week

● In Aix-en-Provence, visit a trio of **museums** (p151), drive out to scenic **vineyards** (p158) and climb up Cézanne's muse: **Montagne Ste-Victoire** (p154).

● In nearby Arles, walk through **Roman ruins** (p164) followed by a visit to the **Fondation Van Gogh** (p161) or the cutting-edge **LUMA Arles art gallery** (p161).

● A day out in **Les Alpilles** (p171) delivers a true village experience with stunning treks.

● From here, head into the Camargue, where you can **ride white horses** (p168), **birdwatch** (p175) and trek to the **wild beaches** (p166) of the Rhône Delta. A final stop in **Stes-Maries-de-la-Mer** (p172) is perfect for coastal cycling and sunbed life.

JUNE
Potentially the best time of year for wine-tasting in Provence: students are still in school, airfares are lower and the heat is more bearable.

JULY
Les Rencontres d'Arles (p161) is an internationally renowned annual photography festival held throughout the city.

AUGUST
Peak heat and peak life: Marseille is on holiday with the residents enjoying a summer of excess.

SEPTEMBER
Visit Mouriès in Les Alpilles for the **Green Olive Festival** on the third weekend in September.

Marseille

GETTING AROUND

Marseille has two metro lines (Métro 1 and Métro 2), two tram lines (yellow and green) and an extensive bus network. Bus, metro or tram tickets are available from machines in the metro, at tram stops and on buses. In general, however, Marseille is a delight to explore on foot.

From April to the end of September, the maritime shuttle crossings from the Vieux Port can also take you to the extremities of L'Estaque and Pointe Rouge.

Rent bicycles at EasyMove and E.Bike Tours Marseille for electric bikes, but know that the roads here are not particularly bike-friendly.

Marseille has an edge. France's second-largest city puts its arms around you as a drunken friend would – passionately and deliriously. Marseille revels in its status as France's underdog. Explore it's hidden corners and it will reveal a beauty that is impossible to capture in a photograph: an urban sprawl with pockets of inspiring nature that can only be experienced first-hand. Founded by the Greeks in 600 BCE, the tremendous influx of immigration in this port city has never ceased. In Marseille, North Africans live shoulder to shoulder with a vast Corsican community, only a skipping stone's throw from northern Italy and Spanish Catalonia.

Greater Marseille is divided into 16 *arrondissements*, which are often indicated in addresses. The city's main thoroughfare, La Canebière, stretches eastwards from the Vieux Port towards the train station, a 10-minute walk away. Just uphill is the neighbourhood Le Panier, the oldest section of the city.

Cours Julien and La Plaine
Drink with the locals

Sooner or later, you'll end up on the **Cours Julien** for a drink, and for good reason. As a pedestrian area slathered with street art and bohemian yearnings, this is the home of some great bars and restaurants, which remain open day and night. Wander the narrow side streets, packed with bookshops, galleries and tattoo parlours, until reach the noisy and elongated main square, long the destination for a solid night out, and you'll find a microcosm of the city itself.

Place Jean-Jaurès, also known as **La Plaine**, is another vast square surrounded by bars and restaurants. For years it has been the battleground for left-wing militants and artists. Closed for urban renewal before the pandemic, it reopened to mixed emotions in 2021, with some claiming the square had become too controlled and sanitised. Unlike many public

☑ TOP TIP

This is a city where we like to joke with everyone. It's what we call t'emboucaner. If we make fun of you, it's to make you feel at home. Don't take yourself too seriously here and you'll do well. – JC, manager of Le Trois Quarts

HIGHLIGHTS
1 Cours Julien
2 Fontaine des Danaïdes
3 La Corniche Kennedy
4 La Plaine
5 Noailles
6 Palais Longchamp
7 Pastis de la Plaine

8 Plage des Catalans
9 rue d'Aubagne
10 Vieux Port

EATING
11 Amandine
12 Au Contraire
13 Bambino
14 Ciao Marcello
15 Jogging

16 La Kaz Kreol
17 La Pépite
18 Limon
19 Razzia
20 Restaurant Fémina

DRINKING & NIGHTLIFE
21 Le Vin sur la Main

22 Data
23 L'Embobineuse
24 Sing or Die

ENTERTAINMENT

SHOPPING
25 Maison Empereur
26 OM Official Store
27 rue Longue des Capucins

areas worldwide, however, it has been redesigned with skateboarders in mind, with long smooth runs and no anti-skate guards in sight. Buzzing day and night in the spring and summer months, it remains a beating heart for locals escaping the tourist traps into the early morning, whether in the bars or in the public seating areas beneath the trees. La Plaine is only a 10-minute walk east from the Cours Julien.

African Food in Noailles

Travel your taste buds

Like Naples in Italy, Marseille is an anomaly in Europe: the poorest residents live in the centre of town, rather than on the outskirts. **Noailles**, a majority African neighbourhood, is only minutes from the Vieux Port.

As with any community, life revolves around the market square. The **Marché des Capucins** is where all the action happens. Sit outside the Cafe Prinder, an establishment serving strong cups of coffee since 1925, and bear witness to the square's energy, overflowing with stands selling fruit and vegetables. You are just as likely to hear Arabic as you are French as the locals come out to shop for essentials.

The long **rue d'Aubagne** acts as the neighbourhood's main artery, where you come down from Cours Julien past the scene of a terrible tragedy in 2019 when two buildings collapsed, killing their inhabitants within the walls of their own homes. The neighbourhood has refused to forget it.

Taking the **rue Longue des Capucins** is essential to understanding where you are. In this narrow street, it's easy to believe that you're in a North African souk. Pyramid-shaped piles of spices, halal butchers, fresh fish on ice and the aroma of rotisserie chicken will send your senses into overdrive. Vegetarian or chicken *pastilla* (a North African pastry) and *kesra* (a round semolina bread served hot) are must-try items, as is West African bissap juice (a type of hibiscus). Do note that pickpockets have been known to operate in this area.

Marseille's Music Scene

The weird and wonderful underground

Marseille's edgier nightlife drags us away from selfies at sunset and nightclubs thumping with generic global hits. If you want to experience the alternative, a stirring underground scene reflects the politics of the street, supported by a large student population and a generally open-minded clientele.

Marseille's residents live their life outside in the summer. You can't escape the humming throb of people on the terraces drinking and smoking into the night, but if karaoke is your thing, then the weekend cult of **Sing or Die** is the place for you: it's run by Jackie (a Scotswoman) and Lionel. Hot and sweaty, it's also extremely raucous. Sing from the stage to a heaving and screaming crowd.

Data feels more like someone's home than a club. The bands play in the front room and people stand in the courtyard smoking and eating the prix libre snacks (pay what you think is right). Expect avant-garde, drum machines and squealing noises, but in a truly bizarre setting. Check their Facebook page for show times.

L'Embobineuse is an institution for underground music in the depths of the Belle de Mai district. A 90s-style club with dark walls and sticky floors, you'll find artists from Texas, Kampala and Berlin all on the same bill here. When

LA CARNAVAL DE LA PLAINE

Every third weekend in March, the raucous Carnaval de La Plaine is held on place Jean-Jaurès. An explosive but joyful affair, the square fills with samba beats and chants for one big party that's essentially an anti-capitalist protest rooted in paganism.

As part of the fight against gentrification, neighbourhood residents dress up in themed costumes and dance, get merry and set fire to effigies of their political rivals.

Be prepared to be covered in flour and insults if you don't look the part. If you do look the part, take care. Without fail, the event ends in a confrontation with the French riot police.

WHERE TO EAT AROUND COURS JULIEN

Chez Gilda
Come here to eat fried seafood and drink white wine with the local skaters. €€

Limmat
The perfect lunch spot: Mediterranean food with a great view from the top of the stairs. €€

Caterine
Gastronomic French cuisine that's served in a canteen-style setting. €€

LE PANIER ON FOOT

The Vieux Port, all boats and bars, is Marseille's centrepoint and places you on the front of a postcard. For a walk that takes you from the port into the delightful Le Panier neighbourhood, begin on the Quai du Port beneath the historic ❶ **Hôtel Bellevue**.

Walking away from town, turn right at ❷ **Passage Pentecontore**, taking the steps up through the arch. The view of the port and Basilique Notre Dame de la Garde in the distance is perfect for a photograph. If you're feeling hungry, this is a great spot to sample ice cream from ❸ **Vanille Noire**, renowned for its charcoal-coloured vanilla flavour.

Not far from here is the steep, narrow corridor of steps of ❹ **rue Beauregard** and rue des Moulins, now emblazoned with street art. These lead to ❺ **place des Moulins**, once home to windmills in the 17th-century. Today,

it offers serenity no matter the time of year.

Descending the ❻ **rue des Muettes** and ❼ **rue du Refuge** takes you into the heart of Le Panier. 'The Basket' is Marseille's oldest quarter, the site of the original Greek settlement and nicknamed for its steep streets and buildings.

Make your way along ❽ **rue des Pistoles** and ❾ **rue du Petit Puits** via rue Antoine Becker, to come to the ❿ **Cathédrale de la Major**.

If you time this walk for sunset – it takes about an hour from the starting point – the square will deliver a blazing view. Below on ⓫ **bd Jacques Saade** are a line of tapas bars, another perfect sunset stop. Taking rue Four de Chapitre to join rue de l'Évêché allows you to get lost in a maze of independent shops, cafes and restaurants or to settle in the buzzy ⓬ **place de Lenche**.

Sadia Chellah, the Algerian-born owner of Le Bar du Peuple (30 bd de Garibaldi) is passionate about her neighbourhood. As she describes it: 'Noailles is the place where people arrive. I love that we now have flower shops in the neighbourhood and tourism.' She shares some of her favourite spots in Noailles.

OM Official Store
There is only one team in this city: Olympique de Marseille. Get your gear here.

Maison Empereur
This hardware store was founded in 1827; it's one of the oldest in France. Walking inside is like entering a museum.

Restaurant Fémina
Not counting my own cooking, this is the best couscous around.

you don't want the night to end, **L'Art Haché**, near La Plaine, opens its doors from 1am to 6 am on Saturdays and Sundays for its extremely low-ceilinged dance party that is guaranteed to kill off your remaining brain cells.

Romantic Views along the Corniche

Catch some rays on les plages

For something a bit more romantic, leave the Vieux Port behind for the **Corniche Kennedy**, which wends its way east along the coast. This is where many visitors first fall under Marseille's spell, bedazzled by the intense, raw energy of the sea, the endless sunshine glinting off the Med and the spectacular coastal beauty. On the way to the beaches, make a first stop at the **Parc du Pharo**, where you can watch the boats sail out of the port or – why not indulge yourself? – stop for brunch at **Le Chalet du Pharo**.

Next you'll pass the crowded **Plage des Catalans** beach and the unreal **Vallons des Auffes** fishing village, with restaurants spread out below. As the road finally bends to the left, head down to the **Port de Malmousque** – a marina from another era where people bring wine and then glide out into

VLASYUK INNA/SHUTTERSTOCK ©

Plage des Catalans

 BEST AFRICAN RESTAURANTS IN NOAILLES

Chez Yassine
No-nonsense Tunisian restaurant with long lunch queues – for good reason. €€

La Jungle
Serves massive plates of Cameroonian food. It's as much a party as it is a restaurant on weekends. €€

Mama Ghana
West African food prepared with love. Also a great spot to watch televised sports events. €€

the waters from the rocks at sunset. Bronzed and exhilarated: this is how the locals do it.

The Mediterranean diet, laid-back culture and a penchant for sleeping late make for a relaxed and healthy trip, so long as you can let yourself go with the flow. Romance should be about passion-driven acts of spontaneity, and Marseille gets your heart beating faster and the dopamine flooding. This is a city to get it on. To show off your tan at sunset to the crowds, head to **Le Cabanon de Paulette**, a sexy hangout overlooking the sea.

Eco-Friendly Cruises on the Med

Take to the water

There is no more joyful escape than to take to the waters around Marseille. Charming captain Jimmy Granger skippers **Les Croisières du Foxy** (lescroisieresdufoxy.com). Docked close to the Mucem, his sloop is ready to zip across Les Calanques (p146) for a swim or enjoy a heady cocktail at sunset.

At the Vieux Port you can find Fanny's barquette **Coco** (capitainecoco.fr) to experience the immediacy of the sea on a Provençal 1960s leisure vessel. You will help run up the sails, learn about biodiversity and enjoy a vegetarian lunch.

Eco-Calanques (eco-calanques.com) is another small company run by local guides. Their eco-trawler is partly solar-powered, and Thibault will entertain passengers with stories about the city's history as he takes you out to the most tranquil bays. While the Mediterranean is blessed with calm, warm waters in summer, the mistral wind may postpone excursions in winter.

Escape to Les Goudes

Seafood at the end of the world

A common insult in Marseille is 'Go throw yourself in the Goudes'. But oddly enough, **Les Goudes** is actually a lovely place to visit: it's a tiny fishing village locked in time, with access to spectacularly rugged coastlines.

Its proximity to the Parc National des Calanques means the village is afforded the same legal protection; thus, there has been no development here. For now, the bygone era remains.

A handful of restaurants and hotels can be found in the village. **Tuba Club** is so exclusive it's almost impossible to book one of its eight rooms or get a seat in its restaurant, but it's worth a shot. **Fashionista Paradise** is another possibility, though you'll need to make reservations to have a drink on the rocks after 5pm.

LE VORTEX

Marseille's underground is furiously anti-fascist and queer-friendly, and the free listings magazine *Le Vortex* vividly captures this spirit.

Each month it meticulously lists concerts whose cover charge is under €10. Whether you're looking for Berlin-style techno, country music, punk, metal, new wave, shoegaze or experimental Middle Eastern beats, it's all here in one place.

It can all also be found under the roof of a former tobacco factory, *La Friche la Belle de Mai*: a huge cultural space with gigs, raves, art exhibitions and a rooftop bar. Tuning in online or to 88.8FM (Radio Grenouille) will give you a flavour of the many musical worlds at play across the city.

 BEST PARTY VENUES

SOMA
Weekend shows bring out the artsy fashion crowd to Cours Julien.

La Mer Veilleuse
Banging techno, electro, Afrobeat and punk in a friendly bar venue.

Le Couvent
The Belle de Mai neighbourhood's venue for rave parties is set in a converted nunnery.

In the heart of the village is Didier's **Le Grand Bar de Goudes**, a welcoming seafood restaurant and bar. As you rub shoulders with those who grew up in these narrow streets, eating fish that has practically leapt out of the ocean and onto your plate, you'll understand the local pride in their enviable lifestyle.

The walk to the **Baie des Singes**, an old smuggling cove, is a surreal sun-beaten experience – don't miss it. The restaurant has sunloungers at €25 euros for the day. Make reservations and return to Didier's later in the day to eat.

Buses 19 and then 20 will get you close to Les Goudes year-round. From the end of May to September, boats leave from the Vieux Port – you will likely need to switch ferries in Pointe-Rouge.

The History of Pastis

The art of the apéritif

Pastis is the apéritif of choice in many parts of southern France, and it's easy to spot: a milky-looking concoction served in a tall glass that adorns outdoor tables in Provençal villages everywhere.

In 1932 in Marseille, Paul Ricard developed his aniseed and liquorice-based liqueur (*pastís* means 'mix' in Occitan) after absinthe was banned in France out of fear that it caused hallucinations and madness.

Since then, pastis has become a drink that is synonymous with the city. Ricard may now be part of a multinational conglomerate based in Lille, but there are still independent pastis producers in Marseille where you can arrange a visit.

The distillery **Cristal Limiñana** is happy to organise tours and tastings. After an in-depth history of anise and the family business, which dates back to 1884, take a walk through the factory to see the automated whir of bottles being filled, capped and packed at surprisingly close range.

The **Pastis de la Plaine** distillery has only been in operation since 2019, but its bottles are already found in bars across the city. This is a much smaller operation, though they also run tours and tastings.

Those who instinctively shy away from aniseed or liquorice can always mix the liqueur with sweet syrup. *Un perroquet* is mint flavoured, *une tomate* is mixed with grenadine and *une mauresque* tastes of almonds. *Santé!*

DATE NIGHT

Nikolaj De L'Ivresse, one of the three owners of Ivresse, a wine bar and the hottest date spot in town, shares his picks for the most romantic spots in the city. *@ivresse.lacave*

Le Vin sur la Main
This is another great natural wine bar. They are cosy, we are hot. €€

Sunset Bar
On the corniche, it's perfect for a drink with a date just after a swim at sunset. Time it right. €€

Jogging
Enter through the back door of a very cool clothes shop for a secret lunch in a quiet courtyard. €€

 BEST VINTAGE SHOPS IN MARSEILLE

Out of Space
A treasure trove of well-selected and chic 1980s and '90s pieces.

Space
Specialist in rare designer sunglasses to take you back to the 1990s in style.

Sepia Swing Club
Cherry-picked Americana that stands out in a street of vintage clothing stores.

BALKANSCAT/SHUTTERSTOCK ©

Pastis apéritif

Escape to the Château d'If

Island life

For a quick and easy trip out to sea, hop on the Frioul-If ferry to Marseille's closest islands: the Château d'If (for historians) and the Îles du Frioul (for nature lovers).

Commanding access to Marseille's Vieux Port, the **Château d'If** was immortalised by Alexandre Dumas in his classic 1844 novel *The Count of Monte Cristo*. A 16th-century island prison with three towers, one giving a great view across the bay, you can wander unaccompanied or visit with an audio or guided tour; the contrast between the cells for the wealthy and the dungeon pit strikes a tone. This is the ferry's first stop; it's 20 minutes from the Vieux Port.

It's another 15 minutes to the next stop, the Port du Frioul, your entry point to two of the Frioul islands, Pomègues and Ratonneau, which are connected by a dam.

Attacking the unspoiled jagged rock of **Pomègues** is liberating. Following the seawall after you dock will lead to the Fort de Caveaux, leaving you lost at sea on an uninhabited island, revisiting ghosts in the bunkers of WWII. Finding a spot to feel utterly alone with the swooping seabirds is easiest in spring.

LES GOUDES' BEST RESTAURANTS

For over 35 years, **Eric Signoret** has been the owner of the only convenience store for kilometres around; you can always find him behind the counter. Here are his favourite places to eat in town.

L'Auberge du Corsaire
Known as Chez Paul to locals, come here for seafood right in the heart of the marina.

Marine des Goudes
A seafood restaurant with great views from above. It's perfect for lunch on the weekend.

La Gelateria
An Italian family business serving 1960s-style ice cream, they're a new addition to our village.

 WHERE TO SLEEP IN MARSEILLE

Hôtel Bellevue Vieux Port
Great port views and home to the historical Caravelle restaurant. €€

Mama Shelter
Friendly boutique hotel with a roof bar; it's close to all the action in the 6ème. €€

Hôtel Le Corbusier
A mastery of modern design with a rooftop pool. A classic. €€

FAVOURITE PIZZA SPOTS

Marc Étienne, the English owner of the natural wine shop Winespirit gives his recommendations for the best pizza places in the city. *@winespirit13005*

Ciao Marcello
Considered by some as the best pizza in Marseille and maybe even France. My personal favourite. **€€**

L'Eau à la Bouche
This is the fashion crowd's choice for pizza on the corniche, with views of the sea. **€€**

Bambino
More than just pizza, this modern Italian restaurant in the Camas (5ème *arrondissement*) also has great cocktails. **€€**

Palais Longchamp

The island of **Ratonneau** has a few small shops and restaurants and is popular for its beaches and tiny village. There's a chapel that resembles a Greek temple and the ruins of the Hôpital Caroline, which once housed quarantined travellers, but the highlight is the St-Estève beach, where you can swim safely, protected from the wind.

The ticket pier for **lebateau** ferries is located at the Vieux Port. When facing the port, get in line at its large booth on the left. Return ferry tickets for one destination is €11.10; a combined ferry ticket for both the Château d'If and the Frioul islands is €16.70. The Château d'If is closed on Mondays.

Another way to get here is with the **Bateau Jaune Club** in the Vieux Port, which organises snorkelling and diving trips.

Pizza, Pizza

From food trucks to the beach

Marseille is famous for its regional specialities: bouillabaisse, aïoli and *panisse*. Yet when you walk around the city, it's hard not to notice that **pizza** is on every corner, and consumed by every ethnicity and age group. Perhaps some of the dish's popularity is due to the city's close proximity to Italy, from which a third of Marseille's inhabitants can trace their roots.

 BEST PASTIS BARS

Bar du Peuple
Left-leaning waterhole on the edge of Noailles that's the authentic place to be in summer.

Bar des Maraîchers
Listen to 1980s radio hits with owner Serge, who also features in his own fresco.

Le Chapitre
Young crowd in a leafy square at the top of the main thoroughfare le Canebière.

The quick fix, pizza by the slice, must be addressed first. Pizza trucks are the obvious place to find such a snack; as grab-and-go as it comes, pizza in Marseille is a spontaneous act: get it on the way back from the beach, the bar, or any other excursion.

From the densely populated African quarter of Noailles to the jam-packed boozy squares of Cours Julien and La Plaine to the beach spots on the corniche, pizza is everywhere waiting to be reheated – the chilli oil sitting in a bottle by the side.

Marseille is also known for its own unique take on a Neapolitan-style pizza: the *moitié-moitié* (half and half). One side has anchovies, the other side has emmental cheese.

Marseille en Vogue

Bohemian quarters

Parts of Marseille look much as they did decades ago. It's easy to imagine you're walking the same streets as Fernando Rey in *The French Connection* (the 1970s noir thriller about heroin smugglers), but it is also impossible to ignore the rapid changes afoot. The global pandemic accelerated many young people's desire to move closer to the Med for a slower pace of life and more sunshine. Unsurprisingly, housing prices over the last few years have been soaring.

To visit some of the hipper neighbourhoods in the city, begin in the green and pleasant gardens surrounding the sublime-looking **Palais Longchamp**, an outrageous 19th-century monument that gushes with fountains in the celebration of fertility. This is a great place to lie on the grass and people-watch.

Walking down the long bd Longchamp and its parallel backstreets, you'll find the new proliferation of bars and restaurants in the area taking centre stage. Despite the slogans on the walls everywhere you go, the rallying cries of a highly organised left-wing community rallying against gentrification, there seems to be more refurbishment going on in this 'new Berlin' neighbourhood than anywhere else.

As you walk, you'll drift past galleries, boutiques, restaurants and bars all the way down to the **Fontaine des Danaïdes**.

In **Vauban** and **Endoume**, much closer to the coast, you'll find an area awash with the bourgeoisie moving in and setting up. Another pleasant amble is the stroll down the rue d'Endoume all the way to Malmousque to enjoy Marseille at a completely different pace.

FOOD FOR THE ISLANDS

Headed out for a day of exploring? Pack your own lunch courtesy of Marseille's best sandwich stops and pâtisseries.

Razzia
A wildly popular lunchtime sandwich maker for the masses in the 6ème *arrondissement*. €

Limon
Vegetarian favourite and an extravagant twist on North African and Mediterranean flavours. €

La Kaz Kréol
Housebaked Creole bread with big fillings. The white fish sandwich is incredible. €

Amandine
Pastries that are as good as they look, for those besotted with sweets in the Camas. €

Au Contraire
Vauban's *tarte* specialists also deliver sumptuous pastry-based wonders. €

La Pépite
Gluten-free, organic and as mouthwatering as it comes in the 7ème. €

 WHERE TO EAT AND DRINK IN LONGCHAMP

Les Eaux de Mars
Michelin-trained chef's cool spot on a quiet corner. Reservations required. €€

Mémé
Outstanding shapes and colours come to your plate; for a meal when you want to splurge. €€€

La Fréquence
Tapas-style plates paired with cocktails and a beautiful crowd. €€

L'Estaque
Niolon • • • Allauch
Carry-le-Rouet • • **Marseille**
• Cassis
Calanque d'En-Vau •
Parc National
des Calanques

Beyond
Marseille

To truly appreciate Marseille, cut loose from its intense energy and explore the nature that surrounds it.

The beauty of leaving Marseille is the overwhelming contrasts that come at you so quickly. The welcome shock at sudden bursts of birdsong or the light breaking through the pine trees in spring will have you breathing differently. Lavender fields, ancient villages and winding mountain climbs with a view to the valleys below are everything you dreamed Provence could deliver.

Head inland to the Provençal countryside, famous for its idyllic charm, or cut yourself off from the world in far-flung beaches on the savage and yet increasingly fashionable coastline that extends in both directions from the city. Either way, the possibilities of vast horizons of time and space are endless.

Outdoor Adventures in the Parc National des Calanques

Kayak, hike, dive and climb

It feels like a miracle to find a refuge like the **Parc National des Calanques** only a short distance from Marseille. In parts of this diminutive 85-sq-km patch of scrubby promontories, it's easy to believe you're far from civilisation. Then a twist in a pine-clad gully reveals the entirety of France's second metropolis spread out within apparent touching distance; Les Calanques appear almost as its uninhabited suburbs.

But with their light-shifting geometry, rich plant and animal life and idyllic hidden coves, the *calanques* are so much more than that. They are beloved of the Marseillais, who come for the sun and to hike over pine-strewn promontories, mess about on boats and generally refresh their souls.

GETTING AROUND

Without a boat, you'll have to drive, cycle or take public transport to visit Cassis and the nearby *calanques*. Be warned that roads are rough, parking scarce and the going slow. In peak summer season, the municipality recommends arriving by bus. In the other direction, the train along the Côte Bleue is cheap and allows you to drink wine with your lunch.

☑ TOP TIP

Wear an OM football shirt when travelling around the region to gain street cred with the locals.

STUDIO EMPREINTE/SHUTTERSTOCK ©

Calanque de Morgiou

Of the many *calanques* along the coastline, the most easily accessible are **Calanque de Sormiou** and **Calanque de Morgiou**. Remote inlets such as **Calanque d'En-Vau** (p148) and **Calanque de Port-Miou** (p148) take dedication and time to reach, either on foot or by kayak. Note that overland access is often limited from June to September due to **fire danger**; always check fist.

There's no shortage of outdoor activities here: hiking, kayaking, stand-up paddleboarding, swimming, diving and rock climbing are all incredible. You'll find guides and gear rental in both Marseille and Cassis. From October to June, hiking trails lead through the maquis (scrub). Marseille's tourist office leads guided walks and has an excellent hiking map of the various *calanques*, as does Cassis' tourist office.

The best way to reach the *calanques* is by sea – either by boat or by hiring a kayak. Operators such as **Destination Calanques Kayak** and **Raskas Kayak** organise sea-kayaking tours while **Calanc'O** rents stand-up paddleboards.

For the most up-to-date info on the park, activities and, most importantly, access, download the Mes Calanques app.

OVERLAND TO THE CALANQUES

Without a boat, you'll have to drive, cycle or take public transport to visit the **Parc National des Calanques**. Be warned that roads are rough, parking scarce and the going slow. The roads into each *calanque* are often closed to drivers, unless you have a reservation at one of the *calanque* restaurants. You must instead park at a public lot, then walk the rest of the way.

For access to the *calanques* closest to Marseille, drive or take bus 19 from Marseille's Castellane bus station down the coast to its terminus at La Madrague, then switch to bus 20 to Callelongue. Note that the road to Callelongue is only open to cars on weekdays from mid-April to May and closed entirely from June to September.

BEST KAYAK RENTALS BEYOND MARSEILLE

Expénature La Ciotat
Kayak with fun guides to the nearby *calanques* and the Île Verte; in La Ciotat, east of Cassis.

Raskas Kayak
Over 20 years of guiding kayaking trips to the *calanques*; located in eastern Marseille.

Sud Kayak/Cleanride Center
Located west of Marseille near L'Estaque. Great sunset trips to the Crique des Aragnols.

Clambering Down to Paradise

From Cassis to the Calanque d'En-Vau

The small port of **Cassis** has lost some of its charm over the years, but the coastline beyond is another story. The village is the perfect staging point for excursions to the **Calanque d'En-Vau**, which lives up to any hyperbole you wish to throw at it. From Cassis, make your way to the **Calanque de Port-Miou** on foot (30 minutes) or, alternatively, park in the Presqu'île car park. This is the start of a difficult, unshaded hike, but it's worth every stretch of sinew. Expect it to take a solid 1½ hours from here.

The first stop is the **Calanque de Port-Pin** for a quick dip. It takes at least 20 minutes to get here as you keep the water to your left and the boats below. From Port-Pin, there are two paths to the Calanque d'En-Vau. Take the blue-coded coastal path, which is longer (around one hour) but more rewarding. Arriving at the cliffs, you'll be glad you made the effort.

Clambering down to the beach is tricky for newbies; you can easily tell who's local, as they look like mountain goats when scampering down the cliffs. If you arrive with good footwear

BEST LUNCHES IN CASSIS

Gabriel Chiesa is a long-time Marseille resident who spends his weekends hiking Les Calanques. Here are his recommendations for eating out in Cassis.

Le Nino
Don't want lunch to be a big ordeal? Look for this local institution in the middle of the port. €

La Presqu'île
Come here for crisp white tablecloths and Michelin stars paired with great views of the bay. Reserve. €€

Le Bistro'Quai
As the French say, this bistro is *correcte* (decent). It's friendly and right on the harbour. €

JANOKA82/GETTY IMAGES ©

Calanque de Port-Pin

THE BEST CALANQUES

Sormiou
Creeks, climbing, a restaurant and a cave adorned with prehistoric paintings dating back to 20,000 BCE.

Calanque de la Crine
Liberating *calanque* with perfect waters on the Frioul islands; get here on the ferry.

Calanque de Morgiou
Pretty port bobbing with fishing boats and sheer rock faces spangled with thrill-seeking climbers.

and take your time the descent is fine, though if you suffer from vertigo, this is not for you. Ideally, plan on arriving by late morning and bring enough water and food for the day.

Cassis is 30km east of Marseille and is best reached by car in low season. At other times of year, taking the train (30 minutes) is advised as you may not be able to find a parking spot. From the Cassis train station, take the M1 bus to the centre of town (15 minutes).

Escape to the Hills above the City

Rural beauty in Allauch

A mere 20 minutes' drive northeast from Marseille – or an hour on public transport – is a unique hotel experience in the village of **Allauch** that offers luxurious romance in a rural Provençe-meets-sci-fi setting. **Attrap'Rêves** (Dream Catching) is an experience that borders on the cosmic.

The rooms here are not your usual hotel rooms: accommodation consists of a series of queen-size beds enclosed in transparent soundproof bubbles. Each pod is secluded from the others, has climate control, chairs and access to a Jacuzzi and shared pool. As you lie down for an all-embracing view of the forest around you, you'll find it's almost like camping, but in an otherworldly style. A nice touch is the telescope through which guests can gaze up at the stars. Order food and Champagne and connect with nature in true serenity.

The village and its celebrated landscape is less than 10 minutes away from Attrap'Rêves. Here you'll find the fully restored 18th-century **Moulin Louis Ricard** windmill. It's well worth the €2 entry to see its inner workings, and when the wind blows, you might be able to catch the milling process in action. Five minutes from here on foot is the 11th-century chapel of **Notre-Dame du Château**. Drop by for outstanding panoramic views of Marseille and its islands.

Ride the Rails along La Côte Bleue

All aboard to turquoise waters

Heading west from Gare St-Charles, Marseille's train station, is the spectacular **Côte Bleue** (the Blue Coast) railway. A 15-minute (€3) journey takes passengers to **L'Estaque**; the views from the train window are the same as the ones that once inspired the impressionists. From L'Estaque's train station it's only a 10-minute walk to the port, where you can sample the regional delicacies of *panisse* and *chichi* (similar to Spanish churros), both staple

PAGNOL COUNTRY

The Garlaban massif, rising 715m above sea level, is where the legendary French writer and filmmaker Marcel Pagnol grew up. His family holiday home, **La Bastide Neuve**, is located in the hills above Allauch.

Pagnol's books and early movies inspired an entire generation to lose themselves in his tales of Provence, most famously the 1986 films *Jean de Florette* and *Manon des Sources*, both adaptations of his novels.

Hiking is extremely popular in the Garlaban massif; from Allauch to the Pagnol holiday home takes about an hour through the *garrigue* – the fragrant Mediterranean scrubland.

Alternatively, a 15-minute drive east of the village is **Château de la Buzine**, a 15th-century castle, made famous in the film *Le Château de Ma Mère* . It's now an interactive museum and movie theatre.

WHERE TO EAT IN ALLAUCH

Restaurant Iod'in
The best sushi in the region is at this young Michelin-starred chef's restaurant. €€

Au Moulin Bleu
A family confectionary business that goes back five generations. Try their famous *suce-miel* honey treat. €

La Quinta Table Provençale
Simple Mediterranean cuisine served by the pool. What summer is all about. €€

ingredients of the Mediterranean. Eat them in paper cones at the *barraques à chichis* (historic food stands) or try one of the region's most authentic seafood restaurants, **L'Hippocampe**. The **Alhambra cinema** is a short cab ride away. Since 1928, it has been standing in a leafy square that's also home to **Denis Bar**, which feels like it has been patronised by fishers and artists for hundreds of years.

The real gem, however, is further up the coast. Another 15 minutes on the train past L'Estaque brings you to **Niolon**, where you'll feel as if you've been transported to a Provençal village. Follow the crowd to make your way along the rocky path to the **Calanque du Jonquier** and swim in the shadow of the spectacular arched viaduct as you gaze across the calm waters back towards the city. Pretty unbeatable.

Coastal Walks of Carry-le-Rouet

Searching for urchins

Only 30km west of Marseille, **Carry-le-Rouet** is another pearl on the Côte Bleue rail line, hitting the sweet spot with its charming port, fragrant pine trees and perfectly rough-hewn inlets. Like many coastal towns, it has gone from being a sleepy fishing village to a thriving seaside resort, appealing to foodies and nature lovers alike. The train here from Gare St-Charles is around €6, and the 35-minute trip passes by in the blink of an eye as you stare out the window at the sea.

Renting a car, however, allows for more freedom to stop in places along the way. You can drive along roads where lime-stone rises all around you and long-horned goats nibble on scrub, but parking will never be easy. The first three Sundays of February are the subject of a grand celebration, when sea-food fanatics descend into the port for the **Oursinade**, a tasting festival offering an abundance of sea urchins that are considered the best in the Med. If you're not crazy about urchins, everything else pulled from the ocean, including platters of shellfish, is on offer too.

At any time of the year, the jaggy promenade from the port to **Sausset-les-Pins** is the perfect coastal stroll, with no shortage of places to stop and take it all in. The beaches are more pebbly than sandy, but the waters are transparent. Every summer during July and August, the **Parc Marin Côte Bleue** (parcmarincotebleue.fr) organises free guided tours in the marine reserve that include a wetsuit, snorkel and mask. Make reservations in advance to learn about the many protected species in the conservation area.

CALANQUE DE L'ÉVERINE

On leaving the train station at Niolon on the Côte Bleue line, turn left and continue walking. After 200m, take the path left into the valley; the path on the right leads up to the Fort de Niolon. This will take you under the last arch of the viaduct above the Calanque du Jonquier. You are now on the sentier des Douaniers, a pleasant but occasionally steep coastal trek that passes beneath a shaded canopy.

From the station, it's around an hour's walk to the gorgeous **Calanque de l'Éverine**. The reward is a cove with crystal-clear waters and only the gentle lapping of the Med and birdsong to keep you company.

WHERE TO EAT AROUND CARRY-LE-ROUET

Rest'o Cap Rousset
Sample French cuisine as sun-worshippers fling themselves into the *calanque* below. €€

La Cal
Stop for great pizza and views between Carry and Sausset-les-Pins. €€

MyPitchu
Relaxed beach bar in Sausset-les-Pins serving fish fresh from the sea. €€

● Aix-en-Provence

Aix-en-Provence

The sun magically lights up centuries-old mansions while fountains gurgle in small squares, hidden at the end of narrow streets. Locals stroll by dressed in understated elegance and stare at you from stylish cafe terraces, coolly sipping espresso. Aix (pronounced like the letter X) is a caricature of French life – that there are no surprises is part of its charm.

It is a city to drift through and observe: precisely what Baudelaire was getting at when he coined the term *flâneur*. But to wander the urban landscape and do nothing is not nothing at all. It is to become part of your surroundings as you take your time. As a university city, Aix is elegant and welcoming, and the streets are arteries for a flood of international students.

Whether you've come to shop, indulge in gourmet meals or use it as a base to venture out into the countryside, Aix will gently guide you on your way.

Art and Architecture in Aix

A stroller's paradise

If you want to get your bearings with a stroll through town, start with **Cours Mirabeau**. No streetscape better epitomises Provence's most graceful city than this 440m-long, fountain-studded street, sprinkled with Renaissance *hôtels particuliers* (private mansions) and crowned with a summertime roof of leafy plane trees. South of Cours Mirabeau, the Quartier Mazarin is home to some of Aix' finest buildings.

Local lad Paul Cézanne (1839–1906) is revered in Aix, and traces of his passage – including at Montagne Ste-Victoire (p157) – can be found on the **Cézanne Trail** through town. Pick up a copy at the tourist office.

For more art in Aix, stop by the Musée Granet or the Caumont Centre d'Art. The intimate **Musée Granet** was established as one of France's first public museums in 1838, on the site of a former Hospitallers' priory. Nearly 200 years of acquisitions have resulted in a collection of more than 12,000

GETTING AROUND

Ask any local and they will tell you that Aix is tiny and you should walk everywhere. The local bus service (aixenbus.com) to the edge of town is a good alternative; tickets are easily purchased on board. Hire bikes (aixpritvelo.com) in the centre of town.

☑ TOP TIP

Being chic is part of cafe culture and an expensive pair of sunglasses are an essential part of the Aix wardrobe. People do not sit across from each other on the terraces but face outward instead, covertly watching who is coming down the street.

AIX-EN-PROVENCE

Pl des Martyrs de la Résistance

Bd Aristide Briand

Av Pasteur

Av Jules Isaac

Av Jean Jaurès

R Boulegon

R.Mignet

R da Suffren

Cours St-Louis

R Célony

Av des Thermes

R Ducancel

R Gaston de Saporta

R Paul Bert

Forum des Cardeurs

Pl des Fontetes

R de la Verrerie

R des Cordeliers

R des Magnans

Pl de l'Hôtel de Ville

R Rifle Rafle

Pl des Prêcheurs

Cours Sextius

Place Ramus

Pl de Verdun

R Manuel

R Éméric David

R des Bernardines

R de la Couronne

R Esperiat

R Nazareth

R Clemenceau

R t'biers

Petite R-St-Jean

R de l'Opéra

R du Maréchal J.

R Victor Leydet

Av Napoléon Bonaparte

Pl Jeanne d'Arc

Pl du Général de Gaulle

Av Giuseppe Verdi

Sq Mattéi

Cours Mirabeau

R Mazarine

R Ferrand Dol

R Itielle

R Frédéric Mistral

R Laroque

Pl des Quatre Dauphins

R Roux Alpheran

R Sallier

R Lapierre

Pl de Navrix

R Cardinale

R Malherbe

Av des Belges

R Gustave Desplaces

R Goriard

Bd du Roi René

Av St-Jérome

City Centre

N   0 ———————— 200 m
    0 ———————— 0.1 mile

SIGHTS
1 Caumont Centre d'Art
2 Cours Mirabeau
3 Musée Granet
4 Parc Jourdan
5 Pavillon Vendôme

ACTIVITIES, COURSES & TOURS
6 Les Thermes Sextius

EATING
7 Brasserie de L'Archevêché
8 Chez Nine
9 Instant V

10 La Brocherie
11 La Maison Béchard
12 La Maison Weibel
13 Le Petit Verdot

DRINKING & NIGHTLIFE
14 Bar des PTT

15 Book in Bar
16 Cafe Caumont
17 Café des Négociants
18 Mana

SHOPPING
19 La Cave des Ours
20 Place Richelme

works, including pieces by Picasso, Léger, Matisse, Monet, Klee, Van Gogh and, crucially, nine pieces by Cézanne. This fabulous art museum, which also hosts top-shelf temporary exhibits, sits right near the top of France's artistic must-sees.

The **Caumont Centre d'Art** is a stellar art space housed inside the Mazarin quarter's grandest 18th-century *hôtel particulier*. While there are three quality exhibitions each year (with additional entrance fees), plus concerts and other events, it's the building itself that's the star of the show. Built from local honey-coloured stone, its palatial rooms are stuffed with antiques and *objets d'art* attesting to the opulence of the house's aristocratic past.

Local Haunts

Drink and dine in timeworn elegance

Before globalisation and high-speed trains from Paris, Aix had an almost mythological status. Many French considered the town to be an obscure and romantic pocket of wealth and sunshine. This was a place where you might catch a famous movie star like Alain Delon drinking espresso. But once the TGV linked the capital with southern France in less than three hours, well-heeled Parisian families relocated here, followed soon after by tourists and retirees from around the world. Nevertheless, some venues have survived for decades. Still beloved by the locals, they have continued to thrive into the 21st century.

Brasserie de L'Archevêché is a restaurant around the corner from Aix' famous Institut d'Études Politiques (IEP), an elite university preparing future diplomats, politicians and journalists. The current owner has been here since 1995, his lunchtime terrace in the historic square buzzing with students under the speckled shade of plane trees.

Within the narrow walls of **Bar des PTT** are people from all walks of life. It's not unusual to find lawyers and market stall owners side by side in this narrow setting. Pass by the sunny terrace on place Richelme to meet the characters in its cool interior.

Hidden away, like all good things in Aix, is **La Brocherie**, which serves grilled meat and seafood in the kind of rustic setting that some may consider old-fashioned, but which rings with integrity. The T-bone steak and lavender-infused crème brûlée will not only transport you to the 1970s, but also cost less than €30.

THE CLINK OF SUMMER

Pétanque, or boules, traces its roots back to the early 1900s in La Ciotat, where it began as a Provençal outdoor bowling game.

It was invented to accommodate a physically disabled player in a wheelchair who could not perform the run-up before releasing the ball.

Pétanque is now the iconic French village sport and is played by people of all ages. The game consists of two teams: the first throws a small ball, the *cochonnet,* across a pitch of gravel or sand. Each player then throws heavy metal boules, trying to get them as close as possible to the *cochonnet* – or to displace their opponent's boules. The team who is closest to the *cochonnet* at the end of the round is the winner.

WHERE TO STAY IN AIX

Hôtel Escaletto
Comfortable and affordable, with inspiring views of Mont St-Victoire. €€

L'Hôtel des Arts
In the centre of town, this simple and unfussy choice is by the Musée Granet. €

Hôtel Cardinal
This hotel is as formal as the gilt-framed mirrors and paintings hanging within. €€

Gourmet Picnics

Bread, wine and a blanket

The market in **place Richelme**, open from early morning until lunch (Monday to Saturday), is the town's premier spot for quality local produce: you'll find fresh bread, speciality saucissons, the usual cavalcade of hard and soft cheeses, plus vibrantly coloured produce, jams and tapenades. In short, it has everything you would expect from a Provençal market and is the perfect spot to find picnic inspiration. For regional wines, try **La Cave des Ours**, which specialises in the natural and biodynamic varieties and is only minutes away from the market. Like all French *cavistes*, they are more than happy to educate you on the stuff.

For green spaces that turn bright orange in autumn, the **Promenade de la Torse** is a wide-open space a half-hour's walk to the southeast of Cours Mirabeau. Wooden bridges pass over a lively stream inhabited by ducks and herons. The grounds of the **Pavillon Vendôme**, only 10 minutes from La Rotonde, are everything you would expect Aix-en-Provence to be: manicured gardens in the shadow of historical opulence built by a love-sick Duke. It's as regal a setting as you could wish for in what is now an art museum. **Parc Jourdan** is a city park the locals are likelier to use to play boules and

BEST CHOCOLATIERS IN AIX

Pâtisserie Philippe Segond
Monsieur Segond claims to be the best in France. Try his chocolates and you might agree.

Les Chocolats Yves Turies
Another artisan who takes chocolate so seriously that your head might spin. Next-level nut bars.

Le Roy René
Famous for making Aix' sweet candied-fruit *calissons*, as well as chocolates.

FRANZ MARC FREI/GETTY IMAGES ©

Saturday market, Place Richelme

where many workers and university students eat sandwiches at lunchtime. What it lacks in beauty is made up for with local authenticity.

Breaking away from it all, only 15 minutes drive north of the city, is a quieter setting. For those who want to be alone for a panoramic sunset, the remains of the 8th-century fortress **La Quille** in Le Puy Ste-Réparade has expansive views over the Luberon and its hills. Only 7km from the city centre and a short drive or taxi ride away is the family residence of **Terre Ugo**, home to the only organic lavender field in Provence that flourishes in late June. For €7, from June to August, you have access to what is essentially a family estate. The gentle murmuring of the countryside fills your ears as you settle on a chaise longue in the shade or play a game of *pétanque*. On Thursdays, a food truck, cocktail service and live music take you into the night from 6.30pm to 10pm.

Thermal Baths

Luxuriate like a Roman

There comes a time on any road trip when you have to scrub yourself free of the tension of travelling, whether you've just arrived and want to wash your problems down the plughole

 WHERE TO EAT GLUTEN-FREE IN AIX

Atelier du Mochi
Hyper-modern French take on the Japanese sticky-rice dessert. Vegan and gluten-free. €€

Ojus
Gluten-free crêpes, vegan rice bowls and lentil dishes: all available to take away. €€

Aux Petits Oignons
Outstanding gluten-free, vegan hot dogs, accompanied by caramelised onions and chips. €€

or pause your journey for an afternoon of indulgence. Aix-en-Provence, originally known as Aquae Sextiae in Roman times, is a great place to immerse yourself in the healing powers of water, reconnecting your body and mind.

It's easy to appreciate the significance of the modern spa **Les Thermes Sextius**, which was built atop the Roman baths of **Aquae Sextiae**, which can be seen beneath glass floors on arrival. Romans settled wherever they found natural springs, and their public baths were a fundamental part of everyday life. Much like the modern gym, this was not only a place to exercise and relax but also to socialise with people of all classes, strike deals and gossip.

The indulgence of steam and massage is a timeless combination. As you lie beneath the vestiges of the Roman empire, within its ancient walls surrounding the pool, you can absorb the sun in peace or choose from one of many hands-on treatments that will loosen those knots. Check their website for drinks and tapas deals.

Art at Fondation Vasarely

The father of op art

Just 4km west of the city is the **Fondation Vasarely**, a cavernous building that catches the eye with its 1970s hyper-contemporary design of glass and metallic geometric blocks. An architectural masterpiece, it has 16 interconnecting, hexagonal galleries purpose-built to display and reflect the patterning of Hungarian-French artist Victor Vasarely's 44 acid-trip-ready, floor-to-ceiling geometric artworks.

As the undisputed father of op art – that's short for optical art – Vasarely feels more relevant than ever in a world of computer-generated images spiralling off into nowhere.

The space he designed overwhelms with sheer colour and scale, the huge psychedelic work pulling you into a world of anamorphic patterns within seven galleries, each containing six works of art. This is a place where art can lead to transcendental meditation in what he described as a 'laboratory of ideas'.

Vasarely's view of the future is timeless. Having been the poster boy for vibrating geometric art, his work in the advertising industry and designing album covers for David Bowie are only some of the examples of how he was ahead of his time. It's a world of pixels before the computer screen – if that's your thing.

WHERE TO BUY SOAPS AND ESSENTIAL OILS IN AIX

Bastide
Artisanal perfumes, candles, potpourri and essential oils that will have you smelling of figs and honey.

Rose et Marius
Deliberately indulgent soaps and perfumes to ensure that well-being is the star of the show.

Agape
Provence-based company with luxurious oils for massage and organic aromatherapy.

Beyond
Aix-en-Provence

Salon-de-Provence

Montagne
Ste-Victoire

Aix-en-Provence

Le
Tholonet

The gastronomical treasures found in Aix hint at
what lies beyond.

As a city that flaunts its abundance of water in its many
fountains and stupefies with the excesses of nobility, Aix' connection to the countryside remains clear. Aromas in town suggest the wide-open spaces of lavender fields and the profusion
of thyme. This is a land of wine, olive oil and bread, which
are so much more than staples. In Provence, these things are
given by the earth but brought to us with a sense of history,
refinement and skill. The journey through the countryside
and to the smaller villages allows travellers to experience for
themselves what a privilege it is to live simply with the land,
from Montagne Ste-Victoire to the Palette appellation vineyards to the olive trees of Salon-de-Provence.

Hiking through Cézanne's Landscapes
From Le Tholonet to Bibemus

Provence is a hiker's dream. Climbing to the summit of
Montagne Ste-Victoire seems like the obvious trek as it
rises in the distance, but it can be excruciating – especially in
the heat. A great alternative, especially for lovers of art and
nature, is a ramble in Cézanne country. A 3½-hour hike from
Le Tholonet with an expert guide can be booked at Aix' tourist office or online at aixenprovencetourism.com.

Le Tholonet provides the perfect starting point with its
waterfalls, windmills, cafes and restaurants. Here, you are
at the mountain's base, with the hike eventually taking you
through the right angles of the Bibemus quarries and beneath
the pine trees. This is the rock that Aix and its monuments
were carved from, and where Cézanne would work from the
old stone house he had built to immerse himself in his work.
As you climb the terrain of dark earth and loose stones, the
views take you into the shapes and colours of his paintings.
The summer treks that set off at 6pm offer magical light.

Reaching the plateau offers the panoramic vistas that
Cézanne made famous in his oil paintings and watercolours.
They largely remain the same views to this day. Returning

GETTING AROUND

Although exploring
by car is the most
practical, there is
a real road cycling
culture in these
parts. Cycling all the
way to Montagne
Ste-Victoire is not for
beginners, but with
an e-bike you can
definitely go a long
ways. Rent one in Aix
at Aixprit Vélo.

☑ TOP TIP
If exploring by car, look
for a farmhouse rental
rather than a standard
hotel for the full-on rustic
experience.

THE GUIDE

BEYOND AIX-EN-PROVENCE BOUCHES-DU-RHÔNE

A Tour of Aix' Vineyards

The countryside that spreads out from Aix in every direction is rich with wineries and notable grape-growing areas. Take a road trip to sample the vintages produced around the imperious Montagne Ste-Victoire, where the hills and valleys shelter the vines and the volcanic earth gives life. The saying goes: 'May the sun be clear and beautiful, and we will have more wine than water'. This tour can easily be driven in a day.

① Domaine des Masques

Head east from Aix-en-Provence on the D17 for 13km, turning south on the rue du Bayon, where a secluded vineyard appears at the end of a potholed track. The landscapes here are as lovely as any in the French countryside. Pass a long line of cypress trees, park the car and then enter a small tasting room to sample a few whites, reds and rosés. Their crisp and floral white wines are the highlight of them all.

The Drive: Return to the D17 and continue east, turning southeast onto the D56C; the Domaine des Diables is only 14km away, but it's a 20-minute drive.

② Domaine des Diables

Thoroughly modern and tasting-friendly, this is the place to learn about rosé wines: the paler and greyer they are, the more delicious. Don't be fooled by the branding; this vineyard has no desire to be on the supermarket shelf. It's a small production of

16th-century cellar, Château Simone

the highest quality. On a tour of the vineyard, you'll learn more about their organic, sustainable wines.

The Drive: Continue south to the D7, then turn west. It's a further 15km (20 minutes) to the next vineyard.

🔴 Château Simone

Wine has been grown here for longer than history records, and this vineyard still produces 80% of the wine bearing the Palette AOC. Vines surrounding the handsome, eponymous honey-coloured château and gardens produce grenache, syrah, cinsault, mourvèdre and the 'secondary varieties' that, fermented in barrels in a 16th-century cellar dug by monks, become Simone's award-winning wines.

The Drive: It's a short 5km drive north to Château Cremade on the D64E (route de l'Angesse).

🔴 Château Cremade

This tiny 9-hectare winery manages to cultivate 25 different grape varieties, many ancient and rare, producing highly respected, AOC-protected whites, rosés and reds. It once hosted Cézanne and Émile Zola; expect a friendly reception and be sure to ask to visit the wine cellar, which feels genuinely historical. Try the fruity reds.

The Drive: One kilometre north is the village of Le Tholonet.

🔴 Le Tholonet

Roman ruins, 17th-century castles, hiking trails and windmills await in Le Tholonet. Finish the day by relaxing at Chez Tomé, a tranquil family-run restaurant with a typically Provençal patio, or Le Table de Boucher, a generous steak restaurant and butcher shop. Alternatively, Ancora Pizza is where the Aixois travel even though they're already spoiled for choice in town.

from the quarries via Lac Zola and Lovers Bench adds an hour to your trek but allows for more opportunities to check out the wildlife. You'll need plenty of water, especially in the arid summer months when forest access may be restricted to protect the region from fires. Check before you set out.

CÉZANNE'S STUDIO

It was not until the end of his life, after years of rejection, that Cézanne began to achieve recognition as an artist. It was also when he painted Montagne Ste-Victoire time and time again. Before retreating from the world in his stone cottage, he painted in his studio to the north of Aix-en-Provence. It's a leisurely walk to the **Atelier Cézanne** at Lauves hill, 1.5km north of central Aix (30 minutes on foot) or you can take the number 5 bus from town.

Here you can be consumed by the same energy the artist would have felt as light floods through the window. Painting tools and still-life models appear as they might have once looked, and his hat is still hanging on a hook, capturing a moment in time.

A Different Sort of Tasting

Liquid sunshine

Olive oil is considered a sacred symbol of eternal life and has been used to signify health, beauty, wisdom and peace since ancient times. As recently as King Charles' coronation in London, oil from hand-picked olives in Jerusalem was used to anoint him.

The key to the Mediterranean diet, olive oil here pours as freely as wine. It's produced and consumed with the same passion, so much so that it remains in the bones of the inhabitants of this sun-drenched basin long after they have passed. The French, Spanish, Italians and Greeks all receive honours in olive oil competitions, but when it comes to France, the oil of Provence – in particular **Salon-de-Provence** – is considered the best.

Salon is less than an hour's drive northwest of Aix, and the **Mas de Bories** olive grove, with its historical dry stone structures, is the ideal stop for anyone interested in the small-scale production of olive oil. When the owner, Claire, talks of her connection to the land, living a life with meaning and her constant search for quality, you feel it. The process from tree to bottle, taking in the super-modern extraction press, is a true education; once you taste it, you'll likely take some home.

In town, Mathieu Ségui hosts tastings of local wines and whiskies on weekends at his wine cellar, **De la Vigne à l'Olivier**. The events can get extremely lively; online reservations are required.

Regional Heritage

A tradition of soap

The tradition of olive-oil production in Salon-de-Provence has meant that it has also played a crucial role in the manufacturing of local soap. The famous **Savon de Marseille** would not exist without it. The **Savonnerie Marius Fabre** in Salon has been toiling away for over 120 years and welcomes you to follow the soap-making process before visiting its boutique. At the **Musée de Salon et de la Crau**, set in the Château de l'Empéri, you are guided through every facet of the rich agricultural life in this region. On a stop here, it is clear that what grows in the earth creates the culture itself.

BEST NATURAL VINEYARDS IN THE BOUCHES-DU-RHÔNE

Villa Minna Vineyard
Organic, unique and not too expensive. Try their vintage.

L'Abri
Wines with great balance and finesse, and particularly affordable.

Château Revelette
Biodynamic wine; their PUR label is a big hit.

Arles

Your arrival in Arles will always be rocked by its inescapable Roman legacy. It is their world that is underneath your feet. As an ancient coastal rival to its neighbour, there is a glory to this town that belies its village intimacy. Indeed, Arles backed Julius Caesar when he wrestled for power and defeated Pompey's Marseille. And then there is its order in the history of art. Some of Van Gogh's finest works were conceived here, too.

Nearly a century and a half later, the contemporary art world continues to boldly uphold the French ideal of straddling both the future and the ancient past at the same time. Art and refinement effortlessly go hand in hand. It seeps into your whole experience as you wander the city, with history spiralling out before you at its own pace, a bastion in the vast wet flatlands of the Camargue.

Capital of Art

Steel, glass and amphitheatres

Frank Gehry and Maja Hoffmann's Tower rises over the city limits, reflecting the south's famous light. It's a steel-and-glass testament to contemporary art and a billionaire-funded funhouse. To be within **LUMA Arles**' walls is to be within its sweeping dream. As a statement, it demands we consign Van Gogh and Gauguin to the past, ushering in a spangly new future within its cutting-edge studios, galleries and performance spaces.

Arles has long been synonymous with the arts: its photography school, the **École Nationale Supérieure de la Photographie**, is one of the best on the planet, and each year the city welcomes **Les Rencontres d'Arles** (July to September), an annual photography festival that began in 1970. It celebrates the big names, discovers new talent and has the art world out until dawn on the festival's big 'Night of the Year'.

It is a city that hosts countless arts festivals, although some locals claim these are a Trojan horse for gentrification, believing art's function is to change the world rather than be patronised

GETTING AROUND

Arles is well connected by train to Avignon, Marseille and Nîmes. Buses leave for Stes-Marie-de-la-Mer and St-Rémy de Provence. Getting around town is easy on foot and bicycle.

☑ **TOP TIP**

Wake up early to wander the streets before Arles wakes. Walking the banks of the Rhône and the quiet alleys that lead through the historical squares unfurls Arles' inimitable spirit.

BEST ARLES EATS

Lucy Cases, owner of the Mazette organic coffee shop (8 place Antonelle), shares her favourite spots to eat.

Le Marché d'Arles
The biggest and best food market in the region; get a *saucisson de taureau* here. €

Le Tambourin
Entirely authentic, this is an important place in the food scene. Many locals eat here all year long. €€

La Chassagnette
If you're going to splurge on a special meal in the region, it should be at this Michelin-starred former sheepfold. €€€

by the wealthy. The **Fondation Vincent Van Gogh** plays a role, staging temporary exhibitions and seminars while keeping a contemporary eye on what has come before.

To return to 1 CE and the remains of the Roman forum, the **Museon Arlaten**, a 15th-century mansion, has been renovated with help from fashion designer and native son Christian Lacroix. It displays Provence's costumes, paintings, arts and crafts across time, with real style.

Life of a Bull

The symbolism of the Camargue

Unlike in Spain, here it is the bull's name on the arena posters, not the bullfighter *(le raseteur)*. The bulls stamp and snort as the stars of the **Course Camarguaise**, a bloodless competition considered less cruel than bullfighting. Races are held in arenas around the city from July to October, with the Cocarde d'Or, in **Les Arenes**, as the main event.

The bull spends 20 minutes in the arena with the *raseteurs,* who show off by dodging and ducking them (rather than attempting to harm them). The following three months are spent grazing in the fields. Although the bulls are not harmed, there are those who argue that the animals still suffer nonetheless and that the spectacle should be avoided.

SIGHTS
1 Fondation Vincent Van Gogh
2 Les Arènes
3 Luma Arles

4 Museon Arlaten

EATING
5 Boucherie Genin
6 Cafe de la Roquette

7 Camargue Social Club
8 Le Gibolin
9 Le Tambourin

10 L'Épicerie du Cloître
11 Monstre

SHOPPING
12 Le Marché d'Arles

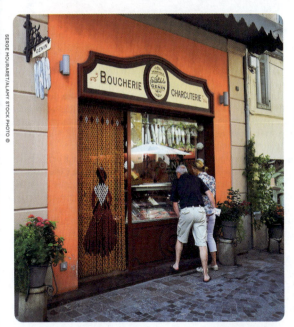

Boucherie Genin

**BEST PLACES
TO EAT IN ARLES**

Monstre
Hip gallery and restaurant that attracts a young crowd, reflected by the art on the wall. €€

**L'Épicerie
du Cloître**
Natural wines and elaborate tapas in a secluded courtyard that has a small shop for you to purchase the finest regional products. €€

**Cafe de
la Roquette**
Laid-back lunch spot where you can watch the world go by. Friendly staff in one of the city's most relaxed squares. €

**Camargue
Social Club**
Vibrant Camargue cuisine accompanied by the headiest of cocktails. €€

Le Gibolin
Small but wholesome Michelin-star restaurant that remains relaxed despite its status. €€

On the other side are the *gardians,* the herders of the semi-feral cattle and horses in the Camargue's wetlands, who dream that their bulls will bring them honour. Bulls are selected by temperament at the age of three. Those chosen may have a career lasting up to 15 years before a peaceful retirement. After their death, they are buried in an almost sacred ritual facing the sea.

Arles Entrées

Local cuisine from local sources

It is no surprise to see the long history of *gardians* farming herds of cattle, sheep and horses reflected in local dishes.

Gardiane de taureau is Provençal bull stew, a slow-cooked comfort dish with red wine that is enjoyed in the winter months with Camargue rice.

The local *saucisson de taureau,* a pork-and-beef dried sausage, is generally enjoyed with pastis for apéritif. Pop by **Boucherie Genin**, an artisanal butcher and deli since 1877, for cold cuts and sausage.

 WHERE TO STAY IN ARLES

Mia Casa
Cosy and centrally located B&B with an art residency and Van Gogh–inspired decor. €

Le Cloître
Spiral staircases lead to 19 distinct, colourful rooms within. Relaxing spa, too. €€

Le Nord-Pinus
Chic landmark with 1930s opulence where Hemingway, Picasso and Piaf all drank. €€€

Arles, originally known as Arelate, is Rome in miniature. Walking its streets, its significance as an economic, political and cultural centre of the Roman Empire is overwhelmingly clear. Many of the city's ancient monuments are not only intact, but within close walking distance from one another.

Start at **1** **Les Arènes**, a well-preserved amphitheatre (90 CE) that today hosts huge concerts and regional bull racing competitions. It once hosted chariot races and gladiators fighting to the death, with as many as 21,000 spectators in attendance. Following the fall of the Romans, the amphitheatre became a defensive fortress and over the subsequent centuries, a 'town within a town' grew up within its walls, containing more than 200 houses and two chapels (now all razed). The amphitheatre is only a stone's throw from the **2** **Théâtre Antique d'Arles** (1st-century BCE), which also remains part of contemporary cultural life in the city. As

a well-curated concert venue, it's a must for any serious gig-goer.

Walking 20 minutes across town, passing through the grounds of the ancient circus, brings you to the **3** **Musée de l'Arles Antique**, which houses impressive archaeological remains, including a marble statue of Augustus found between the pillars of the theatre in 1750.

A quiet walk along the Rhône's banks leads you past the **4** **Thermes de Constantin**; peek into the old Roman baths built for Emperor Constantine's private use in the 4th-century. As you return to the place de la Forum, the Nord Pinus hotel's façade merges into the almost unreal remains of the old entrance to the underground chambers of the **5** **Cryptoportiques**, which once made up the foundations of the forum. If you are into subterranean chambers, have a look around – or choose a spot in the square above them for a cold drink.

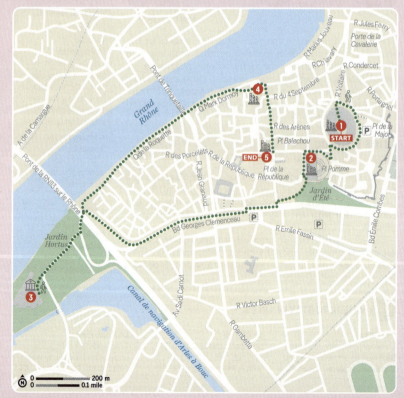

Eygalières

es Baux-de-Provence

Arles

• La Maison du Riz

• Le Sambuc

Domaine de la Palissade

Les Plages d'Arles

Beyond
Arles

To venture into the Camargue is to immerse yourself in another world that is distinct from modern France.

Where the Petit Rhône and Grand Rhône meet the Mediterranean, the Camargue arises: 930 sq km of salt flats, saltwater lakes and marshlands, where the sea and the earth become one. The world here feels completely isolated from our own: it is slow-go country, a timeless wetland chequered with salt pans and rice paddies. It is a land of ancient customs that go back so far that it's easy to suspect the Romans encountered a similar landscape to the one that still exists today. The Camargue is an adventure that takes us through music and food. It is a place where you are forced to exert yourself and discover places that are as welcoming as they are alien.

Wild Beaches

Salt marshes and birdlife

Les Plages d'Arles are found as you follow the River Rhône out of the city and down to the sea. These are savage, windswept beaches that are atypical for the south of France and are as far from the crowded shores of the French Riviera as you could find. To get here, drive south out of Arles to Salin-de-Giraud, which is about 40km south of Arles and is your last chance to purchase water or provisions.

Following the D36D out of Salin to the route de la Mer, don't miss the car park on your right, where you'll find the **points d'observation des salins**, which gives you views of the pink salt pans and a chance to see all manner of birdlife in their natural habitat – a perfect stop for photos.

Close by is the **Domaine de la Palissade**, 12km south of Salin. This remote nature centre organises fantastic forays through 702 hectares of protected marshland, scrubby glasswort, flowering sea lavender (in August) and lagoons on foot and horseback (p168). Before hitting the scrub, rent binoculars and grab a free map of the estate's three marked walking

GETTING AROUND

Touring the tiny roads crisscrossing this flat, wild region is best done by car or bicycle. Cycling from Arles into the Camargue requires long sleeves, long trousers, closed shoes and mosquito repellent. Rent bikes at VélocArles (velocarles.fr).

☑ TOP TIP

Bring insect repellent and binoculars for birding: over 20,000 flamingos nest in the Étang du Fangassier.

trails (1km to 8km) from the office. The birdlife is astounding: you might see spectacled warblers in summer, greylag geese in winter, migrating curlews, and mallards year-round.

From here, the dusty drive to the **Plage de Piémanson** beach gets narrower to the point that you may doubt the road beneath you, but it's worth it. On arrival, the beach gives little indication nowadays of its Burning Man–style past, but part is still famously dedicated to nudists. Greeted by space and dunes, take your time to sink peacefully into the calm white sands.

Another way to get off the beaten track is to get back on it to another off-the-grid beach at the end of a potholed road. The kitesurfer's paradise of **Beauduc Beach** makes the most of its ravaging embrace of the mistral winds, drawing in lovers of the sport from across the globe. More difficult to get to but somehow more populated, it rates highly as a place to lay down a towel with no phone signal for kilometres around.

THE FUTURE OF THE RHÔNE DELTA

The Rhône Delta, where the river meets the sea, is the largest in western Europe. But as the summers grow hotter and sea levels rise, life in the Camargue's marshes and lagoons faces an existential threat. An even more pressing problem than coastline erosion is that droughts have allowed the sea to push inland, destroying pastures and leaving the wetlands infertile.

Tourism has also played its part. Until 2012, these beaches acted as wild, overcrowded campsites that raged all summer. There are now more restrictions against pitching tents overnight. In the national park, the **Musée de la Camargue** has a great permanent exhibition highlighting how pressing the region's ecological issues have become.

NOMADKATE/SHUTTERSTOCK ©

Beauduc Beach

WHERE TO EAT IN SALIN-DE-GIRAUD

Mas St-Bertrand
Cuisine of the Camargue served with great local wines. Rustic and friendly. €€

Restaurant La Grand Ponche
More rice and bull dishes, in a setting overlooking a beautiful lagoon. €€

Bar de Sports
Great seafood with no air of pretentiousness. Unforgettable grilled octopus. €

Horse Riding in the Camargue

Gallop along the beach

Livestock in the Camargue has a reputation for being at least half-wild, but riding the horses of the **Domaine de la Palissade** at the right time of day can be one of the most peaceful experiences you could find in the region.

Riding through the wetlands with the region's iconic flamingos swooping in low patterns all around you, you'll be left with the impression that this is how the Camargue has looked for centuries. Time all but disappears as you go deeper into the marshes along the trails, especially when the early evening sky glows red – an experience memorable enough to write home about.

The local guides are well informed and obviously in love with their job. They are more than patient with first-timers, so you don't need to be wary if you've never ridden a horse before. Children must be at least eight years old. On the three-hour trips down to the Plage de Piémanson (€70), more experienced riders will finally get to cut loose and gallop down the hot sands. There is something quite unreal about the entire experience. Your guide's English is enough to keep you

WHITE WONDERS

The famous white horses of the Camargue, all short necks and thick manes, are one of the oldest breeds of horses and the most visible of the glorious triumvirate of the Camargue's postcard-friendly animals. They have been bred to do a specific job, and they need to be brave, spirited and powerful. Living as semi-wild creatures, they also possess a sharp instinct for survival.

At the **Fête des Gardians** in Arles on 1 May, the day ends at the town's Roman amphitheatre, where the *gardians* demonstrate how they use their horses to round up bulls, displaying the dynamic grace of these iconic animals.

OUTDOOR SPORTS IN THE CAMARGUE

Absolut Kiteboarding
Learn to kitesurf on the famous beaches of Piémanson and Beauduc; based in Salin-de-Giraud.

Manu Kayak Camargue
A relaxing paddle through the wetlands with Manu is educational and fun.

Camargue Autrement Safari
A guided e-bike tour offers the chance to see wildlife and sample the region's delicacies.

safe, but if you want to learn more about the local culture and the flowers and fauna, you will need a relatively good command of French.

All rides must be booked on the phone in advance. Remember to bring mosquito repellent and wear long trousers and closed shoes.

Rhythms of the Camargue

Backwaters of the flatlands

A sleepy village at the heart of the Camargue, **Le Sambuc** epitomises life here. Twenty-five kilometres south of Arles, it is a concentrated vision of proud people living from the land. With birdwatching, ranching and also some of the best places to eat in the region, Le Sambuc will have you tuning in to the rhythm of another world – there are even flamenco evenings to enjoy. Getting close to cattle herders, this experience transposes you to an era that was tougher but arguably more wholesome, with land and climate driving an existence that runs counter to modern life.

BIRDWATCHING IN THE WETLANDS

If you're into birding, don't miss the **Parc Ornithologique du Pont de Gau** (p175) 4km north of Stes-Maries-de-la-Mer, on the far western side of the Camargue.

THE LIFE OF THE GARDIAN

The *gardian's* existence of herding bulls, horses and sheep for the *manadiers*, the landowners, is one steeped in romanticism that goes back centuries. Living in small whitewashed cabins (which can be rented online for holidays), their simple life is today under threat.

New generations are less enthused by a hard life spent on horseback, guiding aggressive bulls that are ready to attack at the slightest provocation. The French government, with all its desire to protect the ecological balance of this land, may struggle to find where to find young men or women to devote a life to it.

BEYONDIMAGES/GETTY IMAGES ©

Flamingos, Camargue wetland

LOCAL DELICACIES IN THE CAMARGUE

Sobrasada
A fatty, soft sausage that's crossed the border from Spain. Delicious spread on toast.

Tellines
These local clams are best sampled at the L'Estrambord restaurant in Le Sambuc.

Fleur de sel
The Camargue's sea salt, rich in minerals and taste. Take a bag home.

ELENA SCHWEITZER/SHUTTERSTOCK ©

Camargue red rice

THE PAELLA OF THE CAMARGUE

In the transition zones between borders, it's not uncommon to see overlap in language, the environment and cuisine. Case in point: the Camargue shares plenty of similarities with Spain, including *paella camarguaise*. It's basically the same saffron-infused dish as you'll find in Valencia, but without the *socarrat* (the crisp, caramelised bottom that gives paella its rich taste).

The local rice means the Camargue's paella has a nuttier flavour, but the inclusion of chicken and large shrimp means it still resembles the Valencia version of the dish. Try it with a local bottle of Guishu, a locally made sake (rice wine), or one of the many local rice-based beers.

Le Mas de Peint is a family-run business steeped in history. This might be the world of the cowboys of the Camargue *(les gardians)*, but their guesthouse with a pool is pure luxury and highly welcoming. For a Camargue experience under one roof, they also organise horseback riding, birdwatching tours and trips down to the local beaches.

The set meals at dinner are a wholesome affair featuring local products that are eaten outdoors; close by is the Michelin-starred **La Chassagnette**, which serves extravagant meals with wine pairings, all set in a glorious space within two hectares of peaceful gardens. The dedication to putting the food on the plate will leave you hard-pushed to eat better anywhere else in the region.

Rice Cultivation in the Camargue

The paddy-field life

The Camargue is the only rice region of France and produces nearly 100,000 tonnes of its three varieties annually. It may only be a tiny percentage of what is produced worldwide, but Camargue rice is nonetheless high quality. Blessed with water from the Rhône Delta and plenty of sunshine to help it grow, the violent mistral wind also arrives at just the right time to dry the grains after harvesting. None of the rice grown here is genetically modified.

Camargue red and black rice is not only slightly crunchier than other varieties, it also has more protein, fibre and vitamins. Importantly, rice cultivation is considered more beneficial to the local environment than salt harvesting, famously popular across the region.

The **Maison de Riz**, less than half an hour's drive west of Arles, encourages travellers to visit their rice production (book online) or stay at their guesthouses. Here, you will see first-hand the Rozière family's way of life where rice is treated with the same attention you would give to livestock. Their boutique sells all varieties of rice grown in the region, as well as rice-based beer, soaps and makeup. Local delicacies from this fertile region are also on sale, from the finest olive oil to bull sausage and terrines, making it more likely that you won't go home empty-handed.

From Les Baux-de-Provence to Eygalières

Atop the Alpilles

Les Baux-de-Provence is the obvious destination for views for days from the Alpilles. Below, the tapestry of vineyards and olive and oak trees will give you feelings of nothing less than exaltation. The carved-up countryside with its sparkling swimming pools and rustic homes is as Provençal as can be, but Les Baux-de-Provence, with its fortified castle and hordes of tourists, may make you wonder if you've made your way to a Mediterranean Disneyland.

Only half an hour's drive northeast will take you to **Eygalières**, a limestone village poking out from the top of a hill where calm is the order of the day. This is a place to wander to the sound of cicadas and gurgling fountains and to appreciate the soft-shoed rhythm of village life in a daze of winding streets and narrow alleys. On Friday mornings, the local market gives Eygalières a gentle buzz, with everything you would expect on display from local cheeses, meats and wines, as does the antique market every last Saturday. **La Banaste d'Eygalières** organise summer events that bring the village to a standstill; collectors travel here from across the region.

For great panoramic views and sacred energy, take the 2km walk to the **Chapelle St-Sixte**, painted by Van Gogh when he stayed in the asylum in nearby St-Rémy. The cypress trees can't help but remind travellers that this was once where an ancient Roman temple stood. To escape even further, a looping hike with thyme and rosemary carrying on the breeze to Lamanon will have the Alpilles embracing you.

VILLAGES IN THE ALPILLES

The mountain range of the Alpilles is an understated destination where old French writers passed on to the next life and Hollywood stars still come wanting the semblance of a normal life. It could be the shady squares when spring has sprung, the colourful shutters of the homes or the treks into nature that make you stop and stare over and over again.

Time slows down in this collection of unique villages – from Maillane to Le Paradou to Mouriès – with their customs and history that all reflect the generosity of Provence in bloom.

For those who want a quiet life, you won't find much better than this.

WHERE TO EAT IN LES BAUX-DE-PROVENCE

Restaurant de la Reine Jeanne
The most stunning vista in town, come here to dine above a tremendous drop. €€

Restaurant Le Mas d'Aigret
Ancient stone interior in a troglodyte dining room and a charming patio with knockout surrounds. €€

La Terrasse Des Baux
Fancy sweet crêpes or ice cream with views down the valley? This is your spot. €€

Stes-Maries-de-la-Mer

Stes-Maries-de-la-Mer

Stes-Maries-de-la-Mer is wrapped up in its own mysticism, rendering it much more than just another Mediterranean coastal town with nice beaches. It mesmerised Hemingway, Van Gogh and Picasso and served as a sacred site for Celts, Romans and Christians.

It is not uncommon to find tourists sitting on the terraces as the locals prop up the bar under bull heads mounted on the wall. There is a lot of bull-fighting memorabilia on view; the bullring in town doubles as a popular summer concert venue.

Nowadays, the town centre resembles a Spanish sea-side resort with bar after bar and restaurants at every turn. It is a place of postcards, stuffed flamingos, summer dresses and fish pedicures, but don't be put off. Each year on 24 May, it holds a celebration for the world's Roma community, who travel from all over to celebrate the spectacular Pèlerinage des Gitans.

GETTING AROUND

Stes-Maries-de-la-Mer is easily explored on foot or bicycle. Envia (tout-envia.com) runs buses to/from Arles (Line 50, €1, 50 minutes).

A Pilgrimage to Notre-Dame-de-la-Mer

The veneration of Ste Sara

Stes-Maries-de-la-Mer has evolved from a fishing village to a town that revolves around its 12th-century Romanesque church, **Notre-Dame-de-la-Mer**, part holy site and part coastal fortress. Climb to the rooftop terrace for tremendous views. Even as a tourist destination, the church remains significant to the small community here, and is likely the first site of Christianity in the Camargue.

In the crypt is the statue of the patron saint of the Roma people, Ste Sara. According to local legend, she was the servant of Mary Magdalene, who landed here with Lazarus, Marie-Salomé and Marie-Jacobé, after fleeing persecution in

SIGHTS
1 Notre-Dame-de-la-Mer

ACTIVITIES, COURSES & TOURS
2 Le Vélo Saintois
3 Le Vélociste
4 Trot'nalex

EATING
5 La Siesta
6 Bambou Palm Beach
7 Boho Beach
8 Glacier Pierre Morere
9 La Bodega Kahlua
10 La Casita
11 Le Jardin des Délices
12 Le Seven
13 Maison Meire Glacier
14 Thaice Cream

the Holy Land in 45 CE; they were all canonised after spreading the gospel. Sara-la-Kâli, or Sara the Black, is adored by her community of Romanies, Manouches, Tziganes and Gitans, who amass here together for their springtime pilgrimage.

This is a time for reunions, and the town comes alive with many people camping out on the streets and the beach – there was even a time when pilgrims slept next to the saint in the crypt. Before the telephone, these disparate communities, who had no other way to stay in touch, would return to Stes-Maries each year to keep up with each other's lives. Their newborn children would also be baptised in the church in intense and noisy candle-lit ceremonies that have changed little over the centuries.

The processions over two days symbolise the arrival of Sara and her companions by boat. It is a dramatic spectacle with the *gardians* galloping their horses into the sea, carrying the statues of the saints. Back at the church, music and bells ring loudly across town.

Cycling the Camargue

Feel the wind in your hair

Coastal cycling is a unique rush. Pedalling away from town, the land turning into the sea before your eyes, is a feeling of liberation. Cycling in the Camargue combines great weather

---

☑ **TOP TIP**

The best way to enjoy Stes-Maries is by exploring its spectacular beaches and surroundings. Getting to know the locals is essential here; they know how to make the most of their region and will pull you into their experiences in no time.

ICE CREAM FOR ALL

Corinne Viala is the owner of Yoko Concept, a home-decor boutique *@yokoconcept*.

She was born in Stes-Maries, and her family's lineage goes back over a century. She shares her favourite recommendations for ice cream.

Thaice Cream
Their Thai-style ice cream and sorbet is natural, organic and has no added sugar. I love it. €

Glacier Pierre Morere
They have the best pistachio ice cream ever. Bonus: there's a wide variety of vegan sorbets, too! €

Maison Meire Glacier
This shop has been here forever, and I've been eating their ice cream all my life. €

with a somewhat unreal landscape speckled with pink flamingos, wild horses and black bulls. While you can see all this through the car windows, the connection with your surroundings is much more intimate as you cycle along with the sea breeze in your hair.

If you have the wind at your back, then you'll speed off to discover the coast, far from peak season crowds. If you're fighting the mistral winds, however, at least know the way back home will be considerably easier. The popular coastal dirt path out of town, straddling the marshlands and the sea, eventually leads to the solar-powered and unstaffed **Phare de la Gacholle** lighthouse, a great place to stop and unpack a picnic.

Rent bikes in town at **Le Vélociste**, and opt for one of the gravel racing bikes. The staff is tremendously helpful and can recommend cycling loops into the national park. Riding on the rte de Méjanes will give you a real sense of open space. Be prepared to see *gardians* galloping on white horses as you follow the inlets inland. For those with limitless energy, combined tours allow you to transfer from a bike to horse or canoe.

Le Vélo Saintois bike shop is in the east of town and

TALJAT DAVID/SHUTTERSTOCK ©

Stes-Maries-de-la-Mer

 WHERE TO EAT BREAKFAST IN STES-MARIES-DE-LA-MER

La Bohème by JF
Well-established hipster spot serving great coffee. €€

Le Fournil Saintois
Easily the best pâtisserie and bakery in town. No competition. €

Rooftop
Enjoy coffee and eggs on the roof above the hot sand. €€

is a good choice for families. They rent bikes for up to a week and are happy to suggest suitable tours. **Trot'nalex**, meanwhile, has a full range of electric bikes if you want to go further with less pedalling.

Birdwatching in the Parc Ornithologique

Where flamingos fill the sky

If you're not already a bird lover, a trip to the **Parc Ornithologique du Pont de Gau** might very well turn you into one. This nature reserve, 4km north of town on the D570, encompasses 60 hectares of wetland beauty and is home to over 200 species of migratory birds year-round. Explore the 7km of trails on foot and make use of the bird hides that allow you to approach the birds as if you're participating in a real-life wildlife documentary. To observe the unreal beauty of flamingos swooping overhead or flocking together on the waters from your observation blind or amid the deep grass is wondrous.

Herons, storks, egrets, teals, avocets, hoopoes and grebes are just some of the birds you may spot, depending on the time of year. Hawks and falcons take to the air with a majesty that is even more appreciated through binoculars.

The park was devised as an almost artificial utopia for Camargue wildlife – some birds have given up migrating and live here full-time in inlets repopulated with the ideal flora and fauna to ensure that they thrive. It is also a place that focuses on educating visitors to understand the fragile balance of our ecosystem, and is a good family excursion.

For the finest photographs, arrive in the late afternoon to avoid the glare. In early autumn, you will be blessed with pastel sunsets and flamingos at their pinkest, making for an unforgettable sight.

BEST BEACH EATS

Alexis Larrazet is the owner of Trot'nalex, an electric-bike rental shop on the seafront. These are his favourite beach spots.

Boho Beach
It's right across from me, so I can be there in minutes with my feet in the sand and tapas to snack on. **€€**

Le Seven
This place is all about seafood. It's a restaurant where you'll want to linger all day. **€€**

Bambou Palm Beach
Bamboo Beach has super comfortable sunbeds – a bit of luxury is always good! **€€**

 WHERE TO STAY IN STES-MARIES-DE-LA-MER

Hôtel Les Palmiers
Great location only metres from the beach and smack in the middle of town. **€**

Mas des Lys
Friendly hotel with simple chalet-style rooms and a swimming pool. **€€**

Hôtel Casa Marina
Bright, modern boutique hotel on the beach. Good family choice. **€€**

Aigues-Mortes

Stes-Maries-de-la-Mer

Beyond
Stes-Maries-de-la-Mer

To immerse yourself in the Camargue is to connect with a unique and timeless way of life.

As your journey into the Camargue goes deeper, you learn more about life on the land as you swat the mosquitoes on your neck. Freezing in the winter and humid as hell in the summer months, it's here that the magical, almost psychotropic fever dream experience can open up to you. Where else can you find a world of knights, biblical characters and tireless animals populating the region with a freedom that cannot be tamed?

The fortified medieval town of Aigues-Mortes is an ideal base for exploring this region. It's actually located over the border from Provence in the Gard *département,* 28km northwest of Stes-Maries-de-la-Mer at the western extremity of the Rhône Delta.

Walk the Ramparts in Aigues-Mortes

The city of dead waters

On the edge of the Mediterranean, in the flat marshes of the Camargue, is the medieval town of **Aigues-Mortes**. A Unesco-protected World Heritage site, the sweeping views from its fortress walls encompass the peculiar pink salt pans that stretch southwards and which have for centuries produced the region's famous salt. Built by Louis IX, this was where the French king's crusade set out in the 13th-century, and with the citadel's towers and battlements you can well imagine the scene.

The first thing to do in town is walk the ramparts and climb the **Tour de Constance**, which provides an education in how a walled city defended itself. Rambling along the 1.6km-long ramparts gives excellent views not only across the rooftops of the town but also out into the pink waters. Climb higher

GETTING AROUND

The beauty of visiting such an untamed and almost trackless region is that you are at times standing alone in a place that feels far from civilisation. It goes without saying that car rental is the best way to navigate this remote part of the Mediterranean.

✅ TOP TIP

Avoid travel in peak summer season. Early June has all the heat you need without the maddening crowds.

HEDI-KUN/SHUTTERSTOCK ©

Aigues-Mortes Saltworks

to the top of the tower, where the angles are a photographer's dream and the sudden tranquillity from its interior is a heart-opening surprise. Once a prison for both the Templar Knights and the Huguenots, it now feels like a chapel, with its breathless vaulted ceilings lit beautifully within.

Tourists in the town have replaced the marauding crusaders, but you can happily walk its long and tightly packed narrow streets, which always seem to lead back to the main square: **place St-Louis**. In peak season, Aigues-Mortes is bubbling with energy, its cafe and restaurant terraces full, but there remains a sense that the town is perfectly preserved – a bizarre rectangular world. Gothic church connoisseurs should spend a quiet moment in **Notre-Dame-des-Sablons**.

FLEUR DE SEL

The pink hues of Aigues-Mortes' surrounding salt pans are astounding from the ramparts. Even before Roman times, the marshes here were used to produce salt, and today Les Salins du Midi continues to extract 500,000 tonnes of the stuff per year.

Water from the Mediterranean is pumped into the reservoirs and left to evaporate amid the strong mistral winds; the crystallised *fleur de sel* is then shovelled into piles and left to bake beneath the hot sun.

You can rent electric bikes at the gate, but hiring them in town and cycling to the salt pans is recommended instead. Race past the flamingos that have settled here as they gorge themselves pink in these magical waters.

The Vaucluse & Luberon

MOUNTAINS, WINE & SUNSHINE

Dig deep into the many faces of the Vaucluse: sun-drenched hilltop villages, leisurely bike rides and scores of local markets.

One thing seems to lead to another in the Vaucluse. Start in Avignon, a city once home to the popes and today home to the largest theatre festival in France. And then think bigger – nearby are the renowned vineyards that produce Châteauneuf-du-Pape. In the distance? That's Mont Ventoux, the giant of Provence and a dream challenge for many cyclists. At the foot of the mountain is the village of Sault and its fields of lavender. Further south, the Plateau des Claperèdes is in bloom too, inside the wilds of the Parc Naturel Régional du Luberon. On the north side of the park are the red, yellow and orange ochres found in the cliffs and rock formations of the Colorado Provençal. And further west is Gordes, the most beautiful village in the world (seriously, it won a prize), which sits perched on a hill. Behind Gordes, the Monts de Vaucluse twist and roll, hiding smaller pastoral villages in their folds. At the bottom of those hills is L'Isle-sur-la-Sorgue, the French capital of antiques. Back in the Luberon, chic villas and innovative restaurants sit below ruined châteaux, where nobility like the Marquis de Sade once retreated on holiday. And that's not the half of it. Even when you live in the Luberon, you can't do it all. But here are the best parts.

FOKKE BAARSSEN/SHUTTERSTOCK ©

Inset: Gordes (p206); Opposite: Weather station, Mont Ventoux (p198)

THE MAIN AREAS

AVIGNON	CARPENTRAS	SAULT
Dense medieval city with a flair for the stage.	Classic Provençal town with truffle and strawberry markets.	Rural bliss on a lush plateau.
p184	**p190**	**p196**

DANIEL DALE/SHUTTERSTOCK ®

L'ISLE-SUR-LA-SORGUE
Canals and antiquing,
history and style.
p202

NORTH LUBERON
The wild side of
the Luberon park.
p209

SOUTH LUBERON
Chic villages surrounded
by vineyards.
p221

Find Your Way

Reach Avignon by TGV and hire a car to discover the villages in Vaucluse, Ventoux or Luberon. There are lots of options for cycling trips, too.

BUS

The Zou! bus system serves the Vaucluse and Luberon. Comfy and clean, the bus is great for a day trip into town. For far-flung villages, though, it's better to have a bike or a car.

CYCLING

With endless backroad options, the Vaucluse and Luberon is one of the best cycling areas in France. Many villages now have a local bike rental shop, and an e-bike can be a great solution for running short errands or side visits.

CAR

For day trips or excursions, consider Blablacar (blablacar. fr), a widely used French ride-sharing app. Prices are reasonable and as long as your stop isn't too much of a detour, folks will usually take you all the way to your destination.

Carpentras, p190

Taste your way around the stalls of one of Provence's best markets, and fill up on strawberries and truffles.

Sault, p196

Fields of lavender, gorges to hike and Mont Ventoux to cycle: nature and sports fiends will love it here.

South Luberon, p221

Epicurean, chic and sun-drenched. Come here for the gourmet cuisine, fine wine and a lively summer scene.

North Luberon, p209

From hilltop villages to ochre cliffs to the prehistoric remains near Apt, the North Luberon is wild and full of mystery.

L'Isle-sur-la-Sorgue, p202

Attracting antique lovers but also the bougie girls of the Luberon, the town is a centre for retail therapy à la Provence.

Avignon, p184

Discover papal history and power struggles in this medieval city. The streets come alive each summer with France's largest theatre festival.

North Luberon

South Luberon

L'Isle-sur-la-Sorgue

Avignon

TOP: GEORGES HANNA/SHUTTERSTOCK ©; BOTTOM: ALEXANDER DEMYANENKO/SHUTTERSTOCK ©

Parc Naturel Régional du Luberon

Montagne du Luberon

Le Grand Luberon

Le Petit Luberon

Mourre Nègre

Plateau de Vaucluse

Colorado Provençal

Gorges d'Oppedette

Durance

Calavon

Coulon

Sorgue

Parc Naturel Régional des Alpilles

Parc Naturel Régional de Camargue

Étang de Berre

Plaine de la Crau

Canal d'Arles

10 km

5 miles

Plan Your Time

With so much to explore, it's impossible to see all of the Vaucluse and Luberon in one go. Plan at least a few days in the region.

Old church, Bonnieux (p217)

Pedalling Provence

● For the leisure cyclist, hopping on an e-bike and cycling the **hill villages** (p216) on the north side of Luberon is unforgettable and accessible.

● A bit more sporty is the **Monts de Vaucluse loop** (p208) through the wild and fragrant hills.

● Or for a real challenge, set your sights on **Mont Ventoux**. Wake up early, strap on your helmet and hop on the bike saddle to pedal up to the mythic summit, the giant of Provence. There are three routes up the mountain (p198, 200, 201) – which is the right one for you?

Seasonal Highlights

Winters are usually mild, but a mistral wind can change that in a second. Summers are hot, but spring and autumn are blissful.

FEBRUARY
Peak truffle season. Visit the **Marchés aux truffes** (p190) in Carpentras to spot traders dealing the black gold.

APRIL
The Luberon reawakens with spring; wild asparagus makes its way onto restaurant menus.

MAY
Warm temps mean hiking, cycling and climbing are at their best until the first heat wave hits, usually near the end of the month.

Four Days to Travel Around

● Arriving in Avignon, visit the **Palais des Papes** (p186) and go for a stroll around the old town.

● The next day, head to the **Dentelles de Montmirail** (p192) to taste the renowned Beaumes-de-Venise wine and watch the sunset over **Mont Ventoux** (p220).

● Drive down to **L'Isle-sur-la-Sorgue** (p203) and hit the antique markets. Take a walk along the river's edge in **L'Isle-sur-la-Sorgue** (p204)or in **Fontaine-de-Vaucluse** (p205).

● Wake up early for a sunrise visit to **Gordes** (p206), and then drive to the **Abbaye Notre-Dame de Sénanque** (p206), hidden away in a small canyon.

● Dine in **Venasque** (p208), on the other side of the Monts de Vaucluse before returning to Avignon.

A Week in the Luberon

● Settle into your village of choice: maybe **Ménerbes** (p216), **Saignon** (p210) or **Bonnieux** (p217).

● Go for a walk in the **Fôret des Cèdres** (p223) before sunset.

● Get out early to visit the ochre hills and take a workshop at the Écomusée in **Roussillon** (p218).

● Visit **Forcalquier** (p214) and **Manosque** (p214), immersing yourself in novelist Jean Giono's Provence.

● Rent a bike and cycle between Luberon villages like **Ménerbes** and **Lacoste** (p216).

● Discover **Lourmarin** (p222), where you can dine in an elegant and ecofriendly restaurant.

● Rent a vintage car and drive through the **South Luberon** (p224) in between vines and medieval châteaux.

JULY
The lavender is in bloom and theatre is in full swing for the **Festival d'Avignon** (p187).

AUGUST
Communities across the Luberon start to hold their annual *fête votive*, a huge village party.

SEPTEMBER
The *vendage*, or grape harvest, begins. In many villages, like **Oppède-le-Vieux** (p220), there is a festival to celebrate.

DECEMBER
After the olive harvest wraps up in November, locals get ready for a Provençal Christmas with the famous thirteen desserts.

183

Avignon

Avignon

AVIGNON FESTIVAL VENUES

Setting the stage is key in performance, and Avignon has no lack of creative settings. Take the **Carrière de Boulbon**, located in a former limestone quarry outside the city, which is absolutely worth the trip if you can get tickets. But the most emblematic stages of the festival have to be those in former papal and abbey courtyards.

Wherever the popes went, vast construction projects followed. During their 100-year reign in Avignon, the popes commissioned the courtyards, gardens and chapels that are now home to some of the Festival d'Avignon's most unique theatres. Try to catch a play at the **Cour d'Honneur du Palais des Papes**, the **Chapelle des Pénitents Blancs** or the **Cloître des Célestins**.

Perched on the banks of the Rhône, Avignon is the gateway to Provence. Stop here at the beginning or end of a visit to get your city break. Inside the rampart-ringed old town, visitors can learn about the story of Avignon as a papal city, visit the numerous Provençal gardens or people-watch from one of the pedestrian-zone cafes and leafy squares. Many restaurants blend the French pastime of eating *en terrace* with seasonal menus that flaunt flavours from the rich agricultural plains alongside the Rhône and the Durance Rivers. And don't discount Avignon's museum scene: with half a dozen museums with world-class Provençal and Italian painting collections, as well as contemporary museums and galleries, Avignon is for lovers of the arts. In July, the city fills to bursting to host the Festival d'Avignon. With theatre troupes walking the narrow streets in costume to promote their plays, the whole city feels like a stage.

Art in Avignon

From the Gauls to the digital age

Stay cool in the dog days of summer with a visit to one, or several, of Avignon's superb collection of museums. They are all within easy walking distance of one another. At the top of the list is the **Musée du Petit Palais**, once the archbishops' palace during the 14th and 15th centuries. Inside you'll find outstanding collections of primitive, pre-Renaissance 13th- to 16th-century Italian religious paintings by Old Masters. The most famous is Botticelli's *La Vierge et l'Enfant* (1470).

Tiny **Musée Angladon** harbours an impressive collection of realist, impressionist and expressionist treasures, including works by Cézanne, Sisley, Manet, Modigliani, Degas and Picasso – but the star piece is Van Gogh's *Railway Wagons*, the only painting by the artist on display in Provence. Impress your friends by pointing out that the 'earth' isn't actually paint, but bare canvas.

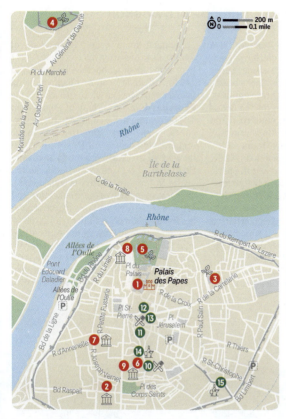

HIGHLIGHTS
1 Palais des Papes

SIGHTS
2 Collection Lambert
3 Jardin des Carmes
4 Jardins de St-André
5 Jardins des Doms
6 Musée Angladon
7 Musée Calvet
8 Musée du Petit Palais
9 Musée Lapidaire

EATING
10 Fou de Fafa
11 Graines de Piment
12 L'Épicerie
13 Restaurant Le Coin Caché

DRINKING & NIGHTLIFE
14 Grand Café Barretta
15 Rue des Teinturiers

The elegant Hôtel de Villeneuve-Martignan (built 1741–54) provides a fitting backdrop for Avignon's fine-arts museum, the **Musée Calvet**, with 16th- to 20th-century oil paintings, compelling prehistoric pieces, 15th-century wrought iron, and the elongated landscapes of Avignonnais artist Joseph Vernet.

The **Musée Lapidaire** is housed inside the town's striking Jesuit Chapel and is the archaeological collection of the Musée Calvet. There's a good display of Greek, Etruscan and Roman artefacts, but it's the Gaulish pieces that really draw the eye – including some grotesque masks and deeply strange figurines.

☑ **TOP TIP**

Need somewhere to stay during peak times? If there's not much on offer inside the walls of Avignon, don't turn up your nose at staying in Villeneuve-lès-Avignon, just on the other side of the Rhône. There are regular shuttles, and the city's bike rental service Velopop' has stations in Villeneuve.

 AVIGNON'S BEST PEOPLE-WATCHING SPOTS

Rue des Teinturiers
A half dozen bars line this narrow street next to a small canal – grab a space and settle in. €

Grand Café Barretta
In the same building as Avignon's first cafe is this sprawling terrace under a large plane tree. €

Restaurant Le Coin Caché
Tucked below the chestnut trees on the north side of the St-Pierre Basilica is this midrange restaurant. €€

A WALK THROUGH OLD AVIGNON

Start from the ❶ **Pont St-Bénézet**, also known as the Pont d'Avignon (buy a combination ticket to visit the Palais des Papes – you'll use it later on this walk). The bridge is unique in its inutility; over the centuries, arch after arch washed away during floods along the Rhône. Cross the outer road and enter the walls of Avignon. Make your way to the shady ❷ **Jardin des Doms** with a view of Villeneuve-lès-Avignon to one side, and, as you work your way down the park, a view of Avignon to the other. Before leaving the garden, visit ❸ **Notre-Dame-des-Doms d'Avignon**. Here lies Pope Jean XXII, who anchored the papacy in Avignon during his lifetime, and his successor, Pope Benoît XII. Continue with the papal theme to the grandiose ❹ **Palais des Papes**. The largest Gothic palace ever built, the Palais des Papes was erected by Pope Clement V, who abandoned Rome in 1309 in the wake of violent disorder after his election. A visit here takes about an hour. Some rooms are not furnished, but can be imagined using interactive tablets. Outside the palace, visit the ❺ **orchards** *(vergers)*, built by Pope Urban V. A dedication to his childhood in the Cevennes, he spent large sums to maintain the orchards and nearby gardens. Walk down the rue Banasterie to reach the ❻ **Basilique St-Pierre**. This Flamboyant Gothic church begun in the 14th-century is considered a good representation of the architecture and artwork of the period. Check out the ornately carved walnut door. Finish your stroll by making your way back to the walls of the city. These ❼ **ramparts** were built during the reign of Pope Innocent VI in the 14th-century to protect the city from English mercenaries during the Hundred Years' War.

Finally, the **Collection Lambert** is Avignon's contemporary arts museum. It focuses on works from the 1960s to the present. Work spans from minimalist and conceptual to video and photography – in stark contrast to the classic 18th-century mansion housing it.

In or Off: The Festival d'Avignon Unlocked

The play's the thing

The **Festival d'Avignon** is among the largest and most renowned festivals in the world for the performing arts. For three weeks in July, the otherwise calm and sometimes sleepy city of Avignon becomes a hive for the theatre world – shows are mostly in French, but some are in other languages or non-verbal.

The official festival, **Avignon In** (festival-avignon.com), takes place across the city, with its epicentre in the Unesco-listed old town. Tickets go on sale in April and sell out fast, although resale tickets are advertised on a noticeboard at the box office in Cloître St-Louis. The unofficial fringe festival, **Avignon Off** (festivaloffavignon.com), runs during the same time. The difference between the two lies in the selection and promotion of performances: the In festival's selection is done by a jury. The Off festival is more boot-strappy – troupes are responsible for signing up their piece into the festival, renting a theatre space and promoting their show. Want to see an acclaimed play? Check out the In. Want to see something more alternative? Go for the Off.

Provençal Gardens

A refuge of greenery

In and around Avignon are a host of Provençal gardens, which are a delight to wander. Inside the city walls, visit the **Jardin des Doms**, overlooking the papal palace and the city; **Jardin des Carmes**, a small quiet garden outside the church of the same name; or the **Square Agricol Perdiguier**, previously the courtyard of an abbey.

Worth the trip across the Rhône, the **Jardins de St-André** and their 10th-century abbey in Villeneuve-lès-Avignon are a breezy way to spend a spring or autumn afternoon.

THE GREAT SCHISM

Avignon first gained its ramparts – and reputation for arts and culture – during the 14th-century, when Pope Clement V fled political turmoil in Rome. From 1309 to 1377, seven French-born popes invested huge sums in the papal palace and offered asylum to Jews and political dissidents.

Pope Gregory XI left Avignon in 1376, but his death two years later led to the Great Schism (1378–1417), during which rival popes (up to three at one time) resided at Rome and Avignon, denouncing and excommunicating one another.

Even after the matter was settled and an impartial pope, Martin V, established himself in Rome, Avignon remained under papal rule. Avignon and Comtat Venaissin (now the Vaucluse *département*) were ruled by papal legates until 1791.

WHERE TO EAT IN AVIGNON

Fou de Fafa
Four-course dinners drawing on Mediterranean and Provençal cuisines. Excellent wine list. Reserve. **€€**

Graines de Piment
This affordable, tasty bistro on place de la Principale gives disadvantaged youth a chance to gain work experience. **€**

L'Épicerie
Classic, rustic French bistro in the heart of old Avignon. Many hearty meat-based dishes; vegan options too. **€€**

Châteauneuf-du-Pape

Avignon

Beyond
Avignon

A sip of a world-renowned Châteauneuf-du-Pape just might deliver you to earthly paradise.

GETTING AROUND

It's possible to catch Zou! bus 992 from Avignon to the Châteauneuf-du-Pape village (about 30 minutes), but getting to the vineyards themselves requires a car.

☑ **TOP TIP**

If you're in a rush, visit a wine bar in town; otherwise, an excursion to the vineyards can't be beat.

Châteauneuf-du-Pape is one of the more famous *terroirs* in the world, and for good reason. The vineyards where this wine is produced are covered in river rocks that absorb sunlight during the day and release it at night, creating the perfect climate for growing the grapes that go into this legendary wine. But there's more to Châteauneuf-du-Pape than just the *terroir*. This wine was the popes' choice in the 14th-century, and today it continues to delight wine enthusiasts with its complex flavours and aromas. From the blend of 13 grape varieties to the climate and soil in which it is grown, there are many secrets that make Châteauneuf-du-Pape so special.

Taste Fine Wines in Châteauneuf
The papal seal of approval

Even in the world of fine wines, **Châteauneuf-du-Pape** retains a special cachet. Only 18km north of Avignon, it's arguably the best-known of the Rhône appellations, prized by oenophiles the world over. The wine blends up to 13 varieties of grape: grenache, syrah, mourvèdre, cinsault, muscardin, counoise, vaccarèse, picpoul, terret noir, clairette, bour-boulenc, roussane and picardon. Most other wines, even in France, are less complex.

Each winemaker has their recipe. Each hectare parcel cannot produce more than 35L of wine; therefore, the grapes are all sorted and only the finest selected to use to make the wine.

Châteauneuf-du-Pape

VINEYARDS TO VISIT

Château Mont-Redon
Three kilometres from Châteauneuf-du-Pape, Mont-Redon is gorgeously placed amid sweeping vineyards. Visit the family vineyard and pick up some bottles for later – these wines get better with age. During your visit you'll learn how long you should keep each particular wine before drinking.

Maison Ogier
Organic wines with lots of personality and freshness, which comes from the large proportion of Grenache in the blend.

Domaine Usseglio Raymond & Fils
Biodynamic family vineyard with a good selection of wines and a friendly welcome to the cellar.

École des Vins Mouriesse
Go beyond wine tasting and take a wine-blending workshop in Châteauneuf-du-Pape.

And, like other Côtes du Rhône wines, the Châteauneuf-du-Pape grapes are grown along the Rhône River, in clay soil topped with river rock, which absorbs the sunlight during the day and diffuses it at night, providing the roots with a constant temperature.

As its name hints, the hilltop château after which the wine is named was originally built as a summer residence for Avignon's popes in the 14th-century, but it's little more than a ruin now – plundered for stone after the Revolution, and bombed by Germany in WWII for good measure. Nonetheless, the village itself is a perfect day trip for honeymooners to pick out a few bottles to take home and enjoy on anniversaries – this is a wine that keeps for a long time.

If you're travelling with kids, **Château Fortia** runs a fun escape game in the vines. The clock is ticking as you follow the history of the domaine to gather the numbers needed for a code that unlocks a special reserve wine. A tasting visit awaits those who succeed.

Carpentras

Carpentras

Known for its serious black truffle markets, Carpentras has much to offer the traveller who is willing to spend a little time getting to know the city. Less touristy than cities like Avignon or L'Isle-sur-la-Sorgue, Carpentras' centre is a good example of a modern Provençal city, where life moves at a relaxed, but not lazy, pace.

In town, narrow streets and plane trees do their best to cast shade during the hot summers, while sharp bends and turns in the roads help block the vicious mistral wind in the winter. Beloved local shops not to miss include La Maison Jouvard for candies and Glory Days Vintage.

In the surrounding vineyards, visitors can go beyond a Côtes du Rhône and try one of the excellent local varieties: Gigondas, Vacqueyras and Beaumes-de-Venise are all excellent. On summer evenings, stay through sunset – many vineyards host weekly concerts and apéritifs.

GETTING AROUND

The centre of Carpentras is quite walkable. Consider parking outside of town and walking instead of trying to navigate the one-way streets. The train station has frequent connections to Avignon and the Zou! bus serves the city and surrounding area.

☑ **TOP TIP**

Travellers who want a base that has a small-town feel with convenient access to essential Provence experiences like wine tastings and Roman ruins should consider Carpentras.

Capital of La Truffe

Observe the secret mushroom market

Have a truffle lover in the family? Then a visit to the Carpentras truffle markets is a must. The Vaucluse region produces an estimated 70% of black truffles in France.

Taking place from November through March, the Friday morning **truffle market (Marchés aux truffes)** on place Aristide Briand is far from the typically busy and buzzing markets of Provence. Here, secrecy and mystery reign as chefs and wholesalers haggle for the best deals of this rare mushroom. Reserve a table at **Chez Serge** to enjoy a dish – or dishes – flavoured with the aromatic truffle.

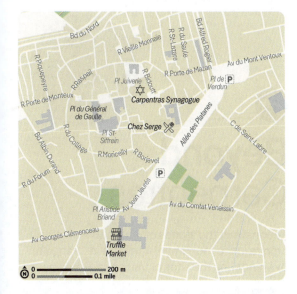

Carpentras Synagogue

Chez Serge

Truffle Market

0   200 m
0   0.1 mile

Summer truffles are less sought-after but still have their fan club. From May to September, try summer truffles grated over salads, atop omelettes or sliced, drizzled with olive oil and enjoyed on toast.

Jewish Heritage in Provence

France's oldest synagogue

During the papal reign in Avignon in the 14th-century, Provence's Jewish community found protection in the Comtat Venaissin, the modern-day Vaucluse region. Although Jews were initially welcomed into papal territory, by the 17th-century they were forced into ghettos in Avignon, Carpentras, Cavaillon and L'Isle-sur-la-Sorgue, and many of the original synagogues were destroyed or left to ruin. The **Carpentras Synagogue**, in the centre of town, is the oldest synagogue (1367) still in use in France. Take a peek into medieval Jewish life in the subterranean level, where you'll see baths, a kosher abattoir and bread ovens. Visit Monday to Friday for self-guided tours, or arrange a guided tour through the tourism office. The synagogue's wood-panelled main level was rebuilt in the 18th-century and is still a place of worship.

Other notable synagogues in the region include the **Synagogue of Cavaillon** and its **Judeo-Comtadin Museum** and the **Mikveh** (baths) of Pernes-les-Fontaines.

REGIONAL SPECIALITIES

Truffles
Black truffles are in season from November to March. St-Jean or summer truffles are in season from May to September. Don't miss a chance to try either.

Strawberries
The Carpentras strawberry has such a sweet and celebrated flavour that an entire guild and festival have sprung up to protect and promote the variety. In season from April to June.

Cherries
May sees market stalls overflowing with the *cerise des coteaux* du Ventoux. It's a protected cherry variety found only in this region.

Vaison-la-Romaine

Gigondas

Orange ● Beaumes-de-Venise
● Vacqueyras ●

Carpentras

Beyond Carpentras

Reconstruct the stories of the Gallo-Romain empire in the monumental theatre in Orange or by wandering the sites of Vaison-la-Romaine.

Discover the Roman vestiges of the Vaucluse with day trips to Orange or Vaison-la-Romaine. Theatre doesn't just run in Avignon's blood – Orange is home to one of the world's best-preserved Roman theatres. Dine on modern Provençal delights before visiting the rest of the city on foot.

Want to take your time? Vaison-la-Romaine sits on a partially excavated Gallo-Roman site of around 15 hectares, making it the most spread-out open-air museum in France. All tickets to the archaeological sites are good for a 24-hour period after purchase. Visit the former farms and follow history as the artefacts tell their story of how the rural settlement became a bustling city complete with its own toll bridge, walled city and castle.

Wine Tasting in the Vaucluse
Go further than Côtes du Rhône

The French generally regard wines from the Côtes du Rhône region as table wines: not bad, but nothing special either. But not all Côtes du Rhône deserve their pedestrian reputation, and it'd be a shame to die without tasting a bottle of Gigondas, Châteauneuf-du-Pape, Vacqueyras or Beaumes-de-Venise.

All four of these appellations grow within a short drive of Carpentras (10km to 20km), making it the perfect city

GETTING AROUND

Vaison-la-Romaine and Orange are both walkable; there are several parking lots around town. A direct bus line from Orange to Vaison-la-Romaine makes visiting the two cities by public transport easy. Orange has a train station that connects to Avignon, Valence and Marseille.

☑ TOP TIP

Vaison is a good base for jaunts into the Dentelles de Montmirail or to Mont Ventoux; reserve accommodation ahead.

WINE FIT FOR A POPE

To taste the most prestigious vintages in the area, head to the village and vineyards of **Châteauneuf-du-Pape** (p188), just 22km west of Carpentras and 18km north of Avignon.

to start a wine tour. Growing in the limestone and ochre hills to the west, these are sun-drenched grapes that rely on water from the Rhône Valley. At the Clos de Caveau vineyard, go for a walk along the marked nature trail to learn more about the geology and climate of the vineyards below the sharp folds of the **Dentelles de Montmirail**, and then stop to taste the aromatic and powerful **Vacqueyras** wine in the cellar. In **Gigondas**, the Caveau du Gigondas represents 100 small producers and offers free tastings.

Most vineyards also host tastings, but some go above and beyond to guide the senses: try Domaine de Longue Toque for a detailed and personalised wine-tasting session. Wine lovers who've seen it all will love the organic and natural wine tastings at the Domaine de Ferme St-Martin on the terraces above the village of **Suzette**. Accompanied by a hypnotist and sommelier, visitors are guided to a state of self-hypnosis before beginning a tasting of one of the finest wines in the region: **Beaumes-de-Venise**, famous for its *or blanc* (white gold) – sweet muscat wines, best drunk young and cold.

Vineyards, Suzette

SLEEP AT A VINEYARD

Domaine de Bellevue
Gîte (guesthouse) and rental cottage outside the village of Beaumes-de-Venise with budget-friendly rooms. Shady grounds, a small pond and the chic vintage style all add to the charm. **€€**

Mas l'Evajade
Farmhouse with regular rooms or the option to sleep in a huge wine-barrel bedroom in the heart of the Domaine du Rocher des Dames. Also in Beaumes-de-Venise. **€€**

Château du Mourre du Tendre
This guesthouse in the garden of the castle grounds is surrounded by Châteauneuf-du-Pape vines; there's pool access too. Don't miss organising a wine tasting of one of the five appellations made by this vineyard. **€€**

 OPULENT PROVENÇAL STAYS BEYOND CARPENTRAS

Château Martinay
Spend a luxurious night in this castle on the western outskirts of Carpentras. **€€€**

Hôtel le Blason de Provence
A 15-minute drive from Carpentras, on the edge of the charming village of Monteux. **€€**

Mas Les Fleurs d'Hilaire
This 18th-century restored farmhouse has five stylish rooms, a garden and a pool. **€€**

WORTH A TRIP: NÎMES

Not far from Orange is one of the grandest Roman vestiges in France: the city of **Nîmes**. An easy day trip from the Vaucluse, stop first at Nîmes' massive arena – which once held 24,000 spectators – followed by a visit to the incredibly preserved Roman temple, the **Maison Carée**.

As the weather heats up, grab some food for a picnic and head to the **Pont du Gard**. A stroke of engineering genius built in the 1st-century CE, this three-tiered stone aqueduct is worth the drive. The site is free to visit; parking is €9.

Afterward, drive a few kilometres down the road to the village of **Collias**. Here you'll find a public beach below the village to cool off in the Gardon River.

Vaison-la-Romaine

Living Roman Heritage
Discover Orange in a day

Two sites may seem like a small reason to visit a city, but ancient art and culture lovers shouldn't skip Orange, 21km northwest of Carpentras. The Unesco-protected **Théâtre Antique**, one of only three intact Roman theatres left in the world (the others are in Syria and Turkey), is worth the visit alone. Its sheer size is awe-inspiring: designed to seat 10,000 spectators, its stage wall reaches 37m high, 103m wide and 1.8m thick.

You don't have to imagine how performances might have been in this theatre during the first two weeks of July, the **Chorégies d'Orange** opera festival takes place on stage. The rest of the year, book ahead an evening at the theatre for an **Odyssée Sonore**, an immersive light and sound performance that travels back in time to meet the gods and celebrities of mythology.

Orange's **Arc de Triomphe** lies less than 1km from the theatre. Once the entrance to the city of

ROMAN RUINS

Gallia Narbonensis, or southern France, was the first Roman province established beyond the Italian Alps. See the amazing arenas, aqueducts and villas in **Arles** (p164), Glanum, **La Turbie** (p67) and at the **Musée d'Apt** (p209) in the Luberon.

Arausio, as Orange was known in 35 BCE, the monument is so ornately decorated that scholars consider it to be an exemplary example of Roman art. Film fans might recognise it from *The Da Vinci Code*.

Day-trippers will also admire the mosaic *Aux Amphorettes,* from the 3rd-century house in the **Musée d'Art et d'Histoire**. Got an early start? The Thursday morning market, one of the oldest in Provence, dates back to the 15th-century and sees more than 300 stalls weekly. For an out-of-the-ordinary lunch, reserve a table in one of the cave restaurants near the amphitheatre.

The Vestiges of Vaison-la-Romaine

From Roman town to fortified medieval village

While Orange and Arles have the monumental Roman sites, **Vaison-la-Romaine**, 30km north of Carpentras, unveils more of the day-to-day Roman lifestyle. The modern city sits atop the old Gallo-Roman city of Vasio Vocontiorum, only parts of which have been excavated.

Visitor passes to the **Sites Antiques de Vaison-la-Romaine** are sold for a 24-hour period, which is just the right amount of time to travel back to Roman days and follow the city's story through the Middle Ages. For younger visitors up to age 12, two of the main sites (Puymin and the Théo Desplans museum) are part of a grand treasure hunt – the game booklet is available for free at the museum.

Start at the ancient **Puymin** site, a former neighbourhood, where a hive of activity once buzzed in the shops and public squares. Also here is the huge Maison à l'Apollon Lauré – a manor with a feasting room, kitchen, private baths and more. Next hit the **Musée Archéologique Théo Desplans** to admire a rich collection of marble statues and other objects. Imagine the sparks of joy and entertainment visitors must have experienced in the nearby 6000-seat theatre. Or check online so that your visit coincides with one of the regular concerts put on by the city.

No more daylight? Wander up to the spectacular walled, hilltop **Cité Médiévale** – one of Provence's most magical ancient villages – for dinner before starting fresh the next morning with a sunrise visit to the 12th-century castle overlooking the valley. If possible, take a guided tour of the **Site Antique de la Villasse**, where local guides are adept at bringing back to life the daily routines of residents.

GOURMET STOPS IN VAISON-LA-ROMAINE

Lunch
Delicious daily specials and local beers at La Caillette, up in the medieval town. €

Apéritif
Specialising in wines from the Rhône region, sample a glass of wine and homemade focaccia at L'Arbre à Vins in the centre of the lower town. €

Dinner
Chambres Du'O's tidy design, private terrace and seasonal dishes put local ingredients and traditions in the spotlight. Reservations suggested. €€

Dessert
Step back into town to try a scoop of homemade verbena ice cream at Léone Artisan Glacier. €

WHERE TO EAT IN ORANGE

La Cantina
Eat inside a natural cave near the Roman theatre. Generous portions for a fair price. €€

La Grotte d'Auguste
Also near the theatre, another cave restaurant has three-course menus starting at €22. €€

La Guingette de la Colline
Typical French fare at this laid-back outdoor restaurant, on the hill above the theatre. €

Sault

Sault

GETTING AROUND

Bikes (or e-bikes) are great for this region. Sault is walkable, but to reach other villages or specific trailheads it's best to have a car.

The breezy plateau of Sault is covered with photogenic lavender fields but somehow has fewer crowds than other parts of the region. Surrounded by numerous hilltop villages and hamlets, Sault itself has been built atop a large limestone outcrop. Visitors who come year-round will undoubtedly fall in love with the friendly folks at the weekly market and the diverse hiking and outdoor adventures. Don't forget to taste some nougat: it's a local speciality, made with honey and almonds.

In the distance, the 'giant of Provence', Mont Ventoux, serves as the end point of the majestic Alps, making it a favourite destination for cyclists, whether on e-bikes or road bikes. Take a leisurely stroll through the lavender fields and savour the sweet fragrances that fill the air. Or, if you're feeling adventurous, explore the deep Gorges de la Nesque where the region's other treasure flows: fresh cold water.

Easy Walks Around Sault

Lavender-scented fields

TOP TIP

For families and adventurers, Sault offers easy access to the outdoors, a relaxed atmosphere and welcoming restaurants. Book a villa or farmhouse here for a week-long stay.

For a family stroll, follow the **Chemin des Lavandes**, just below the village of Sault, in the direction of the Mont Ventoux. The 5.3km lavender-strewn trail is well marked, and information panels periodically share the botanical properties, cultivation, harvesting and distilling techniques of the region's 'blue gold'.

Lavender fields and forests come together on a 10.6km intermediate loop from the centre of Sault

PICNIC PANTRIES

Sault's weekly Wednesday Provençal market has been running since the 16th-century. Other not-to-be-missed markets in the region are in **L'Isle-sur-la-Sorgue** (p202), **Arles** (p161) and **Aix-en-Provence** (p225).

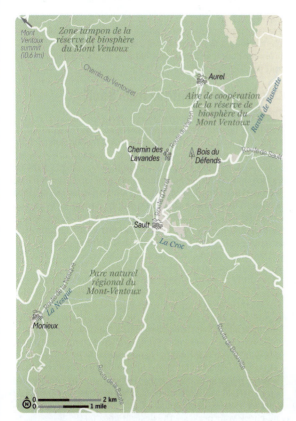

through the **Bois du Défends** north of town. Start on the ancien chemin d'Aurel and follow the yellow hiking signs for Aurel village. The trail loops back to Sault before it reaches Aurel, but if you have the energy, make the detour to visit the village's 12th-century church, perched on a hill.

Leaving from nearby **Aurel**, the 14.5km hike to the **Notre-Dame-des-Anges chapel** takes about three to four hours and is nearly exclusively on trails and dirt tracks. Weaving through lavender fields, pine forests and Provençal maquis or scrub, make a day of it with a picnic lunch.

Better Than a Chocolate Factory

A tasty lesson in making nougat

Generations of Provençal children have enjoyed the sweet nougat made from sugar, honey and almonds that comes from the Vaucluse region. The oldest nougat-making shop is **André Boyer** in the centre of Sault. Keeping ancient recipes alive since 1887, their nougat is made with local lavender honey, which gives it a distinct flavour.

Don't know much about nougat? The *nougatier* workshop hosts tours each Tuesday at 3pm (€1; reservations suggested).

If you can't get a slot on the tour, here's the essentials: there are two types of almond nougat – nougat noir and nougat blanc. Nougat noir is made with caramelised sugar and dark lavender honey, while nougat blanc is made with egg whites and light lavender honey.

Cycling Mont Ventoux from Sault

The easiest way up

Ready to take on the challenge of reaching the summit of Mont Ventoux (1910m) without putting a foot down? This legendary mountain, which is often a part of the Tour de France, is a must-visit destination for cyclists. **Albion Cycles** in the centre of Sault rents both road bikes and e-bikes. The best time to cycle is in spring or autumn when the weather is mild. Winter can be chilly and windy, and summer can be extremely hot. Make a day of it, pack a picnic lunch with a sandwich from the bakery **Aux Saveurs du Ventoux** just outside Sault. Don't hesitate to add a homemade pastry to the picnic from the same shop – they're divine, and the sugar boost might help you reach the top.

The 25.7km route climbs 1152m in elevation and is the easiest of the three classic ascents of the mountain, taking cyclists through stunning lavender fields before the real work begins. It's a climb for sure, but if you need a distraction, just look around and see if you can spot a local bird of prey or a wild boar. Many portions of the road easily lend themselves to becoming an impromptu picnic spot.

Once you reach Chalet Reynard, you'll have completed two-thirds of the climb. Smile for the freelance photographers just before arrival and grab their card to purchase a copy of the shot. At the top, drink a local beer, get comfy on your bike and check your brakes – the descent goes fast!

Note that you can also ascend by car year-round, but you cannot traverse the summit from 15 November to 15 April, or in the case of lingering snow or dangerously high winds.

SCALE MONT VENTOUX ON THE GR4

The GR4 crosses the Dentelles de Montmirail before scaling Mont Ventoux' northern face, where it meets the GR9. Both trails traverse the ridge. The GR4 branches eastwards to Gorges du Verdon; the GR9 crosses the Vaucluse Mountains to the Luberon.

The essential map for the area is 3140ET Mont Ventoux, by IGN (ign.fr). Bédoin's tourist office stocks maps and brochures detailing walks for all levels.

The Carpentras tourist office organises 24km sunrise hikes up to the summit, but they can be gruelling, with over 1500m of elevation gain.

Departure is at 11pm, reservations and hiking boots and a headlamp are all required for this €30 hike. Kids must be at least 12.

SLEEPING IN SAULT

Maison Léonard du Ventoux
Spacious, spotless double rooms and an excellent view in the centre of Sault. €€

La Bastide de la Loge
House rental a few kilometres outside Sault on the plain below Mont Ventoux. €€

Aurel Inattendu
Comfortable, no-frills wooden *roulotte* (caravan), overlooking lavender fields. €

HIKING THE GORGES DE LA NESQUE

For a classic walk that does not involve climbing Mont Ventoux, consider the Gorges de la Nesque. This 10km hike can be done in as little as a morning or it can be drawn out into a full-day trip. It's best in the spring or autumn, when the weather is mild and the foliage is at its most vibrant. Start in ❶ **Monieux**, less than 10 minutes by car from Sault. Follow the ❷**GR9**, a gradual climb that slowly leads up a hill. About 2km in, turn left on the ❸ **Sentier des Chapelles**. This gently descends to the D942 road, where there is ample room on the shoulder for walkers. It's worth detouring to the viewpoint ❹ **Le Castellaras**, from where you'll get a stunning view of the Rocher du Cire, one of the most majestic cliffs in Provence. From here, descend into the Gorges de la

Nesque, which was formed over millions of years as the Nesque River cut through the limestone rock, creating a narrow, steep canyon.

Here in the gorge, travellers will be surprised to find a troglodyte chapel dating back to the 12th-century: the ❺ **Chapelle St-Michel-de-Monieux**. After exploring the chapel, continue along the trail, back towards Monieux. The water levels in the gorges can vary greatly depending on the season and rainfall, so be prepared for a variety of conditions. Before reaching the village, the trail goes by the ❻**Plan d'eau de Monieux**. In summer, a snack bar is open daily, and there's a small market on Sunday mornings. Just a few more minutes' hike brings you back to Monieux.

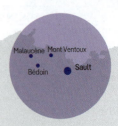

Beyond Sault

Sault isn't the only base for Mont Ventoux excursions; the villages of Bédoin and Malaucène are popular departure points, too.

The area surrounding Mont Ventoux is a paradise for outdoor enthusiasts, with an impressive landscape of rolling hills, towering mountains, canyons, rocky riverbeds and quiet back-roads. Adrenaline seekers will find their joy with a diverse range of activities such as cycling and trail running. The peak can be accessed via three popular cycling routes: one from Sault, one from Bédoin and another from Malaucène. Not in the pedalling mood? Take time off from cycling and explore the charming villages of Bédoin and Malaucène. Both towns have a relaxed atmosphere, with plenty of shops and activities to keep visitors entertained. From sampling local cuisine to exploring historical monuments, the region is great for laid-back day trips.

Cycling Mont Ventoux from Bédoin
The classic way up

On Mont Ventoux' southwestern flanks, **Bédoin** is a typical Provençal village that serves as the perfect starting point for cyclists climbing the peak. Rent a bike from **Provence Cycles** in the village, from €49 per half-day. From here, the route to the peak is 21.3km, with an elevation gain of 1589m. The climbing grade is more consistent than the Malaucène route and the sights are more varied: it begins in the fields, climbs through forests, and then tops out in the moonscape of the wind-shorn summit.

GETTING AROUND

Cycling is the obvious choice for getting around here. Otherwise, your own car is the easiest way to get around. More and more villages have charging stations for electric vehicles; check Chargemap (chargemap.com).

Scan to find your nearest charging station

☑ TOP TIP

Each village below Mont Ventoux has a good collection of rural villas and B&Bs to choose from.

Be sure to check the weather before departure – if the mistral wind is in the forecast, reconsider. This fierce wind, which sometimes reaches speeds of 250km/h, will definitely knock you off your bike. Bédoin is 30km west of Sault.

Cycling Mont Ventoux from Malaucène

The hard way up

Malaucène, 45km northwest of Sault, has deceptively lovely plane tree–lined streets, which hide the challenge that awaits: ascending Mont Ventoux along this northwestern route is considered to be one the hardest routes to the summit. To tackle this climb, rent a bike from **Bédoin Location**, from €25 per half-day. If you've decided on this route because it's the shortest (21.2km), don't think you're off the hook. You'll climb 1535m in elevation, passing a few strenuously steep sections that will put your endurance to the test. There are relatively few flat sections to give you a break.

The landscape on the northwest side of the mountain, which faces the Drome region, is different from the other routes. Conifer forests clothe the mountain slopes, and there is usually less vehicle traffic. Join the hundreds of cyclists who dream of cycling Ventoux three times – once from each direction.

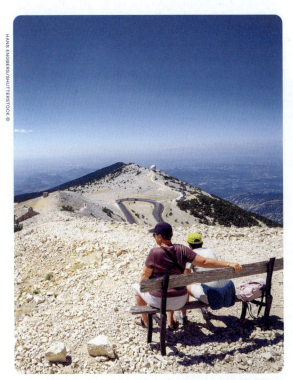

SPORTING CHALLENGES AROUND MONT VENTOUX

Traversée des Dentelles Trail run
Each June nearly 1800 runners come to the Dentelles de Montmirail. Competing in timed marathons or half-marathons, runners cross the rocky terrain of one of Provence's most intriguing natural landscapes.

Ventoux Gravel Tour Trans Massif
Springtime weather in the month of May welcomes hundreds of gravel cyclists, who take to the trails on the range, competing in 50km, 110km, and 220km bike races.

Grand Raid du Ventoux
An ultra-trail that recently joined the UTMB family, the Grand Raid du Ventoux trail race is a 161km race each April, pushing runners to the limits of their craft.

Mont Ventoux

L'Isle-sur-la-Sorgue

L'Isle-sur-la-Sorgue

GETTING AROUND

L'Isle-sur-la-Sorgue's train station has connections to Avignon and Marseille. There is also a Zou! bus for intervillage travels, or try renting an e-bike. Parking in Fontaine de Vaucluse is crowded and expensive in summer – consider taking the bus to avoid the headache.

L'Isle-sur-la-Sorgue is a destination for all the senses. The Sorgue River branches off into several canals throughout the village, and these canals play a key role in the town's identity. It's especially enticing in the springtime, when the village is in full bloom but the summer crowds haven't yet arrived. The town is best known for its antique *brocante* market that takes place every Sunday. All eras of vintage and contemporary finds turn up at the market, and the sellers are as passionate as they come.

For foodies, the Provençal market here is a delight for the palate. The market offers an array of local products, from tapenade to seasonal fruits, like peaches, strawberries and cherries. For those who love to hike, a must-see is the Fontaine de Vaucluse, a village situated at the foot of a cliff at the source of the Sorgue River.

Market Day

France's most bountiful region

The town of L'Isle-sur-la-Sorgue is a must-visit destination for travellers to Provence, and its market is one of the main draws. The market takes place year-round, with vendors setting up stalls on Thursday and Sunday mornings. It's a real pleasure to wander through the alleys and along the canals that run along the Sorgue, with the sound of the water providing a tranquil backdrop to the commercial bustle.

The market is a feast for the eyes and the taste buds, with colourful stalls selling fresh produce, flowers, artisanal crafts and delicious food. Some of the streets where the market stalls can be found include **rue Carnot**, **rue Jean-Jacques Rousseau**, **rue de la République** and **place de la Liberté**.

As you walk through the market, you'll be drawn in by the smells of freshly baked bread, lavender and grilled meats. You can sample local cheeses, jams and olive oil, and pick up a handmade olive-oil soap to take home. The market is a great place to find unique gifts and souvenirs, such as painted ceramics, embroidered linens and handmade jewellery.

HIGHLIGHTS
1 Campredon Centre d'Art
2 Collégiale Notre Dame des Anges

EATING
3 Café de France
4 Grand Café de la Sorgue

SHOPPING
5 Appel d'Air
6 Brun de Vian Tiran
7 Dongier Antiquités
8 Du Côté du Design
9 Le Village des Antiquaires de la Gare

10 L'Ile aux Brocantes
11 Produce Market
12 Quai de la Gare
13 Rives de Bechard

After browsing, visitors can stop for coffee or a bite to eat at one of the many cafes and restaurants in town. The **Grand Café de la Sorgue** is a popular spot, with its outdoor terrace overlooking the river. The **Café de France** is particularly noteworthy for its green decor, which includes antique mirrors, chandeliers and old photographs. The cafe also serves up delicious pastries and sandwiches.

Antiquing in L'Isle-sur-la-Sorgue

Vintage finds await

If your manor house needs that perfect Louis XV chandelier, don't miss L'Isle-sur-la-Sorgue on weekends. Home to one of the largest and most famous **flea markets** in France, most of the antique dealers are open Friday through Monday, with Sunday being the biggest day of all. Twice a year, at Easter and in August, the city hosts an international **Art, Antiques and Flea Fair**, which attracts thousands of visitors.

You can find five main antiques villages along the canals of the Sorgue River. **Quai de la Gare**, located on av de la Libération, is home to galleries like Frédéric Bousquet and Cabanon Design. **Le Village des Antiquaires de la Gare**, located at 2 bis av de l'Egalité, is another great spot to browse. **Dongier Antiquités**, located at 15 esplanade Robert-Vasse, is a

☑ **TOP TIP**

Each village below Mont Ventoux has a good collection of rural villas and B&Bs to choose from.

FARMERS MARKETS

In Provence, there are two kinds of outdoor markets: *marché Provençal* and *marché producteur*. The latter are similar to what are often called farmers markets in English, meaning there's no intermediary. They only offer seasonal, local produce, and are usually only open from June through November, there are dozens in the region. Here are several close to L'Isle-sur-la-Sorgue.

Wednesday:
Pernes-les-Fontaines (night market)

Thursday:
Cavaillon (night market)

Saturday:
Petit Palais

Sunday:
Coustellet
More *marchés producteurs* can be found across the region. Check Provence Guide (provenceguide.com) for a comprehensive map and calendar.

Scan to access Provence Guide

Street antique stand, L'Isle-sur-la-Sorgue

must-visit for antique lovers. **L'Ile aux Brocantes**, located at 7 av des Quatre Otages, is home to shops like Stéphane Broutin and Françoise Aillaud. And last but not least, **Rives de Bechard**, located at 38 av Jean-Charmasson, is another great option to explore for contemporary finds.

There are also a number of independent antique dealers scattered throughout town. Jackie Occelli and Bernard Durand are known for their furniture. Le Magasin Général, Objets de Hasard and La Petite Curieuse are all worth checking out. too.

A Stroll Around Town

Historic sites amid the canals

The exceptional historic centre is contained within canals dotted by creaking waterwheels – the one by the tiny park at av des Quatre Otages is particularly photogenic. In the very heart of the old town, the stately exterior of the **Collégiale Notre Dame des Anges** shows no sign of the baroque theatrics inside – 122 gold angels ushering forward the Virgin Mary. Also of note is the 18th-century riverside mansion, **Campredon Centre d'Art**, a venue for seasonal contemporary art exhibitions.

 WHERE TO EAT IN L'ISLE-SUR-LA-SORGUE

Maison Moga
Sommeliers and cheese experts pair gourmet platters of cheese or charcuterie with the appropriate wine. **€€**

Le Carré d'Herbes
Cédric Brun's table serves an excellent weekday-lunch market menu outside under the arbor. **€€**

Vert Bouteille
Priority to organic, locavore, 100% vegan and mostly gluten-free dishes in this canteen-style restaurant. **€**

Day Trip to Fontaine-de-Vaucluse

The source of the Sorgue River

The village of **Fontaine-de-Vaucluse**, 12km east of **L'Isle-sur-la-Sorgue**, is known for its spring, which gushes out of a chasm at more than 90 cu metres per second, making it France's largest karst spring and the fifth-largest on the planet. Consider this itinerary: starting off at 9am, visitors can head to **La Pointe Noir**, a cosy cafe in the heart of the village, and kick-start your day with a delicious cup of coffee. After that, hike up to the top of the cliffs from the **Font de l'Oule**. The hike is of medium difficulty and takes about an hour to reach the top.

Once at the top of the cliffs, celebrate with a picnic or snack and enjoy the view. Bring plenty of water, as the weather can be quite hot in the summer months. Afterward, wander back to Fontaine-de-Vaucluse and hike 1km up to the **source**. The hike is a bit steep, but the view of the clear water is soothing and the chasm impressive.

After the hike, head down to the river near the **Aire des Vergnes** for a refreshing swim in the cold water. To be precise: the water temperature hovers around 14°C year-round. Time for an apéritif: sip on a cocktail at **La Vanne Marel**, a charming bar with a relaxed atmosphere and stunning views of the surrounding mountains.

For dinner, head to **La Figuier Fontaine-de-Vaucluse**. Reserve a table in advance, as they only have one service per night. Some dishes to try include *dorade au four* (baked sea bream), *pieds et paquets à la Provençale* (stewed sheep offal and trotters with tomatoes) or the classic *confit de canard* (duck thighs preserved in fat).

CONTEMPORARY SHOPS

Appel d'Air
Modern antiques and objects with personality, with an emphasis on postwar lighting and ceramics.

Du Côté du Design
Under the large glass roof at the entrance of the Village des Antiquaires de la Gare is Anne and Jérôme Delor's shop. This store is for lighting professionals: here you'll find everything from 1950s industrial suspension lamps from Russia to cinema projectors recovered in American film studios.

Brun de Vian Tiran
Father and son foster a passion for collecting rare wools: from Arles merino to Kyrgyzstan ibex, infinite soft threads pass through their showroom.

 WHERE TO SLEEP IN L'ISLE-SUR-LA-SORGUE

La Magnanerie de l'Isle
Character-filled guesthouse in a former industrial building in the heart of the historic centre. €€

La Maison sur la Sorgue
Historic boutique hotel with sumptuous suites and a hidden garden with a small stone pool. €€€

Mas la Vitalis
Magali's B&B consists of two inviting bedrooms in a calm, restored farmhouse near town. €€

Abbaye Notre-Dame de Sénanque

Gordes

L'Isle-sur-la-Sorgue

Beyond L'Isle-sur-la-Sorgue

Discover two of the most beautiful scenes in the Vaucluse: the hilltop village of Gordes and a lavender-wreathed abbey.

Get ready for the stunning Monts de Vaucluse, a region known for its picturesque landscapes and rural charm. Along the way, you'll pass through charming Provençal villages like Pernes-les-Fontaines, La Roque-sur-Pernes, Le Beaucet, Venasque and St-Didier. Keep an eye out for the region's famous *bories,* stone shelters used by shepherds and hunters for centuries to hide from the elements, stock equipment or spend a few nights.

If you visit one abbey in the region, make it the Abbaye Notre-Dame de Sénanque, a stunning 12th-century abbey surrounded by fields of lavender. While visitors can explore the abbey year-round, the best time to visit is during the summer months when the lavender is in full bloom.

The Gorges Behind Gordes

The top sights, differently

If you're in the region, the 12th-century Cistercian **Abbaye Notre-Dame de Sénanque** should be at the top of your list. The monks here support themselves by selling honey, lavender and essential oils to visitors. Unlike other abbeys in the region, they also open up their monastic home to visitors at certain times. Self-guided tablet tours are available for non-French speakers. If you're enchanted by the stone halls, the peaceful atmosphere and the spiritual connection, perhaps book a silent retreat for €40 per day and immerse yourself in the contemplative lifestyle of a monk.

The abbey is accessible by car but is also walking distance from **Gordes**. The most iconic hill village of the Luberon,

LUNCH IN GORDES

Clover Gordes by Jean-François Piège
Pop-culture fans will recognise the stunning backdrop from *Emily in Paris*. The cuisine on display is an homage to braised dishes. €€€

La Trinquette
As stunning a view as you can order. Regulars on the summer menu include Provençal aïoli and vegetable platters with homemade chickpea sauce. €€

Petit Palais d'Aglae
Come for the *menu du marché*, a five-star lunch at a much friendlier price (Thursday to Sunday). It's chef's choice, but expect fine fish and bright ingredients like yuzu, orange blossom or, in winter, truffles. €€

☑ **TOP TIP**

Visit Gordes, but don't skip other perched villages of the Monts de Vaucluse. The views always pack a punch.

Gordes seems to teeter improbably on the edge of the sheer rock faces of the Vaucluse plateau from which it rises. It's impossibly photogenic, but also impossibly crowded in peak season; walking a few kilometres out of town, however, is a peaceful diversion. The itinerary passes through Rouguière, Côte de Sénancole, the abbey, Ferme de la Débroussède and Les Boujolles. The route then continues to Croix des Baux, Les Grangiers and a beautiful viewpoint of Gordes before returning to the starting point. In total, the loop is 7km; expect to spend three hours, including a visit to the abbey. Follow the blue and green trail signs.

The hike begins with a slight climb up a hillside. Take a small path that descends towards the abbey if you want to see it from above or visit. Then, go back up and take the path that goes around the plateau above Gordes, which is both shaded and breezy.

WHY DOES THE FONTAINE FILL UP?

Once upon a time there was a minstrel named Basile, who dozed off on his way to Fontaine de Vaucluse. While he was sleeping, a nymph came to him and led him to the edge of the spring. The spring opened up to reveal a meadow full of flowers. The nymph showed the minstrel seven diamonds contained within, which could be lifted up, causing powerful jets of water to gush out, filling the Fontaine de Vaucluse. 'There,' she said, 'is the secret of the spring, of which I am the guardian.' The nymph only lifts all seven diamonds once a year, which sends out so much water that the fig tree high above can drink.

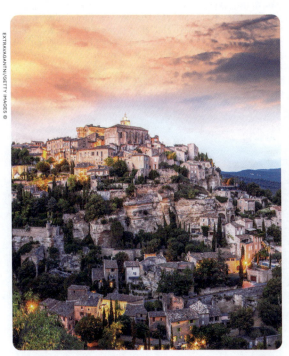

EXTRAVAGANTNI/GETTY IMAGES ©

Gordes

WHERE TO SLEEP IN THE MONTS DE VAUCLUSE

La Bergerie Pradel
Smart hotel in a renovated 16th-century villa surrounded by forests. Close to Le Beaucet. €

Le Cabanon des Secrets
In La Roque-sur-Perne, this cool B&B made from stone is great for week-long stays. €€

Camping La Folie
Simple, choose-your-own pitch campground near Lagnes. €

CYCLING THROUGH THE MONTS DE VAUCLUSE

Experience the countryside of the Monts de Vaucluse with a leisurely 27km bike ride through the nearby villages. With 420m of altitude gain, this is a tour that's best for intermediate cyclists. Rent a bike from Vel'eau Loc in ❶ **Pernes-les-Fontaines**. Before starting, take a moment to admire the Notre-Dame gate, equipped with two towers and a small bridge.

This ride takes cyclists through local fields; depending on the season, you can stop and admire the sheep or goats. The ❷ **Cheverie des Fontaines** has a small shop to sample local goat cheese.

Set your course towards ❸ **La Roque-sur-Pernes**, a Provençal village off the beaten path. La Roque-sur-Pernes was built on a rocky outcrop, which provided natural protection during medieval times. The village square is welcoming and shaded, with the Fontaine du Renard and the church of Sts Pierre and Paul.

Next, cycle through low-growing oak trees, looking for traditional stone shelters called *bories*. A small detour will take you to the ❹ **Borie de la Roque**, a particularly well-restored example open to visitors. Continue cycling along the hill towards Le Beaucet, just on the other side of a small ravine.

From here, take the winding roads to ❺ **Venasque**. There are several local artisan shops and galleries worth a look. Reserve lunch at Le Petit Chose and be wowed by the local flavours like spring asparagus or summer cantaloupe. Plus, the balcony has a spectacular view of a wild gorge.

In ❻ **St-Didier**, cycle through the centre of town and take a moment to admire the Château de Thézan St-Didier. A few cafes decorate the central square. Return to Pernes-les-Fontaines, where you can attend the Wednesday evening farmers market in the summer.

North Luberon

North Luberon

This is the wilder side of the Luberon, where the plains are fed by the Calavon River. On the flanks of the mountains and hills, villages established thousands of years ago still flourish with activity. The fertile plains and a strong agricultural tradition render the Luberon markets some of the finest in France – farm to market is usually less than a half-hour drive. In some ways, tourism has preserved the region's traditions and the resilient, forward-thinking communities of Saignon and Reillanne offer visitors a glimpse into the traditional Provençal life. Adventurers and nature lovers will enjoy the park: hiking and cycling opportunities are endless, and rock climbers will enjoy the challenging cliffs in Buoux. A region with memories waiting to be unlocked, nothing beats a midsummer sunset over the lavender fields of Claperèdes, followed by a glass of rosé on the terrace.

Prehistory and Candied Fruit in Apt

A good base for Luberon visits

For those interested in the prehistory of the Luberon region, start in Apt. The **Musée d'Apt**, located in a former 18th-century mansion built on the remains of an ancient theatre, has a special collection on antiquity in the Annex Apta Julia, where the archaeological treasures of the region are presented.

For those keen on exploring further, **Viens** is a small nearby town that is home to slabs with over 200 types of fossilised animal tracks from approximately 30 million years ago.

GETTING AROUND

Driving is the easiest way to get around, although a bus service does connect Cavaillon, L'Isle-sur-la-Sorgue and Manosque to Apt. There are many secure cycling lanes in the region, and with an e-bike there is hardly anywhere you can't go.

☑ **TOP TIP**

Summer is the high season in the Luberon, but the temperatures can be extremely hot. Plan your busy outdoor activities for the morning and leave time for a mid-afternoon siesta during the heat of the day.

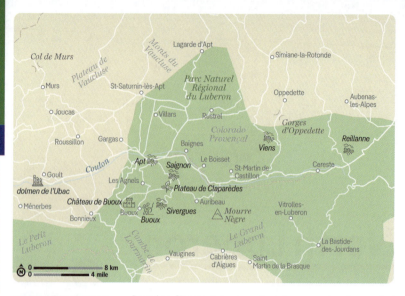

Imagine discovering an ancient funerary chamber sealed off for nearly 5000 years. In Goult, near the Calavon River, that's exactly what happened after days of rain flooded the local river. In 1994 the **dolmen de l'Ubac** was uncovered here, with remains of up to 50 bodies inside. Because the site was so close to the riverbed and at risk of severe degradation, it was carefully excavated. A replica of the site is open to visitors 500m away from the original, near the old gare de Lumières.

Apt has long been an important market town, dating back to the Middle Ages. The town's strategic location at the crossroads of several trade routes made it a centre of commerce and a destination for merchants from all over the region.

Today, the product everyone is after is *fruits confits* (candied fruits). The fruit is preserved in sugar syrup and then dried, creating a delicious and long-lasting treat. Apt is considered the largest producer of candied fruit in the world, and you'll find a wide variety of flavours at the market, from apricots to figs to oranges. A visit to **La Maison du Fruit Confit** unveils the process; the shop is the best place to buy *fruit confit*.

Reach New Heights in Buoux and Saignon

Scale the Luberon cliffs

If you're looking for a thrilling adventure, climbing in **Buoux** is an experience not to be missed. These are some of the most famous limestone crags in Europe, and while the hard routes are *really* hard, beginners can get in on the action as well. It's not for the faint of heart, though – the area is known for its single-pitch sport climbs, with a lot of overhanging and sustained routes. **Vertical Trekking** runs guided sessions for climbers of all levels. The best season to go is in the spring or autumn, when temperatures are cooler and the crowds are thinner.

Above Apt, the village of **Saignon** oversees the valley. Once an important centre for the production of wool and silk (many of the buildings in the village date back to this time period), today Saignon residents live a peaceful routine, and the whole village oozes relaxation. Stop into the *épicerie* (corner shop) of **La Maison près de la Fontaine** to discover curated local products and hear about upcoming events from the in-the-know owner, Julie.

Wander up the streets to visit the **Château de Saignon**, a medieval castle that sits at the top of the hill overlooking the village. Then weave back down to visit the cool interior of the **Église Notre-Dame de Pitié**. Built in the 12th-century, the church features stunning Romanesque architecture and fading frescoes. Dine at **Un Jardin sur le Toit**, a village favourite with a view that spans the horizon.

Small Village, Big Heart
Don't sleep on the Luberon Oriental

Don't let the intimate size of **Reillanne**, a small village in the Luberon Oriental, diminish its character and soul. Reillanne is a vibrant hub of social activity, largely thanks to the **Café du Cours**. This cool cafe situated above the main square is a popular hangout for locals and visitors of all ages. The cafe's Friday night concerts have become the centrepiece of the village's social scene, showcasing the musical talent of both established and up-and-coming artists.

The good news is that the village's music scene is due to expand. Rumour has it that a group of friends who frequent the Café du Cours have purchased the old **Café de la Place** nearby, which is set to host live music concerts every Saturday night. So, if you're a music lover, a weekend in Reillanne is all you'll need to get your fix. Come and experience the soul of the village through its music, food and friendly vibe.

After the music and dancing, shake off the Sunday morning blues with the **Grand Marché de Reillanne**. You can't miss

THE LOVEABLE CHICKPEA
Chickpeas are a Provençal crop that turns up across the region. See the ingredient integrated into surprising manifestations at **L'Auberge de la Fenière** (p221) or try a *socca niçoise* in **Nice** (p61).

APT TO EAT

Café Les Valseuses
Two mains per day: an Asian dish, like pork meatballs with udon and ginger sauce, and a Provençal dish, like buckwheat and grilled veggies with dried fruit and tomato sauce. €

Le Sanglier Paresseux
An established classic, the seasonal mains here might include sea bass tartare with cauliflower pickles or duck stuffed with dried fruits, roasted asparagus, eggplant and tajine sauce. €€

L'Intramuros Restaurant et Rhumerie
Calling the bar's rum and gin menu extensive is an understatement. Vintage and colourful decor, with rotating daily specials like beef cheek, rabbit and citron-limoncello tiramisu for dessert. €€

WHERE TO BUY PICNIC SUPPLIES IN APT

Comptoir de l'Ambroisie
Excellent *fromagerie* with the possibility to build your own cheese plate. €

Le Saint Pierre
Local favourite, this bakery and pastry shop uses high-quality flour for its breads. €

Caillebotte Primeur
Lots of organic fruit and veg, plus local specialities in this corner shop. €

A CURIOUS MAN'S GARDEN

Jean-Luc and his daughter Violette have been collecting and preserving ancient seeds for more than 30 years, and currently grow more than 300 types of plants in their seed garden, **Le Potager d'un Curieux**.

Stop by to wander in the garden or greenhouse or pick up a few packets of seeds: they have over 80 varieties of tomatoes, nearly 50 varieties of lettuce and greens, and dozens of types of peppers, eggplants and herbs.

If you let the plants go to seed, you can collect the grains and plant again next year. The garden is 7km southeast of Apt, just past the hilltop village of Saignon.

it – the stands take over the centre of town. It's one of the most authentic places to buy local olive oil, lavender essence and farm-fresh eggs and chickpeas. Many of the vendors are producers themselves. Don't expect everything to look perfect, but do expect a great selection of organic and biodynamic produce. The beefsteak tomatoes are always full of flavour, which should be reason enough to make a stop here.

Into the Inner Luberon

Go deeper

Explore the folds of the Luberon mountain. The **Château de Buoux** outside the town of the same name is a peaceful and secluded spot in the Grand Luberon, perfect for those seeking tranquillity and natural beauty. Closed to the public for renovations, it serves more as a starting point for exploring the surrounding forests. There are several trails that lead through the nearby hills and forests.

 WHERE TO STAY NEAR APT

La Maison près de la Fontaine
Small Saignon B&B with stylish rooms and a local boutique on the ground floor. €€

Auberge des Seguins
Secluded B&B with a pool and view of the cliffs of Buoux. Restaurant and cafe on-site. €€

Domaine du Castellas
Farm converted into a luxury hotel in Sivergues. Community dining and loads of activities. €€€

Lavender field, Plateau des Claparèdes

ESSENTIAL ESSENCE: LAVENDER

Lavender lovers may already be familiar with the world-famous Plateau de Valensole, but the lavender-growing region stretches much further. Looking for the perfect souvenir? Popular items include soap, bulk lavender and essential oils, all of which you'll find throughout Provence.

Essential oils have a particularly high markup – a tiny vial can sell for €11 to €15. But if you have a number of gifts to buy, consider buying a bulk-sized bottle of essential oil at a local market. Reillane, Sault and Banon all have producers selling 500mL bottles for about €20, which you can transfer yourself to smaller bottles – it's the perfect way to bring home a gift for everyone at an affordable price. Plus, you'll be supporting independent farmers.

If you keep climbing the road after Saignon, **Plateau des Claparèdes** will be your destination of the day. It's known for its stunning lavender fields and remoteness. Unlike the more famous Plateau de Valensole, the Claparèdes is far less crowded, making it the perfect destination for those who prefer a more peaceful and relaxed atmosphere.

Visitors to the area can hike from the hamlet of **Sivergues** to explore the lavender fields and take in the stunning scenery. The hike offers a variety of terrain, from flat meadows to rocky outcroppings, and takes approximately two to three hours round trip.

The lavender fields of the Plateau des Claparèdes are at their most vibrant in late June and early July, when the flowers are in full bloom. Wander through the fields and take in the sights and scents of the lavender, which has been cultivated in the region for centuries. On the drive home, stop at the **Auberge des Seguins** in Buoux for a drink.

WHERE TO LISTEN TO LIVE MUSIC

La Gare
Concerts all year long at Coustellet's former train station, now a cultural centre.

Les Musicales du Luberon
Regional musical association. Check the website for dates and artists (musicalesluberon.fr).

Carrières du Château de Lacoste
Cool acoustics in a former Roman quarry. Hosts the Festival de Lacoste in July.

Beyond
North Luberon

Get out and explore the hills, mountains and plains of the northern side of the Luberon.

No one comes to the Luberon to stay in town. Fan out into the wider north Luberon area to immerse yourself in the history and culture of the region. Cycling enthusiasts can follow the itinerary that takes them through Ménerbes, Lacoste, Bonnieux and Goult, while those seeking a more relaxed experience can explore the hill villages of Maubec, Robion and the Petit Luberon. Wine lovers won't want to miss the cooperatives in the region, where they can sample some of the best wines in the area.

The village of Forcalquier is another highlight, with its charming streets and vibrant market. Art lovers and industrial fans alike will enjoy visiting the ochre-coloured villages of Rustrel and Roussillon.

Follow in the Footsteps of Jean Giono

An icon of Provençal letters

Jean Giono was a French writer who was born in the Provençal town of **Manosque**, 41km east of Apt, and is known for his stories that celebrate the nature and beauty of the region. The **Centre Jean Giono** is dedicated to his life and works, showcasing exhibitions that capture the essence of Giono's Provence. The Centre also offers guided tours of Giono's home for French speakers, providing an intimate look into the author's personal life and the inspirations behind his works.

GETTING AROUND

E-bikes and bicycles are great for getting around. To visit small villages, a car is the best option.

☑ **TOP TIP**

Stay somewhere that's easy to reach from both the east and west sides of the Luberon, like Villars or Gargas.

For nature lovers and literature enthusiasts alike, a visit here is a must-see destination in the beautiful region of Provence.

Love Giono's approach to Provence? His former farm outside **Forcalquier**, 23km north of Manosque, has been transformed into a B&B called **La Margotte**. Writer's block be gone; Giono wrote *Le Hussard sur le Toit* (The Horseman on the Roof) in this house.

Giono waxed poetic about Provençal olive oil many times in his essays. In Forcalquier you can see the **old oil mill of Gouvan** and taste AOC Haute-Provence olive oil produced in Lurs. In bygone days, the olive oil mill was used to crush the olives to make a paste from which the miller could extract the juice. After letting it sit, the water and oil in the juice separated, and the olive oil on the surface was collected.

While in Forcalquier, it'd be a shame not to visit the **Distilleries et Domaines de Provence**, which has been going strong for more than 120 years. Some spirits you may be familiar with, like pastis, but others might be totally new: Farigoule de Forcalquier is a thyme-based spirit, Rinquinquin is a white wine–based peach apéritif, and Orange Colombo is distilled from orange rinds.

Centre Jean Giono

THE MAN WHO PLANTED TREES

For an easy vacation read with a powerful message, pick up a copy of Giono's short fable *The Man Who Planted Trees* (*L'homme qui Plantait des Arbres*; 1953).

This tale beautifully portrays the values of perseverance and love for nature. Lightly mocking society's love of administration, *The Man Who Planted Trees* inspires readers to take a closer look at their surroundings and appreciate the beauty of even the most humble natural environments.

After reading this story, you'll never look at a scrubby Provençal forest in the same way again. It will leave you with a newfound appreciation for the power of nature, and humankind's role in stewarding and rejuvenating the earth.

WHERE TO EAT IN GIONO'S PROVENCE

Restaurant Ma Nine
Stylish Forcalquier restaurant with a terrace and balanced dishes like meatballs and pickled vegetables. €€

Pizzeria Lo Pichotome
Crispy thin-crust pizzas with fresh ingredients and local beers, on a relaxed patio in Forcalquier. €

Pamparigouste
Upscale restaurant at the Couvent des Minimes Hôtel et Spa in Mane, with an emphasis on tradition. €€€

Pedalling the Luberon

With backroads galore, a wink to the agricultural fertility of the valley and twisty switchback turns to reach perched villages, cycling around the north side of the Luberon is the best way to experience what makes this region hum. It isn't just the chirping of the cicadas, but the constant movement of the entire ecosystem in tune with the seasons: from the farmers to the holidaymakers to the wildlife.

❶ Coustellet

Forty years ago, the village of Coustellet was simply a crossroads, but today it's a commercial hub for the hilltop villages flanking it to the north and south. There are a few bike rental shops like **En Roue Libre**, where visitors can get equipped to hit the road.

The Ride: Follow the Calavon greenway east out of town. At Les Beaumettes (km 5), turn right onto route des Écoles to climb up to Maubec.

❷ Ménerbes

Once a sleepy farming village at the foot of the Luberon, Peter Mayle's bestselling *A Year in Provence* brought fame and new blood to the town.

The Ride: Head east out of town on the route de Bonnieux. After km 14, turn left onto route de la Valmasque and pedal up to the top of the hill, which leads down to Lacoste.

CELLIO7/SHUTTERSTOCK ©

Ménerbes

START/
END

0 4 km
0 2 mile

❸ Lacoste

Perched on the east side of the hill, the village of Lacoste has been well-restored thanks to a certain French billionaire (Pierre Cardin). An American art school has a satellite here and outdoor expositions sometimes decorate the town.

The Ride: Hold the course on route de Bonnieux. It's a short descent through cherry and olive groves, followed by another climb up to Bonnieux.

❹ Bonnieux

This rival hill village is a bit more lively than Lacoste. Stop for a housemade ice cream at Glacier Creperie Le Tinel.

The Ride: Leave Bonnieux from the north and pick up the chemin de Gargas until it hits the D36. Turn right and then take the first left onto an unnamed road. On a map the road runs more or less parallel to the larger route du Pont Julien.

❺ Pont Julian

This Roman bridge (3 BCE) is part of the Via Domitia, an important trade route linking Narbonne and Turin. Until 2005, cars were allowed to use the bridge, but today it is pedestrian or cyclist only.

The Ride: Pedal over the bridge and back, because to return you'll need to follow the Calavon greenway for a spell. Turn right on the D36, cross the river and the D900 roundabout to reach Goult.

❻ Goult

A medieval village tucked behind a hill, Goult has loads of character and a tradition of fine dining. It's difficult to choose a restaurant, but try the cool garden and market menu at La Gaudina for a lunch fit for a cyclist.

The Ride: Leave Goult taking the direction 'Lumières', and then follow the Calavon greenway for the last 6km of the journey, taking you back to Coustellet.

ARTISINAL SHOPS

Comptoir des Ochres
Pick up small quantities of ochre pigment and gifts at this shop in Roussillon.

Les Uns et Les Ocres
Hidden in an alley in Roussillon, this little shop sells handmade pottery tinted with the natural pigments of the region.

Atelier Kalayaan
The creative collective in Manosque showcases handicrafts and creations from across the region: ceramics, textiles, soaps, woodwork, honey and medicinal plants.

Il Était une Flamme
Family-owned shop with all the good smells: handmade candles and diffusers in fresh natural scents like cedar, orange blossom and lily of the valley. Nice selection of authentic vials of *parfum de Grasse*.

Painting Workshops in the Ochre Hills
Where art and industry meet

The ochre of **Roussillon**, 13km west of Apt, has brought the region world fame. But for centuries myths have whirled around the village: that the cliffs are red because the lord of the city was tricked into eating his wife and subsequently threw himself into the void. Or that the Titans built a fire cannon in a cave on Mont Ventoux, which burned the hillsides red for all eternity.

Admire the bright colours of the village houses and visit the **Ôkhra workshop**, located in the old factory at the **Écomusée de l'Ocre**. Sign up for a guided visit; in the summer, there is also a two-hour children's workshop to learn how to paint with ochre. The arts aren't only for kids, though – artists can treat themselves to an initiation to decorative painting. The six-hour workshop covers the basic techniques of painting and takes place monthly depending on reservations. The pigments can be purchased in the shop to take home and continue the fun.

Engulfed by visitors during the high season, the **Colorado Provençal** outside of **Rustrel**, 10km northeast of Apt and 21km east of Rousillon, is a former ochre and iron mine. A protected natural site displays the tracks, basins and pipes from the industrial era. Entrance starts from €2 for visitors on foot. Go early in the morning to avoid the heat and the crowds.

For fewer crowds, try an underground spot: the nearby **Mines de Bruoux**, where you can don a helmet and visit the ochre quarries. The roofs of the tunnels reach up to 12m in height. Or go for a short hike on the **Sentier des Ochres** in Roussillon, to see the ochre cliffs dotted with bright green pine trees.

Wine Tasting at a Co-op
Compare Luberon and Ventoux wines

Wine co-operatives are a great way for small farmers to pool their grapes and share the costs of turning them into wine. Historically a region full of small farmers, the Luberon's communities came together at the end of WWI to create cooperatives that have endured, and grown, over the years.

The oldest wine co-operative in the Vaucluse region is the **Cave de Bonnieux**, which includes Bonnieux, Goult, Roussillon, Lacoste and Gordes. The wine produced by these co-operatives is still delicious, and the sale price is often

WHERE TO EAT AROUND ROUSSILLON

Bar des Amis
Don't miss the Hot-Dog du Luberon or the grilled avocados in this bistrot de pays in Villars. €

Ocria
The local microbrewery in Rustrel with a tasting room to enjoy the five types of organic beer. €

Le Grappe de Raisin
Balcony in the centre of Roussillon with cafe fare like steak, housemade chips and Provençal aïoli. €€

Colorado Provençal, Rustrel

lower. Among the recommended wines are the Les Safres white wine (Luberon) and the Domaine Bastide de Rodon red wine (Ventoux).

The second-largest co-operative in the area is nearby: the **Cave du Luberon**. It celebrated its 100th anniversary in 2023 and offers the best white wine in the region, Les Bories, a Ventoux that's perfect for a light apéritif under the trees while snacking on local tapenade. Rosé drinkers can try Ô de Léthé, while red wine enthusiasts will appreciate the complexity of Les Promises.

While tasting, be sure to ask which vineyards have apéritif nights – it's a Luberon summer pastime to visit a vineyard at sunset, taste a glass of wine and take a bottle home to accompany dinner.

Visit Lesser-Known Perched Villages

Near the Petit Luberon

East of Apt, along the northern flanks of the Luberon, you'll find several lively villages tucked into the hillside. **Robion** is off the beaten path and less spectacular than some of the other villages in the region, which has helped keep a friend-

LUBERON VERSUS VENTOUX

Luberon wines are grown in sandy, limestone-rich soil, which gives the wines a light and fresh character. The main grape varieties grown in the Luberon are grenache, syrah and mourvèdre. The wines produced here are generally lower in tannins than those from the Ventoux. They often have notes of red fruit, herbs and spices.

Ventoux wines are grown in rocky soil, which provides excellent drainage and helps to concentrate the flavours of the grapes. The main grape varieties grown in the Ventoux are generally the same as in the Luberon, though because of the growing conditions, the wines produced here are fuller in body and higher in tannins. They often have notes of dark fruit, chocolate and leather.

🍸 VINEYARDS TO VISIT

Domaine de Marie
Elegance and luxury are the standard bearers here; the wines are as opulent as the environment.

Domaine des Cancélades
Independent winemakers with reasonable prices. Fresh apricots, cherries and table grapes, too.

Chateau la Canorgue
Near the Pont Julian, this vineyard was one of the first to go organic decades ago.

KRISZTIAN JUHASZ/SHUTTERSTOCK ©

Église Notre-Dame Dalidon

SUNSET VIEWS

Bistrot le 5
Watch the sunset with a fine cocktail in hand from this patio in Ménerbes. On clear days, you can see Mont Ventoux.

Église Notre-Dame Dalidon
Hike up to the top of Oppède-le-Vieux village and watch the sunset from the church steps. Take a peek behind you to see how the splashes of light change the colour of the building's exterior.

Domaine de La Citadelle Luberon
Let the vines show their true colours as the day slips away in this vineyard. This is the spot to enjoy the world through rosé-coloured glasses.

ly ambience alive here. The ancient theatre, dating back to Roman times, is a popular attraction for history buffs and hosts summer concerts. Nothing on the program? Visit the **Café de la Poste** during the summer for live music, good cocktails and people-watching.

On the flanks of a mountain, **Oppède-le-Vieux** peers over the valley. Park your car below the village and mosey up to **Le Petit Café**, a cosy spot located under the shade of trees, where visitors can enjoy a cup of coffee or a glass of wine.

The main attraction of Oppède is the walk along the old, strikingly narrow staircases up to the ruins of the **château** and the **Église Notre-Dame Dalidon**, which has been extensively restored. The walk is a bit steep, but the views from the top are well worth the effort. Along the way, visitors can admire the thick maquis that covers the mountainside. It's easy to imagine shepherds and their flocks passing through the dense vegetation.

This vegetation is part of the **Petit Luberon**, which is divided from the hills of the Grand Luberon to the east by a deep river canyon, the Combe de Lourmarin. Legend has it that the intricate folds of the mountains can be confusing, and many people have gotten lost here. However, with the right preparation and a good map, hiking in the Petit Luberon can be a rewarding experience.

On a not-too-hot day, walk from Robion to the Gorges de Badarel, which leads to **La Bergerie du Vallon du Colombier**. This well-preserved area shows how shepherds cared for their flocks.

South Luberon

South Luberon

The hot sun, rows of vineyards and dense villages define the South Luberon. The area tends to attract a chic vacation crowd, thanks to its proximity to Aix-en-Provence and the proliferation of excellent gourmet chefs who have taken up residence in the area. But there is an equilibrium here between chic tourism and down-to-earth activities. One of the standout markers of this equilibrium is the agro-ecology movement, spearheaded by renowned chef Nadia Sammut.

For those seeking a deeper connection with nature, a hike up to the Fôret des Cèdres is a must. This beautiful forest is filled with towering cedar trees and permits views of the surrounding countryside. Or get your hands dirty – ahem, colourful – learning about natural dyeing techniques at the Jardin des Plantes Tinctoriales in Lauris. And after a day of exploring the land and the bounty it offers, nothing beats a leisurely stroll through Lourmarin.

Eco-Conscious Dining

Women paving the way

Agroecology is taking root in the Luberon, as the local food community addresses the transition to a more sustainable dining experience. One of the standout restaurants leading the charge is **L'Auberge de la Fenière** in Cadenet, which has held a Michelin star since 1995. Chef Nadia Sammut is known for her innovative approach to cooking and her commitment to using fresh, local ingredients.

GETTING AROUND

If you're planning to explore the region, e-bikes and bicycles are great options. To visit smaller villages, however, a car is best. The Zou! bus lines 8, 9 and 19 connect the southern Luberon villages with Cavaillon, Apt and Aix-en-Provence.

☑ **TOP TIP**

Obtaining restaurant reservations is a local sport in the Luberon. If you want to go to a trendy restaurant, no matter its price point, book a table well in advance.

SOUTH LUBERON

Calavon
Plateau des
Claparèdes
St-Martin de Castillon
Saignon
Calavon
La Viguière
Cereste
Parc Naturel
Régional
du Luberon
Bonnieux
Buoux
Sivergues
Auribeau
Vitrolles-
en-Luberon
Mourre Nègre
Montagne
de Luberon
Le Grand
Luberon
Cabrières
d'Aigues
La Bastide-
des-Jourdans
Cucuron
Vaugines
Saint Martin de la Brasque
Lourmarin
Lauris
L'Auberge
de la Fenière
Ansouis
Jardin des
Plantes
Tinctoriales
Cadenet
La Tour-d'Aigues
La Tour-
d'Aigues
Mirabeau
St-Paul-
lès-Durance
Pertuis
Durance
Le Puy-St-Réparade
N
0
0
8 km
4 mile

NICE WHEELS

Looking to add some extra flair to your road trip? Why not rent a classic car for the day from Yes Provence (yesprovence.com) and ride in style. While you may not have access to modern amenities like air conditioning, the classic charm of a Citroën 2CV, Méhari, VW bug or even a VW minibus will more than make up for it. And if you've been dreaming of cruising around in a classic Renault 4L, Voitures Passion (voiturespassion.com) in Aix-en-Provence has got you covered. Plus, with its convenient delivery service, you won't even have to worry about picking it up yourself.

L'Auberge de la Fenière is oriented around vegetarian and gluten-free dishes, and Chef Sammut uses the restaurant's garden to supply many of her ingredients. Sammut's commitment to sustainability and local agriculture has earned her recognition as one of the pioneers of the agroecology movement in the region. Expect a dining experience that is both delicious and environmentally conscious. The restaurant's menu changes frequently to reflect the seasonal availability of ingredients, and the dishes are designed to showcase local flavours.

Lourmarin's Golden Hour

Go for a cocktail walk

As you pass through the Luberon massif via the deep, cliff-lined Combe de Lourmarin, the first village you'll strike is **Lourmarin**. Once a quiet farming town, it's now a chichi place, its streets lined with upmarket homewares shops and boutiques. Literary pilgrims might also want to peep into the town cemetery, the last resting place of Albert Camus (1913–60), who was living nearby when he was killed in a car accident in 1960.

If you've got dinner reservations here, you might as well go out for a pre-dinner drink too. **La Maison Café** is a laid-back and intimate spot with classic cocktails at good prices. It's a great place for a spritz. **Le Bar du Moulin** is the chicest spot in town for a pre-dinner drink. It offers plenty of creative cocktails, but the homemade mojito with Provençal citrus is a must-try that will reinvent the drink for you.

A WALK IN THE FÔRET DES CÈDRES

The **Fôret des Cèdres** sprawls across a vast plateau in the Luberon mountain range. Established from seeds that originated from the Middle Atlas Mountains in North Africa, the forest is a testament to the beauty and diversity of nature. To explore the area on foot, start at the car park located at the northern end of the ❶ **chemin de Recaute**, northwest of the town of Lauris. The walk is approximately 14km long and involves a total elevation gain of about 500m. It's a moderate trek that takes around four hours to complete at a leisurely pace.

As you begin your hike, follow the signs for the Fôret des Cèdres. To start climbing up, you can take the ❷ **Combe de Recaute**. During the hike, the path sweeps around and runs through the ❸ **Vallon du Gros Ubac**, which is the shaded side of the mountain. At ❹ **Vallon de Lare**, the path splits, and hikers turn right to climb up to the Fôret des Cèdres. Here begins the moment when you will be surrounded by towering trees and the invigorating scent of cedar.

Once you reach the ridge, follow the ❺ **Sentier de la Fôret des Cèdres**, which winds through the impressive and shady forest. As you begin to descend, with ❻ **Vallon de Sanguinette** on your left, the rocky path has a few technical switchbacks. At the split for Vallon de Lare, continue hiking straight south. You will see two paths: one on the left and one on the right. Take the left path down, which hugs a steep hill covered in scrubby forest. You'll pass ❼ **Vallon de Roumias** on your way back down to the parking lot.

Moris Restaurant
In Cucuron, Moris has staked out a space as a top table in the Luberon. Dine on the cool patio where daily specials might include sole fish with sweet potatoes and passionfruit. €€€

Matcha Restaurant
Cucuron's modern restaurant is health-oriented but still satisfying. Vegetable Wellington might be the *plat du jour*, or it could be a homemade hotdog. Either way it's sure to be good. Excellent coffees as well. €€

Lou Pebre D'Ail
Squash tartes, butcher's choice with bearnaise sauce and vanilla panna cotta with fruit coulis – the meals in this little Lauris restaurant are hearty and rich, but oh-so good. €€

Learn to Dye
A garden of colours

The only garden of its kind in Europe, the **Jardin des Plantes Tinctoriales** is dedicated to plants that can be used for dyeing, cosmetics and nutrition. It was founded in Lauris in 2000 by Michel Garcia, a renowned chemist and natural dye expert, with the purpose of preserving traditional knowledge and dyeing techniques.

Today managed by Les Amis du Jardin, the garden includes a vast range of plants such as woad, madder and weld, which have been used for centuries to create a range of colours. The gardens are meticulously designed, and visitors can witness the growing process of these plants and learn about their history and uses. The centre also offers workshops on natural dyeing techniques, where visitors can learn about the process of creating dyes and try their hand at dyeing their own fabrics. The centre is open for visits; for an extra €6 per person it's possible to tour the gardens with a guide (minimum five people).

Every June, the town of Lauris comes alive with plant-based colour, and workshops, guided visits, games, film screenings and live music bring an air of summer festivities to the village and garden.

Road Trip through the Hills
Queue up your Provence playlist

Just have a day in the South Luberon? Rent a vintage car and hit the road to discover the châteaux of the South Luberon and the unique character traits of each village. Start in chic **Lourmarin** – you can't choose a bad cafe as long as it's in the centre with good people-watching. Get the car in gear and make for **Ansouis**. The the part-fortified village's elegant history is still felt in the air today – Ansouis was previously a summer residence for the nobility of Aix-en-Provence. Ramparts, watchtowers and gateways ring the village's old centre, and it's also home to one of the rare Luberon château that's open to the public; reservations are required.

Next on the route is **La Tour-d'Aigues** and its Renaissance château, which today houses a faience (clay pottery) museum. Pick up local olive oil nearby at **À l'ombre de l'olivier** boutique. **Mirabeau** has a fascinating fortress, but it's more famous as the backdrop for the cult film *Manon des Sources* (1986). If you watch one French film before or during your trip to Provence, this is the one. It's based on the novel *L'Eau des collines* (1963) by local writer Marcel Pagnol. In

WHERE TO STAY IN SOUTH LUBERON

La Maison de Lourmarin
Chic, comfortable rooms in this small house in the centre of town. Laundry and kitchen available. €€

Domaine de Fontenille
Bathed in decadence, with a touch of well-being. Friday nights are for BBQs in the garden. €€€

L'Auberge de la Fenière
Comfortable rural hotel linked to the Michelin-starred restaurant and farm of chef Nadia Sammut. €€€

Mirabeau

MARKET DAYS IN THE LUBERON

No need to wait until the weekend to visit a produce market. With so many villages in the vicinity, there is one every single day of the week. Prices are not always cheaper than the supermarket, but the products often come from nearby and are frequently sold straight from the farmer. Think like a chef: choose one of the in-season ingredients and make it the centerpiece of your meal.

Monday:
Lauris, Cadenet

Tuesday:
Lacoste, Cucuron, La Tour d'Aigues

Wednesday:
Coustellet (summer nights)

Thursday:
Mirabeau, Ménerbes

Friday:
Lourmarin, Bonnieux

Saturday:
Petit Palais, Apt

Sunday:
Ansouis, Coustellet, Puyvert

the centre of town sits a statue of Manon on the edge of the fountain. Grab a bite at **Chez Luni** next door if you're feeling hungry.

You'll have to head northward and inward to reach **Vitrolles-en-Luberon**, last on the list. Less celebrated than other villages on this route, the château here is under renovation, but there is a sweet hikers B&B named **Le Vieux Presbytère** that serves simple fare and cool drinks.

WHERE TO EAT SWEETS IN THE SOUTH LUBERON

Pâtisserie Volpert
Inventive desserts like *le mistral,* a swirly treat with walnut ganache, caramel and *chou* pastry. In Ansouis. €

Chez Jarry
In the heart of Cavaillon, this cafe and pâtisserie is the regional go-to for Yule logs and summer desserts. €

La Maison de Gibassir
Come to Lourmarin to try a *gibassir,* the anise-flavoured holiday cookie, or a caramel-apple *lourmarinoise.* €

Alpes-de-Haute-Provence

FROM ALPINE VALLEYS TO FIELDS OF LAVENDER

The Plateau de Valensole, Gorges du Verdon and the southern Alps enchant photographers and the outdoorsy alike with their uniquely dramatic landscapes.

The Alpes-de-Haute-Provence is a largely rural region, extending from the gentle hills of the eastern edge of the Luberon all the way up to the jagged high peaks of the Alps along the Italian border. Visitors tend to concentrate in the adventure-rich Gorges du Verdon and the sunflower- and lavender-speckled fields of the Plateau de Valensole in the southern part of the *département,* but there's so much more to discover. Try out rural village life in the Banon region, enjoying goat cheese preserved in chestnut leaves. Gaze at distant galaxies from one of the observatories; the skies here are some of the darkest in France. Or reach for the stars with a via ferrata excursion in Digne-les-Bains,

followed by a treatment at the town's thermal baths to soothe sore muscles.

Cloaked in snow well into springtime, the mountains of Haute-Provence are divided by six main valleys, connected by some of the highest and most hair-raising road passes anywhere in Europe – an absolute must for road-trippers and outdoor enthusiasts. Head up north to the Ubaye Valley for some of the region's most unforgettable scenery. The uncrowded and unpretentious ski resorts here are great for families or adventurers in the winter, and in summer, the seven mountain passes that lead out of the valley are busy with cyclists and cars following the hairpin switchbacks all the way up to the top of the world.

CACTUS CREATIVE STUDIO/STOCKSY UNITED ®

Opposite: Gorges du Verdon (p237); Inset: Lavender fields (p240)

THE MAIN AREAS

DIGNE-LES-BAINS
Healing waters
and hikes.
p230

GORGES DU VERDON
Outdoor adventure and
lavender fields.
p237

UBAYE VALLEY
Ski resorts and
mountain vibes.
p243

Find Your Way

The A51, which links Aix-en-Provence with Grenoble, is the closest highway and connects to Digne-les-Bains via the N85. The N202, west of Digne, provides access to several valleys and connects to Nice, a few hours southeast.

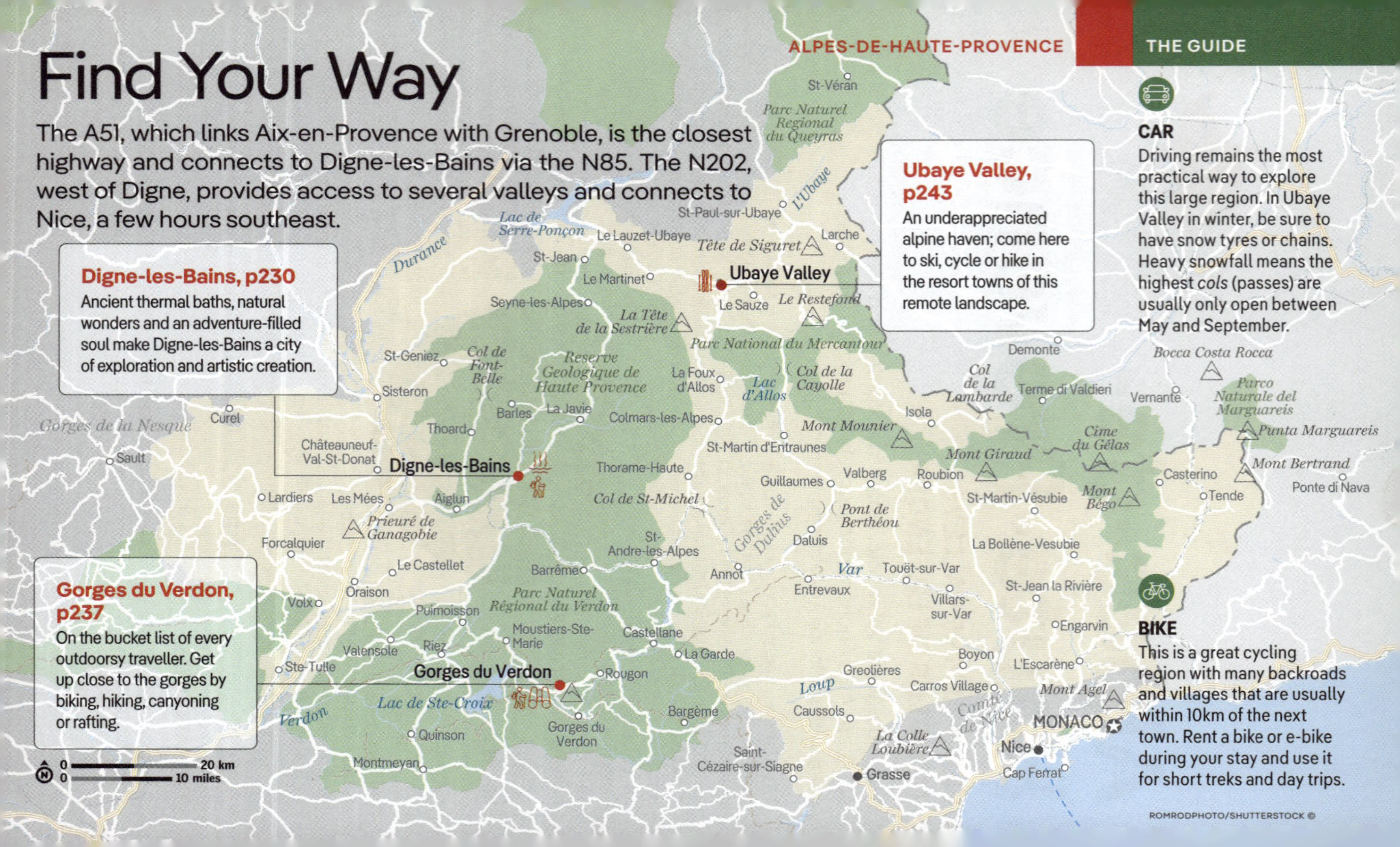

CAR

Driving remains the most practical way to explore this large region. In Ubaye Valley in winter, be sure to have snow tyres or chains. Heavy snowfall means the highest cols (passes) are usually only open between May and September.

BIKE

This is a great cycling region with many backroads and villages that are usually within 10km of the next town. Rent a bike or e-bike during your stay and use it for short treks and day trips.

Ubaye Valley, p243

An underappreciated alpine haven; come here to ski, cycle or hike in the resort towns of this remote landscape.

Digne-les-Bains, p230

Ancient thermal baths, natural wonders and an adventure-filled soul make Digne-les-Bains a city of exploration and artistic creation.

Gorges du Verdon, p237

On the bucket list of every outdoorsy traveller. Get up close to the gorges by biking, hiking, canyoning or rafting.

0 — 20 km
0 — 10 miles

ROMRODPHOTO/SHUTTERSTOCK ©

Gorges du Verdon (p237)

Plan Your Time

Short on time? Hit the Gorges du Verdon for an outdoor adventure or make for the high peaks in the Ubaye Valley.

Pressed for Time

● Hike along the ridge above **Moustiers-Ste-Marie** (p242) and visit the ceramic workshops.

● Spend the next day exploring the **Gorges du Verdon** (p237) on foot, raft or by bicycle.

● In summer, pass through the **Plateau de Valensole** (p240) to see the lavender in full bloom.

● During the other seasons, visit the outdoor **Réserve Géologique de Haute-Provence** (p234) for a journey back to the time of the dinosaurs.

Five Days to Travel Around

● Stay a night or two in **Banon** (p235) to enjoy the village life, going for hikes during the day and spending the evenings **watching the stars** (p234).

● Head to **Digne-les-Bains** (p230) for a night and soak in the **thermal baths** (p230) or try the **via ferrata** (p231).

● Drive up to **Barcelonnette** (p243) to explore the Ubaye Valley: cycle, raft or hike your way through this amazing landscape.

Seasonal Highlights

SPRING

Spring varies by altitude: always check the temperatures and snowpack before you set off.

SUMMER

Lavender everywhere: visit the Plateau de Valensole; by July, the mountain passes in the Ubaye Valley open for cyclists and cars.

AUTUMN

Hiking the Gorges du Verdon in early autumn is the perfect time to admire the canyons and changing seasons.

WINTER

Hit the slopes in the Ubaye Valley. Ski on- or off-piste for adventure without the crowds and glitz of the northern Alps.

Digne-les-Bains

Digne-les-Bains

Sitting at an altitude of 600m, the town of Digne-les-Bains is famous for its healing thermal baths. Napoléon's soldiers were often sent here to recover after campaigns, and a mystical healing spirit hovers over the city. Aside from the thermal baths, travellers can visit the home and association of the intrepid explorer Alexandra David-Néel, who found solace and inspiration here between her pioneering travels, particularly in Tibet.

A 30-minute walk from the centre, the via ferrata along the Rocher de Neuf Heures offers a thrilling ascent and breathtaking panoramas. Work up an appetite and enjoy regional cuisine upon your return to earth: *daube* (beef stew), *tourtons* (fried pastries) or Sisteron's celebrated lamb.

In August, Digne-les-Bains becomes even more magical during the annual Corso de Lavande, which celebrates the beauty and fragrance of the fields surrounding the town. The festival culminates with a parade through town, when locals dress in traditional Provençal costumes and floats are decorated in lavender.

Thermal Cures

Relax in the baths

The town's reputation for natural healing dates back to ancient times; it's believed that the Romans were the first to discover the healing properties of the local **Thermes de Digne-les-Bains**. Throughout history, the town has welcomed visitors seeking relief from a variety of illnesses, including respiratory problems, rheumatism and skin conditions.

Even Napoléon's soldiers recognised the benefits of the town's thermal waters, and many were sent here to recover after their campaigns. Today, visitors can experience the same restorative powers of the waters with a variety of affordable options. The mini-cure programs, which last four days, are a good starting

GETTING AROUND

Digne is one of the most useful hubs for bus transport in the region. The Zou! bus service has frequent connections to nearby towns and cities, with direct lines to Aix-en-Provence and Barcelonnette.

☑ **TOP TIP**

Cruise around Digne-les-Bains on an e-bike rental from Stations Bees. You'll have the freedom to discover the diverse landscape at your own pace, from the valleys and towering cliffs to lush forests and fragrant maquis. It's an exhilarating way to experience the natural beauty of the region.

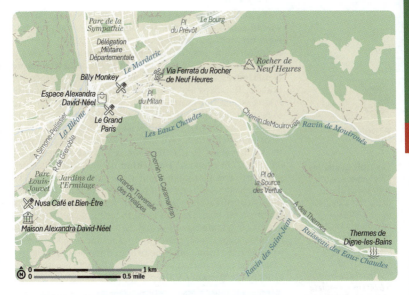

point and are considered a medical treatment. Day trips to the spa are also available, with prices starting at €18 for a half-day, with the possibility of adding on a massage or other spa treatments. The springs are located 3.5km east of town.

In the Footsteps of Alexandra David-Néel

A feminist adventure pioneer

Alexandra David-Néel (1868–1969) was a remarkable explorer, writer and Buddhist convert who lived the last decade of her life in Digne-les-Bains. One of the first Westerners to visit Tibet (1916) and to reach the forbidden city of Lhasa (1924), she accomplished these remarkable journeys by disguising herself as a beggar and monk. Her knowledge of Tibetan and her meetings with the 13th Dalai Lama and the Panchen Lama opened the door for Westerners to learn more about the region's culture and religion. While living in Digne, she wrote several books, including *My Journey to Lhasa* and *Magic and Mystery in Tibet,* which are still read and admired today.

English-speakers can visit the **Maison Alexandra David-Néel**, which has a museum and garden. Bilingual travellers shouldn't hesitate to book a guided tour of the villa itself. In the centre of town is the **Espace Alexandra David-Néel**, which has an excellent book and Tibetan artisanal goods shop. Proceeds go to support villagers in Tibet.

Scale the Heights

Via ferrata fun

How many towns do you know that have walking access to a via ferrata? Developed by the Italians during WWII, via ferrata routes are a mix of mountaineering, high-ropes course and

BEST RESTAURANTS IN DIGNE-LES-BAINS

Le Grand Paris
Enjoy a menu that showcases regional flavours and modern twists, all in a cosy and intimate setting. €€

Billy Monkey
Chow down on a variety of excellent burgers: there's beef, of course, but also chicken filet, pork ribs and falafel. €

Nusa Café et Bien-Être
Vegetarians rule at the Nusa. Whether you stop in for breakfast, lunch or Sunday brunch, this cafe has fresh, seasonally healthy options to enjoy on the terrace. €

PANORAMIC VIEWS

Les Trois Chapelles
This intermediate 3.4km loop climbs to the three chapels overlooking the city, offering access to the Cousson range and the Trois Évêchés range.

St-Pancrace
A 6.1km intermediate out-and-back hike that leads to the 13th-century St-Pancrace Chapel, which overlooks the Durance Valley.

Trou de St-Martin
A 10.8km expert hike leaving from the Forestry Office du Serre inside the Réserve Géologique de Haute-Provence. Follows a ridge until reaching the 'hole' of St-Martin. The sun passes through the hole in the rock twice a year.

rock climbing. If you love the mountains, this is a great, safe way to access huge views and butterflies-in-your-stomach exposure, without needing to master a lifetime's worth of technical know-how. In Digne-les-Bains, the centre of town is just a 30-minute walk from the **Via Ferrata du Rocher de Neuf Heures**. Climbers ascend a mix of steel rungs, suspension bridges, Tyroleans and the sheer rock face on their breath-taking ascent. Don't worry though, your harness is clipped in to metal cables the entire way, making the whole adventure a safe outing (though you still need to be in good shape).

For those with their own harness, helmet and other gear, the via ferrata is free. Otherwise, rent a kit at the tourist office (€17) or the local **Decathlon** outdoor store. It's also possible to arrange a guided tour at the tourist office. If you've never done it before, or even if you've only done it a few times, this is definitely the way to go, as you don't want to risk making a mistake. The cliff is south facing, so get out in the morning or late afternoon to avoid the heat of the day. Essentials include grippy shoes, gloves and water and snacks to keep you energised throughout the two- to three-hour adventure.

Once you reach the top, you'll be rewarded with breathtaking views of the **Durance Valley**.

FRANCOIS ROUX/SHUTTERSTOCK ©

Durance Valley

WHERE TO SLEEP IN DIGNE-LES-BAINS

Le Richelme
This calm hotel is connected to the thermal complex; it's possible to book half-board. **€€€**

Hotel et Pension Village Gaïa
Small hotel for up to 15 people in a 19th-century manor; it's possible to book half-board. **€€**

Ce Nid d'Aigle
Gîte (guesthouse) perched above Digne-les-Bains, with direct access to the hiking trails. **€€**

Réserve Géologique
de Haute-Provence
Digne-les-Bains
Banon
Les Mées
Revest-des-Brousses
St-Michel-l'Observatoire

Beyond
Digne-les-Bains

Each village here has a distinct personality – the challenge is to find which one best suits you.

Get out of Digne-les-Bains and into the rural lifestyle. From the rock formations that tower over Les Mées to the dinosaur footprints in the Réserve Géologique de Haute-Provence, the history of the landscape is everywhere you look. For a more celestial experience, head to St-Michel-l'Observatoire, where visitors can stargaze and marvel at the wonders of the universe. And for a taste of local flavour, make sure to visit the dynamic village of Banon, known for its famous cheese made from goat's milk and wrapped in chestnut leaves. Go for a morning hike to work up an appetite, follow it up with an indulgent countryside lunch and then settle in for a *sieste* beneath a shady chestnut tree.

Hike the Pénitents Trail

A curious landmark

Les Pénitents is a hiking trail that traverses the landscape above the village of **Les Mées**, 26km west of Digne. The hike takes up to 3½ hours, is well marked and begins in the centre of the village. Along the way, you'll pass a long and striking band of puddingstone (conglomerate) cliffs, which formed millions of years ago through sedimentation. It looks like a bunch of riverstone cemented together.

If you prefer the mythical explanation, the cliff is made up of the monks of the Montagne de Lure, who were petrified by St Donat during the Saracen invasions as punishment for falling in love.

The hike takes you through a varied landscape, including dense forests, rolling hills and rocky outcrops, and has striking views of the village and the surrounding countryside. There's parking near the trailhead.

GETTING AROUND

If you've got the time, the roads are great for biking and the villages are usually no more than 10km apart. Otherwise, a car is best.

☑ TOP TIP

Spend a few days outside Digne-les-Bains. The slower pace of life here is good for taking a breather.

VILLAGE DINING

Le Bistrot Gaby
The sister of the nearby Bonne Étape. Come here for local and seasonal dishes without old-world pretension; wonderful attention to detail. Near St-Auban. **€€**

La Trattoria
Outside Malijai, this pizzeria has great pies and frequent live music. Stop on a road trip or come for dinner if staying nearby. **€**

Les Vielles Casseroles
It's a bit in the middle of nowhere near Châteauredon, true, but they do have a great welcome. It's isolated from the road, with a quiet terrace and homemade lasagne. **€€**

Marvel at the Tracks of Time

Explore an open-air geology park

Into rocks? Then **Réserve Géologique de Haute-Provence** should be on your list. Limestone cliffs, volcanic rocks and sedimentary layers are present in the region and highlighted throughout the park, which encompasses 18 sites. The park also contains several important palaeontological sites, with fossils dating back to the Triassic period. Just 3km north of Digne is the impressive **Dalle aux Ammonites** (Ammonite Slab), containing over 1500 fossilised ammonites.

Early dinosaurs once roamed here and their footprints are preserved in the sedimentary rock. Visitors interested in exploring the area can book a guided tour in English. To visit the entire park, you'll need a car and full day.

Need something more recent than a million years ago to hold your attention? Across from the Reserve Géologique, you'll find works from the **Route d'Arte Contemporain**, a Franco-Italian initiative that brings contemporary art to rural spaces.

Stargazing in Provence

Count the shooting stars

Clear skies and low light pollution combine to make the Alpes-de-Haute-Provence a destination for stargazing. One of the best places to observe the distant galaxies is at the observatory outside the village of **St-Michel-l'Observatoire**, a scientific research centre that is 65km southwest of Digne and open to the public. Here, you can join guided tours and peer at the stars through telescopes with the help of experienced astronomers. English-speaking nights are held in the summer.

Another option is to visit the **Observatoire Astronomique de Puimichel**, where you can learn about the workings of the observatory as well as explore the night sky with telescopes.

For those who prefer to stargaze on their own, clear skies across the region offer plenty of opportunities to see the stars, and some planets, like Venus and Jupiter, with the naked eye.

Walk Up an Appetite

Small village character, big city quality

The plan: hike to work up an appetite. The starting point: the village of **Revest-des-Brousses**, 62km west of Digne and home to the **Lupin Blanc**, a *bistrot de pays* (a rural restaurant where great-value meals are made with local produce). The well-marked hike takes between two to three hours and covers

 VILLAGES BEYOND DIGNE-LES-BAINS

St-Étienne-les-Orgues
At the foot of the Lure mountain, small village with a cafe and easy access to the hills.

Puimichel
Sleepy village near an observatory with a *bistrot de pays* and friendly locals.

Entrevennes
Dense little hill-village with one restaurant and surrounded by lavender fields.

Dalle aux Ammonites, Réserve Géologique de Haute-Provence

BRUNO M PHOTOGRAPHIE/SHUTTERSTOCK ©

VILLAGE HOPPING

True to its *paysan* (farmer) past, the western part of the Alpes-de-Haute Provence is marked by frequent villages with tight and tidy centres, surrounded by rolling fields. This makes the region perfect for village-hopping by electric bike or car – usually you're never any more than 10km away from the next village.

From Banon, it's easy to explore the perched village of **Simiane-la-Rotonde**, the flourishing **Jardin de l'Abbaye de Valsaintes**, or a bit further down the road, the mysterious **Lure mountain**, with its family-friendly ski station (when there is enough snow).

All year round, each village helps you to explore Provençal culture, countryside and gastronomy.

BISTROT DE PAYS

The Alpes-de-Haute-Provence has the highest number of *bistrots de pays,* which play an important role in keeping small villages alive. *Bistrots de pays* can be found elsewhere in Provence, too. Outside Menton in Castillon, try the **L'HarTmonie** (p73).

about 13km of rolling terrain, weaving in and out of forests and fields. While on the trail, hikers might spot birds of prey circling above the fields. The loop starts and ends at the town square, leading to Aubenas-les-Alpes before circling back to Revest-des-Brousses for a much-anticipated lunch. The *bistrot* offers a nice selection of local spirits and a fresh menu every day. Reservations are recommended.

Cheese and Chestnut Trees in Banon

Visit on market day

There is no cheese more cottage-core than Banon AOP, a soft goat cheese wrapped in chestnut leaves. Named after the small village of **Banon**, the cheese was made as early as the Middle Ages, though it may be older still. A typically French story attributes the death of Roman emperor Antoninus Pius to indigestion: allegedly, he gorged himself on too much Banon. A strong flavour radiates from this raw goat's milk cheese, but the most distinctive feature is the packaging. The cheese

BANON CHEESE DIRECT FROM THE FARM

Le Petit Troutouil Farm
Located 7km from Banon in Simiaine-la-Rotonde, Valérie still milks her goats by hand each day at 6.30pm. Buy the AOP Banon cheese on the farm or at the Banon market on Saturdays.

Fromagerie GAEC du Grand Jas
Near St-Michel-l'Observatoire, this farm shop is open 8am to noon and 3pm to 7pm daily. In summer it's possible to organise group tours.

Fromagerie Domaine de la Haute Lèbre
In Revest-du-Bion, pick up Banon cheese and other fresh and aged goat cheeses.

Banon AOP cheese wrapped in chestnut leaves

is preserved by wrapping it in chestnut leaves that have been soaked in *eau-de-vie,* a type of brandy made from fruit.

Banon cheese is typically only produced during the summer months, when the goats are grazing in the lush mountain pastures. The cheese is then left to mature for several weeks before it is ready to be enjoyed. It is often served as a dessert cheese, paired with fresh fruit and a crisp white wine.

The cheese's fame has likely helped keep the village of Banon so dynamic, despite its isolation. The weekly market is a must-visit, taking place every Tuesday and Saturday morning in the town square. Here, visitors can find fresh produce, artisanal cheeses and handmade crafts from local vendors. For the ambience of an old-fashioned French cafe, stop by **Café de l'Union**. Wine lovers should try **Les Vins au Vert**, a well-curated wine bar that offers a selection of local and international wines.

The village is also home to the popular blue bookshop, **Librairie le Bleuet,** which is a must-visit for bibliophiles. Each May, the village hosts a Fête du Fromage and a literature festival, which is sure to be a good time.

GIONO'S PROVENCE
Provençal writer Jean Giono had a farm in **Forcalquier** (p214), where he wrote his novel *Le Hussard sur le Toit* (The Horseman on the Roof). Just 20km east of Revest and 25km southeast of Banon, the farm is now a B&B.

WHERE TO EAT BEYOND DIGNE-LES-BAINS

La Chouette Gourmand
With a view over Digne-les-Bains, this family restaurant fuses Provençal, Corsican and Armenian cuisine. €€

Les Lavandins
Chic *bistrot de pays,* with *pieds et paquets* (trotters and tripe) and *alouettes sans tête* (rolled beef). €€

D'Ici et d'Ailleurs
Simple, hearty fare from here and there in the village of St-Étienne-les-Orgues. €€

Gorges du Verdon

Gorges du Verdon

For sheer, jaw-dropping drama, few sights in Provence can match the Gorges du Verdon. It's at the top of many visitors' to-see lists, and rightly so. To get the most out of a trip here, pick an outdoor activity and come prepared to immerse yourself in and around the gorges. Hikers will love the trails on the canyon floor, and will certainly get their feet wet. Cyclists can challenge themselves with a steep climb along the balcony road, followed by an exhilarating descent. And adventure seekers will be forced to make some tough decisions: do you want to go canyoning, climbing or whitewater rafting? If that's too much excitement, opt for wildlife watching.

The main gorge begins at Rougon, near the confluence of the Verdon and Jabron Rivers. The most useful jumping-off points are Moustiers Ste-Marie in the west, and Castellane in the east.

Cycle the Balcony Road

Climb the Verdon heights

Cycling the **Balcony Road** (Route des Crêtes) above the -century is probably about as good as it gets. Originally built as a 24km loop road for tourists to drive from **La Palud-sur-Verdon**, the park service is now beginning to limit the number of cars per day and on special occasions the route is reserved for cyclists. All the more reason to visit by bike. E-bike rentals are available from **Verdon E-bike** in La Palud. Pedalling the balcony road (655m of elevation gain), cyclists will be looking down on the turquoise waters at the heart of the Gorges du Verdon. As you cycle along the route, keep an eye out for vultures flying high above the cliffs. The best time to cycle the route is in the spring or autumn, when the temperatures are cooler and there are fewer tourists – in winter a section of the road is closed.

GETTING AROUND

Traffic gets crazy in the Verdon during high season. Best to park your car as soon as possible in Moustiers-Ste-Marie or La Palud and get around by bike, foot or raft. Bus 450 runs from Moustiers-Ste-Marie through La Palud to the departure point of many hikes, and on to Castellane. Hikers might reserve also the Navette Blanc Martel (navette. parcduverdon.fr) for drop-off and pick-up at the start and exit points of the famous hike of the same name.

☑ **TOP TIP**

Consider camping during high season. Evening temperatures are comfortable and the views from your tent can be out of this world.

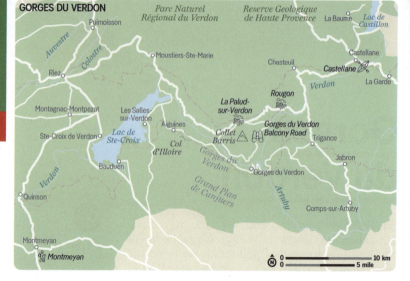

Hiking the Basses Gorges du Verdon

The canyons up close

For those who love hiking, the **Basses Gorges du Verdon** is a classic route that promises up-close discovery of the canyons from the valley floor. The parking lot for the trail is just after the village of **Montmeyan**, about 37km south of Moustiers – this is a totally different direction from access to the Balcony Road. Expect to spend around three to four hours on this 12km hike. Inexperienced trekkers and kids can come along, but know that there are a few technical sections, including a passage through a tunnel. Expect to get your feet wet. Summer hikers should aim to be on the trail before 9am. Bring a picnic and plenty of water.

Dozens of other blazed trails traverse the wild countryside around Castellane and Moustiers. Tourist offices carry the excellent, English-language *Canyon du Verdon*, detailing 28 walks, as well as maps of five principal walks.

Canyoning in the Gorges du Verdon

Follow the river's flow

There is no better place in France to try **canyoning**. If you've never done it before, you're in for a treat: expect all the fun of a water park, but in a gorgeous natural landscape where you can get up close and personal with the gorge along every bend in the river. The tourism office at Moustiers-Ste-Marie is a good place to book a tour.

Participants navigate through the river canyon by jumping, sliding and rappelling (abseiling) down waterfalls and rocky terrain. Most trips are a half-day. A bathing suit and grippy shoes are all that's needed – your guides will provide wetsuits, harnesses, helmets and rope.

While canyoning does require a certain level of physical fitness and agility, it is suitable for beginners and experienced adventurers alike. Guides will provide instruction on proper techniques and safety measures, and will tailor each experience to the skill level of the group.

Whitewater Rafting

A splash of adrenaline

Rafting on the Verdon River is an exciting adventure for thrill-seekers of all levels. From April to June, water levels provide an exhilarating ride downstream. Rapids range from Class I to Class IV – or, to put it another way, from flat water (beginners) to the gnarliest of rapids (experts). Most departures leave from the village of **Castellane**, at the gorges' eastern edge. Book at least a week ahead of time with a rafting company like **Yeti Rafting**.

Requirements differ depending on the difficulty of the route: easier options have a minimum age of seven, while more extreme trips require participants to be at least 16. Everyone needs to be able to swim.

WHY I LOVE THE GORGES DU VERDON

Ashley Parsons, writer

Despite the Gorges de Verdon being on nearly everyone's bucket list, and despite the bumper-to-bumper traffic on the main road during summer, I love that it's still possible to explore, get lost, explore, and get lost all over again in the Verdon.

Between the canyons, the hiking trails, and the area beyond the canyons, each time I visit it feels like I discover something new. The air is clean, the people are kind and, inevitably, I leave the Verdon more centred and invigorated than when I arrived.

CHRIS HELLIER/GETTY IMAGES ©

Rafting, Verdon River

WHERE TO EAT NEAR THE GORGES DU VERDON

Ferme Ste-Cécile
Enjoy country specialities like slow-roasted chicken in between the Gorges and Moustiers-Ste-Marie. €€

Chalet de la Maline
Restaurant attached to the Club Alpin Français, with a terrace overlooking the gorges plus local beer. €

Chez Steph
A snack joint in Rougon with hip decor and a relaxed vibe. Personal pizzas, cheese plates, soft drinks and beer. €

Beyond
Gorges du Verdon

Visit the most famous lavender fields in the world on the high plateau above the Gorges du Verdon.

While the Plateau de Valensole is the most famous spot for lavender fields, the charming village of **Moustiers-Ste-Marie** is a laid-back chic destination. Known for its iconic chapel perched high on a cliff, Moustiers-Ste-Marie offers much more than just lavender fields and stunning views. The village is also home to a thriving ceramics industry, with shops and studios lining the narrow streets.

And for those seeking a more active experience, a hike to the star above the village is a challenging but rewarding detour. Meanwhile, the Plateau de Valensole offers an exciting opportunity to explore sustainable agriculture by visiting an organic lavender distillery.

Sustainable Lavender Visits

A picture of lavender's future

Dive into the new face of ecologically responsible lavender production by visiting an organic lavender farm on the **Plateau de Valensole**. To start with, look for the lavender fields that have let golden grass grow up between the rows of purple – these farms are doing their part to preserve the soil for the next generation. Many farms are open year-round to guests, but run special tours during the harvest season. And no visit would be complete without trying some lavender-based products

GETTING AROUND

The Zou! bus service runs regular lines between Moustiers-Ste-Marie, Marseille, Manosque and Nice. Visiting the Plateau de Valensole by bike is lovely but should be avoided in the middle of the day in summer because of the heat.

☑ **TOP TIP**

The lavender harvest can start as early as 1 July, so to be safe, plan to come mid- to late June.

straight from the source, such as essential oils, soaps and perfumes produced on-site using sustainable methods.

Practically begging for aesthetic photoshoots, the lavender fields of Valensole are usually the highlight of a photography tour of Provence. Visit in late June or early July, but no later. During this time, the fields are alive with colour and fragrance, providing a stunning backdrop for your photos. To get the perfect shot, you'll have to get up early – sunrise has the longest 'soft-light' period, which reduces shadows and harsh light.

Don't go tromping in the fields, but tread carefully between rows – these are precious crops for local farmers. What to wear? Consider colours that will complement the lavender fields. Soft pastels, earthy tones and neutral colours work well in this setting. Avoid wearing bright colours that may clash with the lavender or draw too much attention away from the landscape's natural beauty.

LAVENDER FAR AND WIDE

For more perfectly symmetric rows of lavender, check out the village of **Sault** (p196) in the Vaucluse and the **Plateau des Claparèdes** (p213) in the Luberon.

LACS DE STE-CROIX & DE QUINSON

The largest of the lakes in Parc National Régional du Verdon, **Lac de Ste-Croix** (southwest of Moustiers Ste-Marie) is a reservoir formed in 1974. It has scads of watercraft to rent – windsurfers, canoes, kayaks – try L'Étoile. Pretty Bauduen sits on its southeastern banks.

Lac de Quinson lies at the southernmost foot of the lower Gorges du Verdon. In the village of Quinson, taxidermy-rich **Musée de la Préhistoire des Gorges du Verdon** explores the gorges' natural and archaeological treasures. From March to October, it organises monthly expeditions to the **Grotte de la Baume Bonne**, a prehistoric cave. Several campsites dot the lake shores, such as the Domaine du Petit Lac, a large activity-oriented campsite.

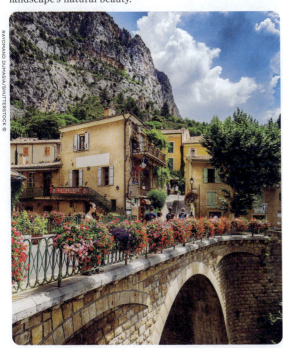

Moustiers-Ste-Marie

RAYOMAND DUMASIA/SHUTTERSTOCK ©

CHAPELLE NOTRE-DAME DE BEAUVOIR

Flanked by two cliffs, the Chapelle Notre-Dame de Beauvoir is located in a peaceful area above Moustiers-Ste-Marie. Built between the 12th and 16th centuries, the style is partially Roman, partially Gothic.

Follow a winding staircase up to the chapel for epic views over the surrounding plains; it's about a 20-minute climb from the centre of town.

Allegedly, the chapel has special powers. There were a number of cases recorded in the 17th-century of villagers bringing stillborn infants here, only for them to come back to life long enough to receive their baptism.

On 8 September, Mass at 5am celebrates the nativity of the Virgin Mary, followed by flutes, drums and breakfast on the square.

Moustiers-Ste-Marie from Above

A kingdom of cliffs, lavender and canyons

Suspended between the cliff walls above **Moustiers-Ste-Marie** is a golden star. Legend says the original was hung by a knight in 1210 in honour of the Virgin Mary. Climb above the village to get a better view of the star and the Gorges du Verdon in the distance. There are two ways to reach the path (the **Sentier de la Chaîne**): by foot or by electric mountain bike.

By foot from the centre of town, pick up the trail at the Parking Haut, which leads to the chemin de Courchon (the old Roman road). After 1.5km, pick up the Sentier de la Chaîne until you reach the star. This is a steep hike not recommended for young children.

By electric mountain bike, take the main road out of town towards Puimoisson. Turn right towards En Naups and Le Castillon. The route passes above Le Castillon and hugs the hill until it comes back around nearly full circle to Moustiers-Ste-Marie, just on the other side of the hill. After the campground, turn on the bike's motor to help you climb up to the top of the hill via the old Roman road. It's marked with yellow-and-white VTT (mountain bike) trail signs.

Ceramics in Moustiers-Ste-Marie

A time-honoured tradition

A craft practised in Moustiers-Ste-Marie since the Middle Ages, the decorative faience (glazed earthenware) made here once graced the dining tables of Europe's most aristocratic houses. Typical decoration of a faience piece includes shades of blue (like porcelain), aux Guirlandes, which usually depicts a single scene in the centre of the dish and the 'grotesques', which usually incorporate animal or even fantasy figures. Seven workshops still sell ceramics today, including **Atelier Serrailler**, **Atelier du Barri** and **Atelier Bondil**. For antique masterpieces, visit the small **Musée de la Faïence**, adjacent to the town hall.

LAVENDER FARMS ON THE PLATEAU DE VALENSOLE

La Ferme du Riou
This organic farm runs distillery visits during the harvest season and farm visits year-round.

La Marché du Plateau Producteur Valensole
Organic producer with a cabin in the fields during harvest season.

Lavandes Angelvin
Runs distillery visits during high season and guided visits on Tuesdays at 3pm.

Ubaye Valley

Ubaye Valley

The Ubaye Valley, nestled in the heart of the southern French Alps, is surprisingly underrated. The valley is steeped in history, with curious destinations like the town of Barcelonnette, which still holds a close link with Mexican culture, hosting festivals year-round that celebrate everything from music to local cuisine. And on that topic, the Ubaye Valley does not shirk from its duties in creating hearty mountain dishes. Visitors can sample local specialities such as *fondue d'Ubaye*, local honey and spirits. The Ubaye region is also home to two notable ski resorts: Pra Loup and Le Sauze. These resorts have excellent skiing and snowboarding, but without the crowds that can be found in the more well-known resorts of the northern Alps. Whether you're looking to explore the valley's history and culture, indulge in its delicious cuisine, go rafting on the river or hit the slopes for some winter fun, the Ubaye Valley is waiting for you.

Barcelonnette: C'est la Fête

Secluded town with diverse celebrations

The Fête de la Morte is an annual celebration in **Barcelonnette**, taking place on the first two days of November and sharing similarities with Mexico's Día de los Muertos. This vibrant event has a long-standing history in the city, ever since emigrants from Barcelonnette to Mexico returned in the late 19th-century. The festivities involve a range of activities, from colourful parades and street performances to traditional rituals and offerings.

In addition to the Fête de la Morte, the nearby town of **Jausiers** hosts the Fête de la Transhumance in early June each year to mark the beginning of the grazing season in the

GETTING AROUND

There are free shuttles to the resorts during ski season and summer. Check the tourist office for hours. If driving in winter, be sure to have snow tyres or chains.

☑ **TOP TIP**

The southern Alps are less bling-bling than the northern resorts, with a laid-back attitude and pride in the local traditions. This is a region where actions speak louder than words; locals are welcoming but not overly outgoing.

 WHERE TO EAT AND DRINK IN THE UBAYE VALLEY

Villa Morelia
Reserve a table at this Mexican villa in Jausiers, with tall bay windows and spectacular dishes. €€€

Maison de Pays
On the outskirts of Jausiers, come here for a selection of local cheeses from the cooperative. €

Brasserie des Hautes Vallées
The local microbrewery in St-Paul-sur-Ubaye; tasting rooms and fabulous Alpine views. €

high pastures. Visitors and hikers alike can witness this impressive migration as they explore the surrounding woodlands and pastures, taking in the views of the Parc National du Mercantour. The festival also showcases local cuisine, traditional music and cultural activities, making it a must-visit event for anyone interested in the unique history and traditions of the region.

Rafting the Ubaye River

Splash your way downstream

Late spring through autumn, rafters of all levels come to the Ubaye River above Barcelonnette for an adrenaline rush. Depending on the combination of rainfall and snowmelt, rafters will leave from Jausiers, Barcelonnette or further down the river. Age and experience are important too: starting at four years old, children can give baby-raft a go, but they need to be older to give the class IV rapids a try. Book an excursion with the team at **Anaconda Rafting** to race down the river in a raft, two-person kayak or hydrospeed, a type of miniature raft.

THE MEXICAN CONNECTION

Mexican Colonial-style homes, a celebration of Día de los Muertos and more than one Mexican restaurant in this small mountain town – what's going on in Barcelonnette?

In the 19th-century, emigrants who left the region to seek their fortune in the New World returned, their pockets bursting thanks to a successful textile business they built in Mexico. This new bourgeoisie built around 50 'Mexican Villas' from 1880 to 1930.

Drop into the **Villa La Sapinière**, which is home to the **Musée de la Vallée**. The exhibition follows not only the entrepreneurial Barcelonnettes in Mexico, but the comings and goings of the valley communities between Italy and France, and the travels of notable locals around the world.

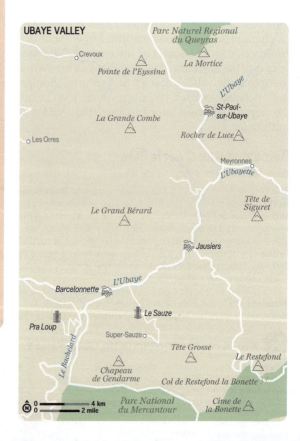

UBAYE VALLEY

Parc Naturel Regional du Queyras

Crevoux

Pointe de l'Eyssina

La Mortice

L'Ubaye

La Grande Combe

St-Paul-sur-Ubaye

Les Orres

Rocher de Luce

Meyronnes

L'Ubayette

Tête de Siguret

Le Grand Bérard

Jausiers

Barcelonnette

L'Ubaye

Le Sauze

Pra Loup

Super-Sauze

Le Bachelard

Tête Grosse

Le Restefond

Chapeau de Gendarme

Col de Restefond la Bonette

0   4 km
0   2 mile

N

Parc National du Mercantour

Cime de la Bonette

PETER GUDELLA/SHUTTERSTOCK ©

Skiing, Pra Loup

Ski the Southern Alps

For families and adventurers

The Ubaye is a hidden winter hotspot. Besides being home to two popular ski resorts, Pra Loup and Le Sauze, the valley's microclimate, which ensures abundant snowfall even during dry winters, makes it an ideal destination for skiing enthusiasts.

Pra Loup, the larger of the two stations, is 9.5km southwest of Barcelonnette and has an extensive network of pistes spanning 180km, with an elevation ranging from 1600m to 2575m. With 80% of its runs higher than 2000m, Pra Loup is guaranteed a longer season, even during mild winters. In addition to skiing, the resort also has three marked ski touring trails, providing access for adventurous skiers to ascend towards higher summits for a more exhilarating experience. There are two main areas: Pra Loup 1500 (sometimes called Les Molanes) and Pra Loup 1600 (with more infrastructure and nightlife). Together they form the southern Alps' largest snowsports destination, and in summer the lifts haul mountainbikers and hikers up to the summit.

Le Sauze, a mere 5.5km southeast of Barcelonnette, is another skier's playground with 65km of runs and 1000m of elevation gain, topping out at 2400m. The resort also has five marked trails for snowshoeing, providing a more relaxed way of exploring the valley's winter landscape.

Apart from skiing and snowshoeing, the valley also has the usual run of other winter activities, including snowmobile rides, sledding, ice skating and the spa.

UBAYE CHEESES

Wherever you go in the French Alps, you can expect to find a local version of one of the holy trinity of cheese dishes: tartiflette, raclette and fondu.

For a *fondu à la vallée d'Ubaye,* head to the **Cooperative Laitière**. There, you can pick out the perfect combination of *meule, miche gavotte* and *carline* to make your own fondu.

The cooperative also produces other cheeses, such as *tomme de chèvre* (goat cheese), *bleu d'Ubbaye* (blue cheese) and *tomme au Génépy.*

The *tomme de chèvre* is perfect for adding a tangy kick to salads or pasta dishes. *Bleu d'Ubbaye* is rich and creamy with a sharp taste, ideal for pairing with a glass of red wine.

Tomme au Génépy is often cooked in the oven and served over potatoes.

Col de Vars

Col de Pontis

Ubaye Valley

Col St-Jean   Col de la Bonette

Col d'Allos

Col de la Cayolle

GETTING AROUND

Local buses service Barcelonnette from Digne-les-Bains and from Gap. By car be wary of the narrow roads, especially if you're in an RV. In winter most of the passes are closed, but even before they close, the roads can be snowy or icy near the top, so be sure to have appropriate tyres.

☑ **TOP TIP**

Bring some cash with you to stop for a coffee or a beer at the top: *Après l'effort, le reconfort.*

Beyond
Ubaye Valley

Embark on a celebrated bike or motorcycle ride to cross a mountain pass.

The Ubaye Valley is surrounded by seven mountain passes, and is part of the famed Route des Grandes Alpes. This famous route through the French Alps spans over 700km, going from Thonon-les-Bains on Lake Geneva to Menton on the Mediterranean coast, and crossing 17 passes along the way, including the highest paved road in the Alps, the Col de l'Iseran (2764m). Near the end of the journey, the route passes through the Ubaye Valley at St-Paul-sur-Ubaye, the low part of the valley after Barcelonnette. Even if you check just one of these passes off the bucket list, it's worth discovering the southern Alps from the saddle of a bike or motorcycle.

Mountain Passes on Two Wheels

Epic climbs

The Ubaye Valley attracts adventure seekers all summer long to conquer its seven mountain passes – usually on a bike or motorcycle.

For the perfect photo, try the **Col de la Cayolle**. This pass is one of the most postcardy in the area. Cycling up to the pass is challenging, with numerous steep sections and tight hairpin turns.

Try the **Col de la Bonette** for one of the highest passes in the Alps; it tops out at a height of 2715m. It's sometimes featured in the Tour de France – pretend you've joined the peloton.

If you feel a need for speed, then it's the **Col de Vars**. Cyclists love this pass for its fast and exhilarating descent.

Headed to Italy? Then it's the **Montée de Ste-Anne** (cyclists) or **Col de Larche** (bikers). The former is the replacement climb for cyclists, who are forbidden to ride the latter.

The **Col de Pontis** is small but mighty. There is less hype around this pass, but it still provides a challenging climb sure to get your quads burning.

At the west end of the valley is the **Col St-Jean**; a long portion of this ride passes through a scenic forested area.

And the most classic ride of all is the **Col d'Allos**. The descent from the top of this pass goes all the way to the Gorges du Verdon.

Head to **Cycle Ubaye Sports** in Barcelonnette for good rental bikes and advice. On a motorcycle and have a problem? **Sport Moto** can get you out of a pinch.

Cycling, Col de la Cayolle

BEST ALPINE ACTIVITIES IN UBAYE

Sylvain Boudou is a mountain guide in the southern Alps. @sylvainboudou

As a guide, it's my job to spend time in the mountains – it doesn't matter where. But the southern Alps will always be a special place for me. Here are my favourite activities by season.

Winter
Ski touring in the high Ubaye and ice-climbing in the Vallon de Maljasset.

Spring
Mornings are for ski touring; in the afternoon, it's warm enough to go rock climbing in a T-shirt on the valley floor.

Summer
Mountaineering rules. There are summits and ridges suitable for all levels of mountaineers, and there are no queues like in the northern Alps.

Autumn
Climbing takes over again, and the skis come out of storage and get tuned up for winter.

MOR65_MAURO PICCARDI/SHUTTERSTOCK ©

247

TOOLKIT

The chapters in this section cover the most important topics you'll need to know about in Provence & the Côte d'Azur. They're full of nuts-and-bolts information and valuable insights to help you understand and navigate Provence & the Côte d'Azur and get the most out of your trip.

Arriving
p250

Getting Around
p251

Money
p252

Accommodation
p253

Family Travel
p254

Health & Safe
Travel
p255

Food, Drink
& Nightlife
p256

Responsible
Travel
p258

LGBTiQ+
Travellers
p260

Accessible
Travel
p261

How to Visit
the Markets
p262

Nuts & Bolts
p263

Tram, Nice (p54)

Arriving

Aéroport Nice Côte d'Azur is an important intercontinental gateway to the region, and Aéroport Marseille-Provence is connected to many European destinations as well. Seasonal routes link smaller airports at Avignon and Toulon with European hubs. Avignon, Aix-en-Provence and Marseille are connected to Paris on the TGV high-speed rail network. Many services continue along the coast to Nice, but at a slower pace.

Border Crossings

As part of the Schengen zone, there are no formalities to complete when crossing into France from elsewhere in Europe. ID checks at the Italian border at Menton are rare.

Visas

Travellers from the UK, Canada, New Zealand, the US and Australia can stay up to 90 days in any 180-day period with no visa. See schengenvisainfo.com for updates.

Wi-Fi

Follow the prompts to connect to free wi-fi in airports and many train stations. It's now commonplace for cafes, bars and hotels to offer complimentary wi-fi. Look out for free public hotspots in Nice and Marseille.

Tax Refunds

Non-EU residents can claim VAT refunds on purchases made in France over €175 in value at self-service machines or at Interchange offices inside both Terminal One and Two at Aéroport Nice Côte d'Azur.

Public Transport from Airport to City Centre

	Nice	Marseille	Monaco
TRAIN	4 mins €2.10	n/a	40 mins €5.40
BUS	30 mins €1.70	25 mins €10	60 mins €19.40
TAXI	15 mins €32	30 mins €50-60	45 mins €95
TRAM	30 mins €10 return	n/a	n/a

ETIAS

In 2025, the European Commission's new electronic vetting system – European Travel Information and Authorisation System (ETIAS) – will begin operation. All nationals from non-EU, visa-exempt countries, including the UK, US, Canada, Australia and New Zealand, will have to fill in a pre-arrival online form. Once approved, travellers will be able to remain up to 90 days in all 27 Schengen-zone countries. ETIAS will be valid for three years and will cost €7, payable online via the official ETIAS website or mobile app. For updated information, see etiasvisa.com.

Getting Around

You can't beat the value of the combined Zou! train and bus regional network when travelling between the main tourist centres. Elsewhere, it's best to have your own wheels.

TRAVEL COSTS

Rental
**from
€48-60/day**

Petrol
**approx
€1.90/litre**

E-Bike rental
€40/day

Train ticket
Nice–Marseille
from €30.50

Bikes & E-Bikes

From breezy coastal tracks to pro-level mountain passes, the region is a cyclist's dream. Both road bikes and e-bikes are readily available to hire in most towns. Nice, Monaco, Marseille and Avignon have user-friendly public bike and e-bike share schemes.

Taxis & Rideshares

You can't just hail a taxi in the region; when in doubt, there will always be a taxi rank at the train station. Uber is a well-established rideshare platform in the bigger cities. Note Uber can drop off but not pick up in Monaco, but this may change.

TIP

Carpooling app BlaBlaCar was born in France and is the country's favourite app for connecting drivers with travellers heading in the same direction.

STRIKE THAT!

The public transport system in Provence and the Côte d'Azur is great when it works, which is 95% of the time. However, the French love a good strike and, unfortunately, the first thing to be hit are trains and buses – sometimes with only a day or so notice. On these occasions, a very reduced timetable still operates; it is usually back to business as usual the next day. Intriguingly, if they do happen, most strikes take place on a Thursday.

DRIVING ESSENTIALS

Drive on the right

Priorité à droite means you must yield to vehicles entering from the right.

.05

Blood alcohol limit is 0.05%

Speed Limit

The motorway speed is 130km/h across the region, except in the Alpes-Maritimes where the speed limit drops to 110km/h. Be aware of speed cameras, roadworks, traffic jams and other obstacles; calculate the best route by turning on community navigation app Waze.

Parking

Parking in big cities and popular tourist destinations is becoming increasingly difficult, although new Park + Ride options on the edge of city centres are springing up. Many towns offer 30 minutes to an hour of free metered parking, but a ticket is still required.

Peak Hour

During morning and afternoon commuter rush, the motorway exits around Aix-en-Provence, Toulon and everywhere between Nice and Antibes can be gridlock; expect the same in Monaco. Between Menton and St-Tropez, local English-speaking radio station 106.5 FM Riviera Radio provides live traffic updates.

Money

CURRENCY: EURO (€)

Credit & Debit Cards

Many, but not all, businesses accept credit or debit card payments. That said, always carry a small reserve of cash, particularly in small towns or in the markets. Small businesses may ask for a minimum spend to pay with card. Tap payments are authorized up to €50.

Digital Payments

It's increasingly common to use your phone's digital wallet to pay for things in France (average limit of €300 per purchase). Still, it's worth having an alternative mode of payment at hand (cash, physical credit or debit card) for occasions when the facility is not available.

ATMs

There are no shortage of ATMs, known as distributeurs automatiques de billets (DAB), particularly in more populated areas. However, bank charges may apply to withdraw cash – check with your bank. Obtaining cash back at a supermarket or another point of sale is not practiced in France.

HOW MUCH FOR...

a French Riviera Pass (48hr)
€40

a sunlounger on the beach
€20-50

a boat from Ste-Maxime to St-Tropez
from €8.40

a museum entry
free-€20

HOW TO... **Save Money**

Eating out
Savings are to be made by ordering the plat du jour (daily special) at lunch. Often it is combined with either an entrée or dessert (or both) in a similarly well-priced menu du jour.

First Sunday of the month
Many state-run museums are free.

Public transport
Multi-ticket and day passes work out cheaper than individual tickets if you're taking more than one trip by public transport.

TIPPING AND HAGGLING

France doesn't have a tipping culture similar to the US; in fact, as is indicated by the phrase service compris on the bottom of your restaurant or cafe bill, a 15% service fee is already included. To show your appreciation for good service, however, a *pourboire* (gratuity) in the form of a few coins is always welcome – but never mandatory.

Find a treasure at the Isle-sur-la-Sorgue antique markets? Go ahead and bargain. Price tags are firm everywhere else except *brocantes* and *marchés aux puces* (antique and flea markets).

LOCAL TIP

Always keep some coins handy to pay for public toilets (between 50c and €1), a coffee, a cool drink or to buy a ticket on the bus.

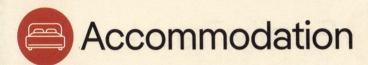

Accommodation

Chambre d'Hôtes

Whether surrounded by lavender in the Luberon or lemon trees in Menton, cosy *chambres d'hôtes* are the French equivalent of a B&B: a handful of guest rooms inside a private home. Breakfast is included in the nightly rate; rooms are usually doubles so families will need to book two. Amenities can vary; pools and parking are popular add-ons in Provence.

Gîtes

To live out your Provençal holiday dreams, nothing beats the romance of a stone gîte, or a rural self-catered cottage. Usually rented by the week in the summer months, or for shorter durations the remainder of the year, gîtes come in all shapes and sizes, from rustic barn conversions to sprawling villas with private pools, townhouses and mountain chalets.

Refuges & Gîtes d'Étapes

Hikers bunk down in *refuges* (mountain huts) and *gîtes d'étapes* (rest houses) dotted strategically atop mountains and beside lakes on popular trails. Facilities are basic; usually just bunkbeds in shared dorms and hot showers, but new friendships are often struck up over evening meals. Most shutter up outside of summer or open on reservation only. Booking in advance and sleeping bags (for refuges) are strongly recommended.

Camping

Wild camping is technically illegal in Provence and the Côte d'Azur, but there is no shortage of designated campsites across the region. Many lean towards the holiday-park definition of camping, with mobile homes and evening discos; *campings municipaux* (municipal campsites) can be smart options if you are looking for flat, uncluttered spaces to pitch a tent or park a campervan.

HOW MUCH FOR A NIGHT IN...

a *chambre d'hôte*
€50–150

a mountain refuge
€20–30

a *hôtel de charme*
€110 and up

Hôtel de Charme

Provence overflows with *hôtels de charme*, an unofficial definition for intimate, independently run hotels that offer a uniquely regional flavour. Expect sublime design, personalised service and a high-quality restaurant, all set inside set inside character-filled buildings such as manors, châteaux, priories and hôtel particuliers (private townhouses) with manicured gardens and friendly hosts.

HIDDEN COSTS

All accommodation providers (including Airbnb) are obliged to collect a tourist tax on behalf of the local municipality. Exactly how much depends on the rating of the property: budget for a little over €1 per night extra for one-star establishments and around €4 when living it up in five-star glitz. Bedding and towels aren't usually included in holiday park-style campsites; if you don't bring your own, you can pay extra for a linen pack. Don't assume you'll find sheets in your gîte rentals either. An end-of-stay cleaning fee often applies, too.

Family Travel

Laze on a sunlounger at the beach while the kids play with a bucket and spade in the sand, or stretch out on the grass in one of the many gated parks and gardens – for sleep-deprived parents of young children in particular, the outdoor lifestyle and year-round sunshine of Provence and the Côte d'Azur provides a welcome, Vitamin D–infused respite.

Reduced Rates

Children under four travel for free on the region's Zou! train and bus networks, assuming they sit on your knees.

Admission is free for under-12s (and sometimes under-18s) at many state-run museums and sites; otherwise, a reduced rate usually applies for children's tickets. Keep your eyes peeled for family-entry tickets for two adults and two children.

Eating with Kids

Most restaurants have a set-priced *menu enfant* (children's menu) at lunch and dinner; expect to pay between €10 and €12 for a burger or nuggets with chips, plus a drink and dessert. Dinner service rarely starts before 7pm. Boulangeries abound with all-day supplies of croissants, pains au chocolat and other delights for snack times. With their unique array of flavours, the region's legion of ice creameries are a crowd-pleaser for all ages.

Not So Pram-Friendly

The narrow pedestrian streets that make the villages of Provence and the Côte d'Azur such a photographer's delight make pram-wrangling bumpy. Smaller, lighter prams, such as the fold-up types that can be carried on planes as hand luggage, fare best on the cobblestones.

No Change

Nappy-changing facilities are the exception rather than the rule, and it's a welcome surprise when you chance upon a restaurant or cafe with a change table. Carry a changing mat and be prepared to improvise. Dedicated breastfeeding spaces are almost non-existent.

KID-FRIENDLY PICKS

Musée Océanographique de Monaco (p96)

Four floors of wonder, including a vibrant aquarium and mesmerising multimedia show.

St-Martin-Vésubie (p72)

Indoor fun at Vésubia Mountain Park and outdoor adventures in the majestic Mercantour.

Plage de Pampelonne (p107)

With a long curve of fine buttercream sand, there's no better beach in the region.

Gorges du Verdon (p237)

From rafting to rock climbing, canyoning and hiking, energetic teens are all set in France's answer to the Grand Canyon.

CAMPING COOL

Camping in France can mean many things besides pitching a tent. As a general rule, campsites are hybrid holiday parks where you can pitch your tent, park your camping car or book a stay in a mobile home on-site. Since it can feel like the entire country migrates south in summer, the region overflows with options from the water's edge deep into Provence Verte. Blessed with space and on-site facilities such as swimming pools, restaurants and play areas, there's plenty of chances for kids to find playmates. During the high-season months, most operate a weekday kids' club led by a trained team .

Health & Safe Travel

HEALTH CARE

- The French love their pharmacies and you are never far from one: a lit-up green cross indicates that a pharmacy is open. Call here first to treat cuts, infected insect bites, grazes and burns.
- Nice's Pharmacie Riviera (66 ave Jean Médecin) is open 24/7.
- On Sunday, find out which one is open closest to you at 3237.fr.
- Dial 112 for an ambulance.

Hunting Season

Hunting is France's third-most popular sport and the hunting season – la chasse in French – runs from September to February. Signs reading chasse en cours are put up on forest tracks to make walkers, hikers and joggers aware that a hunt is underway, although it's probably best to postpone your planned outing for another day.

Forest Fires

Over a third of the Provence-Alpes-Côte d'Azur region is covered by natural forest, and sizzling heat can spark fires from early July to mid-September. The Var publishes daily fire danger updates during summer on its social media accounts (see @Prefet83 on Facebook and X). The My Calanques app is similarly up to date.

ON THE BEACH

Never leave valuables unattended when in the water. Keep your eyes peeled for purple jellyfish; particularly during summer and autumn.

SWIM SAFELY

Green flag Safe to swim	**Yellow flag** Proceed with caution; potential hazards in the water.	**Red flag** No swimming allowed	**Purple flag** Pollution or other danger.	**Red & yellow stripes** Area under lifeguard supervision if first-aid post open	**Black & white chequered** Watersports zone; swim with caution.

Petty Crime

Keep handbags and phones carefully guarded as pickpocketing is rife, particularly in busy tourist areas and on crowded trains of the Côte d'Azur during the holiday period. Lock your doors and wind up your windows while driving in bigger cities as thefts have been known to happen at red lights. Leave nothing valuable on display in parked cars.

STORM ALEX

In October 2020, Storm Alex swept through the mountain communities of the Côte d'Azur, in particular the valleys of the Vésubie and the Roya. The force of the storm washed away homes and killed 10 people. Recovery has been slow, not least because of damage to the road infrastructure connecting these towns and villages to the coastline. As these communities rebuild, tourism is a key driver.

Food, Drink & Nightlife

WHEN TO EAT

Petit déjeuner (7–10am) French breakfasts are simple: think a toasted baguette or croissant with coffee.

Déjeuner (noon–2.30pm) Lunch can be a baguette sandwich enjoyed on the run or a sit-down meal accompanied by a glass of wine. Restaurants are strict on service times.

Dîner (7–10pm) Dinner in France is never rushed, usually involving three courses (starter, main, dessert) and sometimes four (cheese).

Where to Eat

Brasserie Casual restaurant open all day with a menu of traditional favourites.

Snack Might have a couple of tables but mostly does take-away. Budget-friendly food to eat on the run.

Kiosk A roadside hut, often known for regional specialities such as panisse and pan bagnat.

Boulangerie Bakery for bread and pastries.

Pâtisserie Specialises in cakes of all sizes.

Cave A wine shop; can sell wine by the glass.

Bistrot de pays A rural restaurant where great value meals are made with local produce.

MENU DECODER

Entrée A starter or appetiser
Plat The main course
Dessert Dessert
Plat du jour Daily special
Formule A meal deal, usually in bakeries
Carte A menu
Menu Two or three courses at a fixed price
Fait Maison Homemade
Menu Dégustation A tasting menu (high-end restaurants)
Menu Enfant Set-price kid's menu (meal, drink, dessert)
Viande Meat
Fruits de la Mer Seafood

Légumes Vegetables
Glace Ice cream
Gâteau Cake
Boisson Drink
Pichet de vin A carafe of wine
Bouteille de vin A bottle of wine
Vin blanc White wine
Vin rouge Red wine
Vin rosé Rosé wine
Pression Draught beer
Démi 25cl draught beer
Carte des vins Wine list
Eau plat Still water
Eau pétillante Sparkling water
Carafe d'eau Tap water (free)
Soft Soft drink

HOW TO…   **Order Rosé**

Although synonymous with warmer months elsewhere in the world, it's always rosé season in Provence. This is the region that sparked the world's love affair with the pink drink. You can order it *au verre* (by the glass), *au pichet* (by the carafe; 25/50cl), or *à la bouteille* (by the bottle) from the *carte des vins* (wine list). A *pichet* costs less, but expect a more rustic wine. No one will bat an eyelid if you ask for a couple of *glaçons* (ice cubes) to be added in your glass – in fact, it's quite common to drink a *piscine de rosé*, or a glass of rosé wine served over a generous scoop of ice-cubes (you can also ask for a *piscine de vin blanc* if you'd prefer). Côtes de Provence is the largest AOP, or geographically defined wine-making area in the region. Don't expect to find much rosé made anywhere else on the menu here, either.

HOW MUCH FOR...

a croissant
€1–1.50

an espresso coffee
€1.50

a glass of wine
from €3–5

a pint of beer
€7

a pizza
€10–15

a plat du jour
from €10–15

dinner at a Michelin-starred restaurant
€100 and up

a single scoop of ice cream
€2.50

HOW TO...

Drink Pastis

Nothing screams summer in the south of France more than a highball glass of cloudy pastis, the anise-flavoured drink born in Marseille. For purists, there's only way to sip it: *à l'ancienne*. To prepare it just right, you'll need a 20ml shot in a tall glass, a carafe of water and a pot of ice cubes. For one part pastis, add five parts water to dilute the amber-coloured drink. Watch the liquid turn opaque as the water mixes with the spirit. Add ice cubes last – any earlier and it stops the release of delicate aromas (plus, it's a surefire way to be labelled as *un parisien* by friendly locals). Order pastis by the brand; Pastis 51 (Ricard) is the original, and for many it's still the best.

Once you've got the hang of the basics, it's time to add a twist, so stock up on a collection of sirops (cordials). For a *mauresque*, add 10cl of *orgeat* (almond) syrup to your 20cl shot, before adding the water and the ice. A *perroquet* shimmers green from a similar pour of mint cordial, while *la tomate* takes its name from the red colour the drink turns once a 10cl serve of grenadine cordial has been mixed in. Or go all out and swap the water for a can of Coca-Cola: et voilà, you've got yourself a *pétrole* (also called *mazout*).

Mixology

Across Provence, a new wave of craft distilleries is adding an artisanal twist to this classic drink. Marseille's Distillerie de la Plaine runs pastis blending workshops near Cours Julien. In Nice, keep your eyes peeled for the local *Pastis de Nice*.

COFFEE, TEA HOUSES & CAFÉ GOURMAND

Order *un café* (a coffee) and most people will assume an espresso, the shot of choice for kick-starting mornings or rounding off a meal. For an espresso with a dash of milk, ask for *une noisette*. As a blanket rule, the milk added to coffee, whether poured in cold, heated or frothed, is long life. On the menu, a cappuccino or a *café crème* (milk coffee) is often as adventurous as it gets.

Thankfully, coffee culture is trickling through the region, and it's becoming easier to find a latte or flat white, or a quality brew to take away. Australian owners have made Lorgues Coffee Roasters worth the detour when in the Var; Nice's cyclist cafes (p65) are similarly sure bets.

If tea is more to your taste, stop by a *salon de thé* (tea room). Chances are the setting will be wonderfully boho-chic, with hot drinks and accompanying sweet treats served up on mismatched china. Take your pick from a multitude of sachets of herbal teas (*tisanes*); tracking down a milky English tea is more difficult.

The restaurant menu conceals a sweet secret: a coffee and dessert combo called the *café gourmand*. An espresso (or *noisette*) is served with a selection of mini desserts of different styles, textures and colours; this pretty dish is made for indecisive dessert diners. No *café gourmand* is ever the same; the selection changes daily, even in the same restaurant. And this variety is where, for most, the attraction lies.

Responsible Travel

Climate Change & Travel

It's impossible to ignore the impact we have when travelling, and the importance of making changes where we can. Lonely Planet urges all travellers to engage with their travel carbon footprint. There are many carbon calculators online that allow travellers to estimate the carbon emissions generated by their journey; try resurgence.org/resources/carbon-calculator.html. Many airlines and booking sites off er travellers the option of off setting the impact of greenhouse gas emissions by contributing to climate-friendly initiatives around the world. We continue to off set the carbon footprint of all Lonely Planet staff travel, while recognising this is a mitigation more than a solution.

Flexible Approach

In a first, community navigation app Waze is working with the PACA region to notify users if a site is seeing a surge in tourists and direct them to an alternative nearby.

Best Beach

Relax on a sunlounger at Baia Bella in Beaulieu-sur-Mer, France's first carbon-neutral beach according to Allcot. Solar panels, recycled water, wooden furniture and seabed cleaning are some of the sustainable initiatives at play in the sun.

0km

Dine at restaurants sourcing from local producers. Many menus specify the provenance of their ingredients.

Local Meets

See the region through local eyes on a walking tour with a city Greeter (p82). In Marseille, Nice and Cannes, these passionate volunteer guides show you the lesser-known side of their cities. The experience is free, although tips are appreciated. See greeters.fr.

Scan to book your walking tour.

Support Rural Bistros

Dig into local flavours at great prices at a bistrot de pays. Born in the Alpes-de-Haute-Provence, the association champions France's under-threat rural bistros. Find them across the region. See bistrotdepays.com.

Scan to find a bistrot de pays

A CHANGING AESTHETIC

The purple explosion of blooming lavender fields is emblematic of Provence, but the image as we know it has to change. Rows of lavender with cover crops in between are the sustainable vision of the future.

Green Touch

Find unique stays and other experiences with Mercantour Ecotourisme (mercantourecotourisme.eu), an association regrouping sustainably minded accommodation providers, restaurants, producers and artisans in the Parc National du Mercantour.

E-Dreams

Plug your electric car into charging points scattered across the region, from five-star hotels to campsites and at public networks operated by Eborn (Alpes-de-Haute-Provence, Var), Wiiiz (Alpes-Maritimes), larecharge (Bouches-du-Rhône) and Vauclus'elec (Luberon).

Solar Power

Enjoy a sunny serve of solar cuisine at Le Présage, a 100% solar-powered restaurant in Marseille. More relaxed in nature than a formal restaurant, the cuisine is flexitarian and fresh. A more permanent building is coming.

Keep Cool

Closed can still mean open when shopping, especially in summer. In the face of rising energy prices, shops are now legally required to close their doors if they want to leave their air-con running.

Ride Green

Say yes to Uber Green to ride in an electric or hybrid vehicle for little extra charge.

Water Fountains

Save on single-use plastic by carrying a reusable water bottle. In Nice, public drinking-water stations offer the choice of still or sparkling water. The app Free Taps (freetaps.earth) directs you to the nearest fountain.

Scan to find your nearest water fountain

Too Good to Waste

Find nearby bakeries, supermarkets, cafes and restaurants selling 'surprise bags', or end-of-service food bundles for a heavily reduced price, by downloading the Too Good to Go app (toogoodtogo. com).

Scan to find food at reduced prices

Mind Your Trash

Take your rubbish back to the mainland after a day trip to the Îles des Lérins; the two islands off Cannes no longer have any garbage bins after tourist trash led to a proliferation of rats.

RESOURCES

laclefverte.org
An international label for sustainable accommodation.

bienvenue-a-la-ferme.com
Your stay, meal or visit will support an independent local farmer.

blablacar.com
Hitch a ride with France's incredibly popular rideshare app.

LGBTIQ+ Travellers

The French have long considered people's private lives just that: private. This laissez-faire attitude means that France is one of the most LGBTIQ+-friendly countries in the world. The rainbow flag flies high in Nice; it's more discreet in Marseille. There are also gay bars in Cannes, Aix-en-Provence and Avignon. As always, rural areas tend to be more conservative than bigger cities.

Nice Events

Nice is the undisputed hub of the LGBTIQ+ scene in the region. Plan your visit to coincide with one of the following community events. Glitter and confetti cover Nice in February during France's first queer carnival, **Lou Queernaval**. Expect live bands, energetic dancers, dazzling floats and drag queens.

The queer film festival **Rencontres In&Out** spans a week in April. Look for autumn editions in Cannes and Toulon.

Crowds swarm Nice's main streets for July's **Pink Parade** (Pride).

The dress code is white for the Centre LGBT de Nice's loud and proud **Dolly Party** street fiesta in August.

MONACO PRIDE

Monaco Pride is still in its infancy – 2022 marked the inaugural edition. The formal event lacks flamboyant flair, but it's a step in the right direction: in 2022 Monaco was called out by the European Commission against Racism and Intolerance (ECRI) for unjustified differences in treatment between same-sex and heterosexual couples.

Neighbourhood Watch

Painted in the colours of the rainbow flag, rue Bonaparte is Nice's LGBTIQ+ HQ. Despite a host of gay bars, gay saunas and gay-friendly restaurants, Marseille lacks a gay quarter – in fact, the city's first LGBTIQ+ centre only opened its doors in 2023. The city's underground music scene is anti-fascist and queer-friendly.

Best of the Rest: Events

Pride spills onto the streets in June with **Marche des Fiertés** parades in Arles, Toulon and Avignon. July's Pride Marseille is thirty years strong; the day itself is now prefaced by two weeks of debates, exhibitions, workshops and shows.

Queer acts take to the stage during summer's **Festival Off Avignon**.

Autumn's **ZeFestival** LGBTIQ+ film festival takes over cinema screens in Nice, Marseille, Toulon, Avignon and Seillans.

NICE IRISÉE NATURELLEMENT

Easily identify Nice's gay-friendly restaurants and hotels by the Irisée Naturellement (Naturally Iridescent) label on display; browse the city's gay-friendly guide (explorenicecotedazur.com/en/prepare-your-holidays/my-nice-cote-dazur/gay-friendly) for a comprehensive list of establishments, shops, theatres, bars, clubs, saunas and cruising bars.

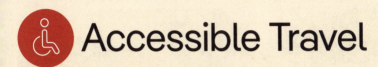

Accessible Travel

Travel across Provence and the Côte d'Azur still presents accessibility challenges, although efforts are underway to make tourism more inclusive. Many offices de tourisme publish a comprehensive mobility guide in English. Pick up a map of Monaco's extensive network of lifts to navigate the principality's hilly terrain.

Cobblestone Streets

High-walled medieval villages and historic city neighbourhoods are characterised by uneven cobblestone streets not adapted for wheelchair use. Paved sidewalks often turn into defacto car parking spaces or restaurant terraces.

Airport

Both Aéroport Nice Côte d'Azur and Aéroport Marseille-Provence provide a comprehensive range of services for travellers requiring special assistance; notify your airline at least 48 hours before departure of your requirements.

Accommodation

Lifts and accessible rooms are harder to find in older hotels and small B&Bs. Gîtes de France (gites-de-france. com) filters B&Bs and self-catering accommodation by accessibility.

TRAIN

For train journeys, arrange special assistance in advance through the Zou! Accès Plus service (zou.maregionsud. fr/en/accessibility). Bookings 48 hours in advance are essential. Audio announcements advise passengers of upcoming stops.

GRAND PRIX

The Automobile Club de Monaco reserves a grandstand for spectators with reduced mobility to watch the Monaco Grand Prix, Monaco ePrix and Grand Prix Historique de Monaco. Pre-registration is required through the Monegasque Association of Motor Disabilities (AMHM; amhm98.com).

Car Hire & Transfers

Rent adapted cars for the duration of your stay through Libertans (libertans.com). MCMobility's (monaco-mobilites.wixsite.com) fleet of adapted vehicles provides airport and train station transfers among its transport services.

Bus & Tram

Ligne d'Azur's dedicated mobility service offers an on-demand bus in and around Nice and nearby villages, including Villefranche-sur-Mer, Èze, Vence and into the Vésubie. Most buses and all trams have retractable platforms. See mobilazur.org.

RESOURCES

tourisme-handicaps.org
Accessible hotels, restaurants, tourist operators, hiking trails and nature sites are regrouped under the label Tourisme & Handicaps

visitmonaco.com
Visit Monaco's Access Monaco brochure covers practicalities including getting around, where to stay and suggested itineraries across the principality.

info.urgence114.fr
114 is the French emergency number for the deaf and hard of hearing. Send a text message, connect through the website (info. urgence114.fr) or download the app.

Provençal market

HOW TO...

Visit the Markets

Bright, busy and brimming with colours, scents and flavours, markets are an essential ingredient in the intoxicating recipe for life in Provence and the Côte d'Azur. More than a chance to fill your basket with fragrant fresh produce to take back to your kitchen, the market is a highly social occasion. It's a chance to catch up with neighbours and friends, as well as on all the local gossip. The best value lies in shopping for what's in season; bio means organic and commands a higher price tag. Some markets repeat daily; others are once-a-week affairs.

On Special

Plan your shopping list around local specialities in season: summer screams sweet melons from Cavaillon and juicy strawberries from Carros while winter kitchens warm up with pungent truffles from Carpentras and candied chestnuts from Collobrières.

Inside Out

Covered food markets are a treasure trove of culinary delights come lunchtime, where you can feast on regional fare at wallet-friendly prices cooked to order. Eat in at Monaco's Marché de la Condamine, or take away at the Marché Forville in Cannes.

Market Dos

- **Early bird catches the worm** Do arrive early. Not necessarily before 8am, when stalls are still setting up, but aim for around 9 to 9.30am for your pick of the produce. Vendors start to pack up around lunchtime. By 1pm, the scene can feel like the markets never happened.
- **BYO bag** Do bring your own bags, whether a woven basket, canvas tote or reusable supermarket bag.
- **Small change** Do carry some cash; the stallholders that accept cards often have a minimum spend.

Market Don'ts

- **Don't be afraid to ask for advice** It's OK to let the stallholder choose your fruit and veg; perhaps a ripe melon for today and an avocado ready to be cut open tomorrow. Same goes for serving suggestions and cooking tips for fish, meat and cheeses – you name it!
- **Bargaining** Save it for antique and flea markets; haggling is a no-go.

WHAT'S IN A NAME?

Marché Provencal
More than fruit and veg, here you can pick up tasty tapenade, runny cheeses and spicy sausages for a picnic, fresh flowers for home, or a floppy sun hat or new linen shirt.

Marché des Producteurs
Farmers market where zero-kilometre produce reigns.

Marché de Nuit, also known as marché nocturne, these come alive as the sun starts to set. Expect local arts and crafts accompanied by a live band and food trucks.

Marché à la Brocante Antique market; scour for a one-of-a-kind souvenir on the Cours Saleya in Nice and along the canals in L'Isle-sur-la-Sorgue.

Nuts & Bolts

OPENING HOURS

Banks open around 9am, close for lunch for at least an hour between 12 and 2pm and for the day by 5.30 or 6pm. Can be closed Mondays.

Shops open at 10am and close around 7pm. Smaller boutiques may still close for lunch.

Outside of shopping centres, shops close on Sundays.

Supermarkets usually open Sunday morning only.

Smoking

Smoking is forbidden inside restaurants, cafes and bars as well as on public transport and near forests in summer. Certain beaches are now smoke-free.

Public Toilets

Carry some small change to pay for public toilets. Expect to pay either 50c or €1. In cafes, order a drink.

GOOD TO KNOW

Time zone
GMT+1

Country code
33

Emergency number
112

Population
5.1 million

Electricity 230V/50hz

Weights & Measures

France uses the metric system. Decimal places are indicated by commas, and thousands by points.

Type C
220V/50Hz

Type E
220V/50Hz

PUBLIC HOLIDAYS

Good Friday and Boxing Day are not public holidays in **Provence and the Côte d'Azur**.

- **New Year's Day** 1 January
- **Easter Sunday & Monday** Late March/April
- **May Day** 1 May
- **WWII Victory Day** 8 May
- **Ascension Thursday** May (40th day after Easter)
- **Pentecost & Whit Monday** Mid-May to mid-June (7th Sunday after Easter)
- **Bastille Day (*Fête Nationale*)** 14 July
- **Assumption Day** 15 August
- **All Saints' Day** 1 November
- **Remembrance Day** 11 November
- **Christmas Day** 25 December

Monaco shares some, but not all, public holidays with France. Differences include
- **La Sainte Dévote** 27 January
- **Corpus Christi Thursday** 60th day after Easter
- **Monaco National Day** 19 November.

STORYBOOK

Our writers delve deep into different
aspects of Provence & Côte d'Azur life

A History of Provence & the Côte d'Azur in 15 places

In many ways, Provence and the Côte d'Azur feels like one large open-air museum.

Chrissie McClatchie

p266

When Italy Inspired Nice

A city with a foot in two countries.

Chrissie McClatchie

p270

Le Mistral Gagnant

The famous and fearsome wind of Provence, so intrusive it penetrates even the tiniest crevices

Ashley Parsons

p273

Heat in Marseille

The heat transforms Marseille's personality in the summer and forces residents outdoors.

Michael Frankel

p276

A HISTORY OF PROVENCE & THE CÔTE D'AZUR IN

15 PLACES

Mysterious prehistoric cave paintings, grand Roman arenas, thick-walled papal palaces, glittering Belle Époque buildings and modern architectural marvels. In many ways, Provence and the Côte d'Azur feels like one large open-air museum. Are you ready to buckle up and embark on a fascinating adventure spanning more than 3000 years? By Chrissie McClatchie

WELCOME TO A corner of the world that brings the history books of your childhood instantly to life, starting with a slab of fossilised ammonites, 200 million years old, cast for eternity in the Alpes-de-Haute-Provence. After that, the mysterious rock engravings that haunt the Vallée des Merveilles seem positively modern, until you learn they date back to between 1800 and 1500 BCE. Fast forward to the Greeks, who colonised Marseille in 600 BCE and brought with them wine grapes and olives. The Romans weren't far behind and left the imprint of their grandeur in towns and cities across the region.

In the Middle Ages, much of the population fled to the hills, taking refuge in thick-walled hilltop villages that offered protection from invaders, while the papacy swapped Rome for Avignon. Wars and plagues followed, as well as Napoléon, who marched across the region to reclaim his throne in Paris. Then came the first tourists in search of winter sun and the Côte d'Azur was born. Whether your favourite bedtime reading was stories of the earliest humans or more recent tales of power-hungry emperors, Belle Époque characters or charming rural traditions, Provence and the Côte d'Azur has all bases covered.

1. Réserve Géologique de Haute-Provence

WHEN OCEANS COVERED THE LAND

Over one hundred million years ago, the Alps were covered by a vast temperate sea. Today, a mammoth 230,000-hectare

stretch of the mountain range is Europe's largest protected geological reserve: the Réserve Géologique de Haute-Provence. While the park stretches across three Provence départements (Alpes-de-Haute-Provence, Var, Haute-Alpes), its most emblematic site is just outside of Dignes-les-Bains in the Alpes-de-Haute-Provence. Known as La Dalle aux Ammonites (the Ammonite Slab), this wall is a geological marvel, with over 1500 ammonite shells from 200 million years ago frozen in time. The largest specimen is an incredible 70cm long!

To see the ammonites of the Reserve Géologique de Haute-Provence up close yourself, see page 234.

2. Vallée des Merveilles

ANCIENT ART

Over 40,000 mysterious petroglyphs – ancient pictures carved into rock – cover the red stones of the Vallée des Merveilles and give this narrow canyon its name: the Valley of Wonders. Much mystery surrounds the identity of the artists behind them, but what's not up for question is just how important these prehistoric etchings of animals, weapons, tools and even people are when it comes to giving us a glimpse into Bronze Age life in the region. You really need to plan for two days to do it justice; because access is limited unless you are accompanied by a qualified guide, this remains one of the Côte d'Azur's blissfully untouched sites.

For more on the Vallée des Merveilles, see page 74.

3. Roman Arles

VENI, VIDI, VICI

Arelate (Arles) owes its ancient prosperity to Julius Cesar, who elevated the status of the town as a reward for its support when his troops plundered nearby Marseille in 49 BCE. Befitting its new status as a regional Roman darling, Arles welcomed high-society events like gladiator fights, chariot races and plays in its 20,000-seat amphitheatre and 12,000-seat theatre. Modelled on the Colosseum in Rome, Les Arènes d'Arles, as the amphitheatre is known, stands tall as the largest Roman monument in France. A block away, centuries of looting have taken their toll on the Théâtre Antique, but it's still a majestic setting for summer events.

To walk in the footsteps of the Romans in Arles, see page 164.

4. Théâtre Antique, Orange

PAX ROMANA

Louis XIV called Orange's Théâtre Antique 'the finest wall in my kingdom' but he owed his gratitude to the stability of the Roman empire, specifically during the reign of Augustus (27 BCE–14 CE), who commissioned the theatre's construction. A magnificent setting fit for an emperor, the ingenious venue was built to host 10,000 spectators. The natural acoustics are so superb that even those in the furthest corners could hear the action from the stage. In the centuries since, the site has been pillaged, used as a prison and a place of refuge. Today, it's under Unesco protection, and once again the site of summer performances.

To step back in time in Orange's Théâtre Antique, see page 194.

5. Monastère Notre-Dame de Clémence de la Verne, Collobrières

A REFUGE FROM THE WORLD

Just an hour from St-Tropez but a world away from the flash of paparazzi cameras, the Monastère Notre-Dame de Clémence de la Verne rises up on a ridge in the Massif des Maures, surrounded by little more than chestnut and oak trees. The 12th-century monastery is said to have been built on the site of a pagan temple to the goddess Laverna, who protected the brigands who took shelter within the mountain ranges' leafy folds. Three fires in three separate centuries couldn't drive out the monks, but the French Revolution did. Almost two hundred years would pass before another religious order moved in.

To hike marked trails through ancient chestnut groves to the Monastère Notre-Dame de Clémence de la Verne, see page 128.

6. Palais des Papes

GAME OF THRONES

A series of seven French-born popes put Avignon on the map in the 14th century when they made the city on the Rhône River the centre of the Roman Catholic universe. It may have been the seat of power for less than 70 years – during the Great Schism (1378–1417), rival popes resided at Rome and Avignon, denouncing and excommunicating one another – but the papal presence can still be felt in the immense Palais de Papes, the largest Gothic palace ever built, as well as the prized red wine that flows through the cellars of nearby Châteauneuf-du-Pape, the site of the pope's summer residence.

To visit the Palais des Papes, see page 186.

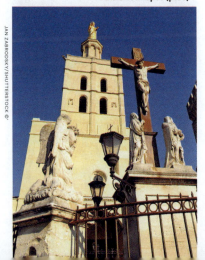

Palais des Papes (p186)

JAN ZABRODSKY/SHUTTERSTOCK ©

7. Palais Princier de Monaco

A HOLLYWOOD LOVE STORY

Set in their palace on Le Rocher, Monaco's oldest neighbourhood perched high above the Mediterranean Sea, the Grimaldis – aka the royal family of Monaco – stand firm as the longest-ruling royal family in Europe. Within these gilded walls, Prince Ranier III met Grace Kelly, Hollywood royalty, in

1955. But that's only part of the story that unfurls on a visit to the ornate Grands Appartements, or staterooms, the only section of the residence open to the public. A new chapter is being written as painstaking restoration works continue to bring sweeping Renaissance frescoes hidden under layers of paint for centuries back to the surface.

To admire art old and new in the Palais Princier de Monaco, see page 94.

8. Route Napoléon
THE BEGINNING OF THE HUNDRED DAYS

In February 1815, Napoléon Bonaparte returned to home soil after fleeing exile on the Italian island of Elba. From Cannes, he set off on a route into the French Alps and then onto Paris. Once he arrived in the capital, just two and a half weeks later, he swept back to power with a legendary military comeback. The 325km path he took from the Côte d'Azur to Grenoble is now considered one of France's epic road trips, passing through destinations such as the potter's village of Vallauris, inspiration for Picasso, and the perfume-scented town of Grasse, before flattening out on the alpine plains of the Alpes-de-Haute-Provence.

To learn about the highlights of his route through the Côte d'Azur, see page 91.

9. Casino de Monte-Carlo
PLACE YOUR BETS

If you need an example of a building that changed the course of a nation's history, look no further than the Casino de Monte-Carlo. Built on an arid plateau dotted by olive and citrus trees, this Belle-Époque beauty's opening in 1863 heralded the arrival of a new destination for Europe's elite – and a new direction for the tiny principality on the Mediterranean Sea that had, until that point, relied on agriculture as its main source of income. Not long after the casino threw open its doors, the similarly lavish Hôtel de Paris was inaugurated and the glitzy neighbourhood of Monte-Carlo was born.

To marvel at the glittering Casino de Monte-Carlo gaming rooms, see page 96.

10. Barcelonnette
FROM THE ALPS TO MEXICO

In the early 19th century, a wave of young men left the villages of the Vallée de l'Ubaye in the Alpes-de-Haute-Provence in search of a new life in Mexico. They found success in the textile and banking industries, and many eventually returned to Provence with money to spend. And spend they did, building large villas as a visible testament to their wealth. Around 50 of these villas, mainly built between 1890 and 1930, still remain in Barcelonnette and Jausiers. Collectively, these elegant bourgeois residences are known around the valley as the 'Mexican Villas'.

To learn more about Barcelonnette's Mexican Villas, see page 243.

11. Nice
STROLL THE PROMENADE

Everyone from aristocrats to artists were drawn to the mild winters of the Côte d'Azur on doctor's orders – the sunshine was thought to cure tuberculosis in particular. Visitors returned every year for the colours, the light and the mild climate, making its wide waterfront boulevards and Belle Époque gambling dens the place to be seen. During the late 19th- and early 20th-centuries, winter was the high season in Nice, and the rich architectural legacy that remains has conferred a new distinction on Nice: it's now a World Heritage-listed Winter Resort Town of the Riviera.

To learn more about Nice's Unesco World Heritage buildings, see page 54.

Promenade des Anglais, Nice (p56)

TRAVEL-FR/SHUTTERSTOCK ©; RIGHT: BEGIR/SHUTTERSTOCK ©

Ménerbes (p216)

12. Villa Ephrussi de Rothschild
LIFESTYLES OF THE RICH AND FAMOUS

On the leafy millionaires' peninsular of St-Jean-Cap-Ferrat, the Villa Ephrussi de Rothschild is one of the Belle Époque jewels of the Côte d'Azur. Appearing like a two-tiered, candy-pink wedding cake, the building brims with ornate architectural detailing and is framed by manicured gardens. Commissioned as a winter residence for Baroness Béatrice Ephrussi de Rothschild in 1912, the rooms are filled with objects from her personal art collection. Just before her death in 1933, she bequeathed the villa and all its collections to the Académie des Beaux-Arts who have maintained it as a splendid museum of the era.

To visit the Villa Ephrussi de Rothschild, see page 68.

13. Auberge St-Martin
TRANSHUMANCE CUISINE

Provence's pastoral traditions run deep and transhumance – herding the flock to summer pastures – still takes place in certain areas of the region. In the tiny village of La Brigue, tucked in the northeastern nook of the Côte d'Azur, chef Patrick Teisseire is bringing the culinary heritage of the practice back to the kitchen at Auberge St-Martin, his hotel and restaurant. Named cucina bianca for the colourless nature of the ingredients that were once collected en route, staple recipes include sügeli, a pasta shell fashioned out of little more than flour and water, as well as plenty of uses for sheep milk cheese.

To tuck into a plate of freshly-cooked sügeli at Auberge St Martin, see page 76.

14. Ménerbes
TOUJOURS PROVENCE

It's the classic tale: busy city professional throws it all away to embrace rural life in a new country. But Peter Mayle wrote the script when he swapped his advertising career in London for a ramshackle farmhouse in the Luberon. The book that followed – A Year in Provence – not only put the sleepy village of Ménebres on the map and triggered a slew of copycat travel writers. More than that, his work crystallised the Provençal idyll that still defines the region today and draws visitors in ever-increasing numbers.

To see Ménebres, the village that started it all, see page 216.

15. LUMA Arles
FUTURE PAST

The chrome facade of LUMA Arles can be seen from all angles, its 11,000 stainless-steel panels shimmering in chorus against the southern French sun. The Frank Gehry–designed structure rises 56m high (it's the tallest building for miles) and is a bold statement of the future in a place so often defined by its past – although the architect drew inspiration from both the artist Vincent Van Gogh and the Romans. The creative campus is a new hub for the arts as well as a centre promoting future-forward thinking about topics such as sustainable design.

To set foot inside the visionary LUMA Arles, see page 161.

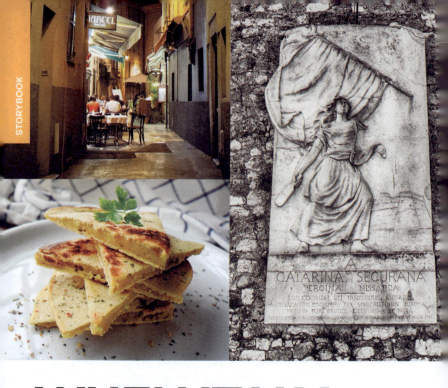

WHEN ITALY
INSPIRED NICE

A city with a foot in two countries.   By Chrissie McClatchie

NICE IS THE belle of the Côte d'Azur, and France and Italy have long been engaged in a tug-of-war for its affection. France ultimately emerged victorious, but from the street-food culture to the colourful façades of the old town, the Italian influence remains especially strong.

The capital of the Côte d'Azur is less than 30km from the border, and from here it's quicker to drive to Rome than to Paris. So it makes sense that Nice can often feel as Italian as it is French. You'll see it as you walk the narrow streets of Vieux Nice, the shaded alleys lit up by the warm yellows and rich reds of the Italianate façades. You'll taste it as you bite into a portion of socca, the thin chickpea-flour pancake that is closely related to Liguria's farinata. And you'll hear it in the voices of the shopkeepers, who seamlessly switch between the two languages, depending on their clientele.

Just over 160 years separate Nice from the time it actually was, for all extents and purposes, Italian.

Pictured clockwise from top left: Vieux, Nice (p54); Catherine Ségurane Memorial (p57); Socca (p61)

History Lesson

The tug of war for Nissa La Bella, as the city is affectionately known, has its roots in the late 14th century when a civil war broke out in Provence, triggered by a succession tussle fit for modern TV. In 1388, the County of Nice pledged allegiance to the House of Savoy, a county of the Holy Roman Empire, in a classic play for protection. The deal was a solid one for both sides: the previously landlocked duchy, which extended from Geneva into northern Italy, could finally lay claim to a few kilometres of precious coastline.

Of course, the Savoy's territory wasn't Italian, as Italy only became a nation in 1861. However, the house would acquire more land and rule in Piemonte in the early 15th century. In the 18th century, a treaty brought Sicily into the fold, although eventually the island was swapped for another: Sardinia. A Savoy duke, Victor Emmanuel II, was crowned the first king of unified Italy.

As they expanded their own domain, the Savoys were there at landmark points of Nice's history: none more so than in 1543, when they fought alongside the residents as French and Turkish forces besieged the city. The invaders managed to take the town (today's Vieux Nice neighbourhood), but they couldn't take the citadel (the Colline du Château); legend has it that it was thanks to the actions of a local washerwoman, Catherine Segurane, who knocked out a Turkish attacker with her laundry bat. You can still see a cannonball in Vieux Nice today if you know where to look.

In 1561 the Dukes changed the official language of Nice from Latin to Italian.

Game On

The French kept coming, however, and the next time the ending was different. In 1691, the troops of Louis XIV seized Nice and the ping-pong match was on. He handed it back over in a treaty five years later, but returned for a second serve in 1705. This time he razed the citadel, as evidenced by the ruins atop the Colline du Château today. But in 1713, he signed Nice back to Italy – again.

At the end of the 18th century, French revolutionary forces occupied Nice. For the first time ever, the population was allowed to have a say in its sovereignty. The vote fell in favour of 'reattachment' to France. The result was that the département of the Alpes-Maritimes was established and Nice named its capital.

But the tussle for Nice would go into extra time. After Napoléon's abdication, Nice was handed back yet again to the House of Savoy in the Treaty of Paris in 1814. And so it would remain until 1860, when Nice was dangled as France's reward for coming to the defence of the soon-to-be Italian king, Victor Emmanuel II, against an invading Austria.

Another referendum on whether or not to join France was held in a show of democracy that was just that: a show. As the story goes, on the day of the vote, the 'no' ballots were nowhere to be seen.

That was the final whistle, however, and for France, the victory quickly started to pay dividends. Four years later, the newly forged train line unfurled from the west, bringing with it tourists in search of the winter sun. The mythical Côte d'Azur was born.

THE NEWLY FORGED TRAIN LINE UNFURLED FROM THE WEST, BRINGING WITH IT TOURISTS IN SEARCH OF THE WINTER SUN. THE MYTHICAL CÔTE D'AZUR WAS BORN.

Train line and beach, Villefranche-sur-Mer (p64)

LILIGRAPHIE/SHUTTERSTOCK ©

Art Walk

If you take the art walk along the Promenade des Anglais, one of the sculptures you'll come across is the towering 9 Lignes Obliques. It's an installation that has divided the residents of the city: for some, it's just a rusty collection of long metal rods. For others, it's a masterpiece to celebrate. The artwork was installed in 2010 to commemorate the 150th anniversary of Nice's 1860 annexation. Why nine lines? That's one for each of the nine valleys of the County of Nice.

Only a few minutes away, in the Jardin Albert 1 overlooking the Baie des Anges, another testament to this history stands tall. Erected in 1896, the winged Victory, cloaked in a French flag, is sculpted from bronze atop the Monument Centenaire. The statue commemorates the first reattachment of Nice in 1793 and the creation of the Alpes-Maritimes.

Part French, Part Italian, 100% Niçois

In the century and a half since it returned to French hands for the last time, Nice has grown into the country's fifth-largest city, and its second-most visited. Visitors flock not only to the palm-fringed beachfront, but also to the many cafe-lined squares for a morning espresso or a glass of chilled rosé. It all epitomises the city's relaxed, outdoor lifestyle. In the restaurants, you can dine on all-you-can-eat moules frites or find the perfect plate of pesto pasta. This history has made Nice the unique destination it is today, and also created a fiercely proud and independent people with rich traditions and a language, niçois, that is still taught in schools.

But that's a whole other story.

Moules frites

POWERED BY LIGHT/ALAN SPENCER/ALAMY STOCK PHOTO ©

LE MISTRAL
GAGNANT

The famous and fearsome wind of Provence. By Ashley Parsons

ON THE FIRST day of the mistral, a feeling of reassurance sweeps across Provence. A good wind has come to blow away the humidity and the clouds. Its arrival will bring clear blue skies and a brilliant sun that defines the picturesque Provencal landscape. Farmers are pleased for what it means for their crops, and people recount legends and sayings about the wind to each other. No one really has to listen, though; they've heard them all since childhood.

The mistral wind, renowned for its ferocity and persistence, has been an integral part of Provence's identity for centuries. The first mention of the mistral dates back to 700 BCE when it was described as a 'horrible force'. The Albique people, a Celtic tribe, believed that the wind was the child of Vintur, a Gaulish god, and an Albique woman.

THE MISTRAL WIND, RENOWNED FOR ITS FEROCITY AND PERSISTENCE, HAS BEEN AN INTEGRAL PART OF PROVENCE'S IDENTITY FOR CENTURIES.

Mistral (p34), Provence
MASLENKA/SHUTTERSTOCK ©

In one legend, villagers barricaded the mistral inside a cave with planks made from century-old olive trees – a tree that is notably resistant to the mistral's temper. When the mistral awoke, it warned the people that without its presence, desolation would befall the land. Mosquitoes would infest their fields, water would putrefy, and fevers would claim the lives of their children and elders. However, the villagers remained steadfast in the desire, and left the mistral confined.

The mistral turned out to be right, of course, and during a night of debate among the villagers, the wind spoke up and pledged to show clemency if the villagers granted it its freedom. It promised to not uproot fruit trees, dismantle rooftops or destroy the fences in the fields. And so the villagers agreed to free the wind.

273

When the last plank was lifted from the cave, the mistral rushed out and began to blow with all its might. The villagers stood frozen in place, uncertain of how to react. At that moment, a courageous child stepped forward and reminded the wind of its promise. Instantly, the ferocious gusts subsided.

On the Second Day of the Mistral

Yesterday's laundry freshly put away, today people might wash their sheets or even a carpet. The incessant wind will dry wet linens on a line in less than an hour. But by midday, weariness is starting to creep in.

Born from the convergence of anticyclones and depressions, the mistral possesses a chilly and arid nature. It sweeps across the region with an average speed of 50 km/h, occasionally unleashing gusts exceeding 100 km/h. With such an intrusive nature, it penetrates even the tiniest crevices, causing windows and doors to rattle. Dust devils whirl across the countryside, inciting a resigned frustration among inhabitants.

The mistral's arrival is often met with mixed emotions. While it brings the challenges of strong gusts and unsettled weather, it also cleanses the air, providing clarity and vivid colors to the landscape. The wind's cooling effect on hot summer days is welcomed, as it offers respite from the scorching sun. It becomes a dance of emotions – a waltz between joy and frustration, appreciation and annoyance.

Does it remind the inhabitants of their interconnectedness with nature and the challenges they must face? As the wind howls through the narrow streets, it weaves stories and bonds. Touching all aspects of life in Provence, where the forces of nature coexist with human existence, a simple wind shapes the character of the land and its people. Protection from the mistral in Provence goes as far as to influence rural architecture: old Provençal mas, or farmhouses, are usually south facing, and there are few, often tiny, windows on the north side.

THE WIND PENETRATES EVEN THE TINIEST CREVICES, CAUSING WINDOWS AND DOORS TO RATTLE. DUST DEVILS WHIRL ACROSS THE COUNTRYSIDE, INCITING A RESIGNED FRUSTRATION AMONG INHABITANTS.

On the Third Day of the Mistral

Shouldering a thick coat, one might meander to a village cafe while waiting out the wind. Across Provence, dozens of bars, tabacs and bistros bear the name of the mistral (lou mistrau – the master – in Provençal).

This powerful wind not only shapes the physical environment but also plays a crucial role in the region's viticulture. The mistral's influence on vineyards is significant and beneficial. As it blows through the grapevines, it helps to dry the leaves, reducing the risk of fungal diseases such as mildew. This drying effect, combined with the wind's ability to prevent excessive humidity, creates favorable conditions for grape cultivation. A natural ally to the renowned vineyards of Provence, the mistral contributes to the production of high-quality Côtes du Rhône wines, including the famous Châteauneuf-du-Pape.

In the face of the relentless gusts, the Provençaux find solace in their cherished traditions. The local cafes and brasseries become sanctuaries where friends gather to find camaraderie and share their grievances over a glass of red wine or pastis. The clinking of glasses and the lively chatter form a symphony of frustration and resilience, echoing the spirit of Provence.

With a nod to the wind, to the time and to nostalgia, the bar owner might play a Georges Brassens album, the one with 'Le Chapeau de Mireille' on it. This action is with the hope that tonight the wind will calm, and that three days will not stretch into six.

As they say: Le mistral qui dit « bonjour » (débutant le jour) est là pour 3, 6 ou 9 jours, alors que celui qui dit « bonsoir » (débutant le soir) est là jusqu'à demain soir. The mistral who says 'good day', (starts in the morning) is here for 3, 6, or 9 days, but the mistral who says 'good evening', (starts in the evening) is here until tomorrow night.

Opposite: Vineyard, Châteauneuf-du-Pape (p188)

HEAT IN
MARSEILLE

La canicule, or 'heat wave', transforms Marseille every summer as residents and visitors spend time outside.   By Michael Frankel

THE HEAT TRANSFORMS Marseille's personality in the summer and forces residents to adapt to life outdoors. This is a rebellious city, where people claim the streets as their own. When night falls, they commune in the thronging squares until late or lean over balconies and stare into each other's lives above the narrow passages. From the cobbles, you hear the intimate sound of a thousand living rooms: televisions on blast, erupting laughter, mangled conversations over music, the lonely scraping of chair legs on tiles or a fork across a plate. All these sounds ring out from open windows after a day spent horizontal on the rocks and pebbles that lie at the edge of the gently agitated waters of the Mediterranean.

Summer in the City

Heat forces the molecules around us to vibrate faster as life slows down, altering what we choose to eat, the liveliness of our energy levels and the regulation of

Marseille (p136)

our sleep patterns. Over time, it begins to define who we are. It affects our bodies and minds as we wake up in a daze of late mornings to the sleepily hypnotic whirrings of a fan, stretched out on bed sheets, deeply tanned and still. The duvet will have long been packed away, forgotten and unimaginable. Reaching for water, the idea of anything touching your skin becomes abhorrent; even the proximity of another body radiating next to you can be too much.

Opening the shutters to blue skies and white light, we soon venture outdoors to a sun that scorches us, the heat punishingly reflecting up from the concrete that has absorbed as much as it can take. It's like living in a furnace with the temperature penetrating your existence in the same way that gravity does: completely.

Yet, these summers force many of us to rise gratefully. If you visit in July or August, be prepared to sweat. There is no escaping how close and hot it is, even indoors or in the shade. Large beads of perspiration

> **HEAT AFFECTS OUR BODIES AND MINDS AS WE WAKE UP IN A DAZE OF LATE MORNINGS TO THE SLEEPILY HYPNOTIC WHIRRINGS OF A FAN, STRETCHED OUT ON BED SHEETS, DEEPLY TANNED AND STILL.**

pour from your body and explode at your feet, your brain sending blood racing to the skin's surface, regulating your temperature, to keep you cool, to keep you alive.

Showers are taken cold; inadvertently, you awaken the reptilian brain. Water spraying over your head and neck invigorate your system. Soon, you make your way to the coast to stare at the summer crowds that lie prostrate on the rocks or vividly coloured sunbeds as the temperatures climb, causing your vision to become wavy and your brain confused. This may be what people describe as 'too hot' – when decisions are made that may not feel like your own. It is the point where your cognitive function becomes languorous as your body overheats.

Those not from Marseille may be taken aback to see the tanned, lithe bodies, semi-nude or completely naked in the sun. These bodies disappear into the waters to return energised, golden, wet. Where do you look? It becomes normalised; there is a timeless pagan connection to it all – worshipping the sun and its effects. Your afternoon becomes meditative or even spiritual as you become an offering to the gods, as wave after wave of infernal heat forces you to retreat into an inner world of glory. Thoughts get pushed away until you are only a voice saying, 'Wow, it's so hot'. You are incredulous as you suck from a bottle of cold beer. It can become a challenge, but out of your pores streams the cleansing of your inner world, allowing everything bad and unwanted to escape. You can sweat so much it is almost at a cellular level. Your body is a universe unto itself.

You wait as long as you can before you plunge into the sea, unable to take any more of the sun burning into your skin. Diving into the Mediterranean can feel like being reborn, with the colours of the water and the stillness below. You get to let go of it all. Removing all static and connecting with your inner voice. It leaves you fortified, ready to brave the chaos of real life again, back to a sweltering city of a million people packed together with lots of personality on display. Back to a city

Calanques, Marseille (p146)

SUFIYAN GANGAT/SHUTTERSTOCK ©; FAR LEFT: DEMAN/SHUTTERSTOCK ©

277

that is reactive, provocative and as short-tempered as it is wildly expressive and bold, whether you like that or not. Marseille's character has been forged in fire.

In such sweltering heat, you are luckily forgiven for doing nothing. It would be impossible to expect anything from anyone in such conditions. Life is on pause; in the intensity of no future and no past, there is only the blistering moment. A long hot summer where your ambitions become over-ridden, when all you need to do is lie down with your friends and laugh for days on end. To float through it in a haze. Everything becomes more straightforward and lighter, even what is found on your plate.

The spaces we love the most, where we go to escape the heat, are also those that are most at risk; preserving nature together is also preserving a whole culture. In the summer months, there is a ban on trips into the *calanques,* so it is essential to download the Mes Calanques app to keep you informed on navigating the region's most precious natural spaces. The app encourages us to be responsible,

report incidents and ask questions. The national park has become a tinderbox, rendered so arid that a single cigarette butt can destroy the biodiversity of acres of scrubland, the flames wildly driven on by the furious mistral winds.

The heat's effects on the ecology strike you the most as you return from the beach to see end-of-the-world images on the news, where nature has been eviscerated and entire regions destroyed. The weather reports become red maps and exclamation marks. There are interviews from families fleeing and crying, their tears salty tracks down soot-covered faces. Desperately, you watch people fighting the flames, as planes overhead drop tons of water and fire retardants. It's as regular as summer itself and seemingly inescapable. Marseille watches the news as the media reaches a boiling point. It is a city neglected by the state; it is the poorest in France and one of the poorest in Europe. Summer was once the great leveller, where all you needed was a hat and a cold drink to survive. Now, it threatens to engulf us all.

> **THE SPACES WE LOVE THE MOST, WHERE WE GO TO ESCAPE THE HEAT, ARE ALSO THOSE THAT ARE MOST AT RISK; PRESERVING NATURE TOGETHER IS ALSO PRESERVING A WHOLE CULTURE.**

Calanques (p146), Marseille

INDEX

281

Map Pages **000**

Map Pages **000**

Map Pages **000**

It's always rosé season (p158) in Provence and the Côte d'Azur.

The village of Fontaine-de-Vaucluse (p205) is known for it's spring. It is France's largest karst spring and the fifth-largest of its type in the world.

Mapping data sources:
© Lonely Planet
© OpenStreetMap http://openstreetmap.org/copyright

THIS BOOK

Destination Editor
AnneMarie McCarthy

Cover Researcher
Marc Backwell

Production Editor
Jennifer McCann

Book Designer
Dermot Hegarty

Cartographer
Bohumil Ptáček

Assisting Editors
Sofie Andersen, Alison Killilea, Kate Mathews, Christopher Pitts

Thanks
Ronan Abayawickrema, Karen Henderson, Darren O'Connell

MIX
Paper from responsible sources
FSC™ C021741

Paper in this book is certified against the Forest Stewardship Council™ standards. FSC™ promotes environmentally responsible, socially beneficial and economically viable management of the world's forests.

Published by Lonely Planet Global Limited
CRN 554153
11th edition – May 2024
ISBN 978 1 83869 934 5
© Lonely Planet 2024 Photographs © as indicated 2024
10 9 8 7 6 5 4 3 2 1
Printed in Malaysia